PENNSYLVANIA IN PUBLIC MEMORY

PENNSYLVANIA *in* Public Memory

Reclaiming the Industrial Past

Carolyn Kitch

THE PENNSYLVANIA STATE UNIVERSITY PRESS
UNIVERSITY PARK, PENNSYLVANIA

Library of Congress Cataloging-in-Publication Data

Kitch, Carolyn L.
Pennsylvania in public memory : reclaiming the industrial past / Carolyn Kitch.
p.   cm.
Summary: "Looks at sites and events in Pennsylvania to explore the emergence
of heritage culture about industry and its loss in America. Traces the shaping of
public memory of coal, steel, railroading, lumber, oil, and agriculture, and the
story it tells about both local and national identity"—Provided by publisher.
Includes bibliographical references and index.
ISBN 978-0-271-05219-9 (cloth : alk. paper)
ISBN 978-0-271-05220-5 (pbk. : alk. paper)
1. Industrial archaeology—Pennsylvania.
2. Historic sites—Conservation and restoration—Pennsylvania.
3. Collective memory—Pennsylvania.
4. Heritage tourism—Pennsylvania.
5. Industries—Pennsylvania—History.
6. Working class—Pennsylvania—History.
7. Deindustrialization—Pennsylvania—History.
8. Pennsylvania—Economic conditions.
9. Pennsylvania—Social conditions. 10. Pennsylvania—History, Local.
I. Title.

T22.P4K57 2012
338.09748—dc23
2011029070

This book is dedicated to my grandfathers,

Arthur James, who was an anthracite miner in the Williamstown Colliery of the Susquehanna Coal Company,

{ *and* }

John Kitch, who worked out of Harrisburg's Enola Yard as a freight conductor for the Pennsylvania Railroad.

Contents

Acknowledgments

This book came to be through the help and kindness of very many people. I'm grateful to Temple University for awarding me a research and study leave to work on this project, as well as two travel grants-in-aid. I have been especially fortunate to have the support and encouragement of my friend and boss, Department of Journalism Chair Andrew Mendelson. I appreciate the research assistance of Temple doctoral students Eliza Jacobs, Amanda Scheiner McClain, and Siobahn Stiles as well as the many insights I have gained from other graduate students who have taken my Media and Social Memory class over the years. Librarian Rebecca Traub at the Temple Harrisburg campus also was a key research ally on this project.

Over the three and a half years I've been working on this book, I have received dozens of suggestions on places I should see, and many friends and colleagues have steadily sent me articles and links of interest. Denise Graveline was always on the lookout for industrial heritage news; Matthew Lombard, who shares my enthusiasm for trains, directed me to numerous articles, websites, and events; and Rick Popp offered valuable insights as he pursued his own study of tourism history.

Other academic colleagues provided advice along the way. Even before I knew I was working on a book, Kurt Bell, archivist at the Railroad Museum of Pennsylvania, accompanied me on the Road of Anthracite in the summer of 2004 when I was a Pennsylvania Historical and Museum Commission (PHMC) scholar in residence, an opportunity that was made possible by PHMC historian Linda Shopes, who directed that program. Robert Weible, former director of public history for the PHMC and the State Museum of Pennsylvania, now the state historian and chief history curator of the New York State Museum, patiently listened to me try to articulate this idea in its early stages and provided valuable suggestions. Simon Bronner, Distinguished Professor of Folklore and American Studies at Penn State Harrisburg, has opened many doors for me in the study of Pennsylvania public history and took an active interest in this project. I received valuable feedback from other scholars when I presented parts of this research at conferences of the Pennsylvania Historical Association and the Mid-Atlantic American Studies Association.

A large cast of public history and tourism professionals contributed to this book, sharing their time and expertise with me by answering my interview questions in person, by telephone, by e-mail, or by letter. I would like to thank them here (realizing that some of their titles or jobs may have since changed), in alphabetical order: Christopher Barkley, director, Windber Coal Heritage Center; Brenda Barrett, director, Bureau of Recreation and Conservation, Pennsylvania Department of Conservation and Natural Resources (DCNR); Marilyn Black, vice president for Heritage Development, Oil Region Alliance of Business, Industry, and Tourism; Anita Blackaby, former PHMC director of special projects and former director of the State Museum of Pennsylvania (now director of The House of the Seven Gables in Salem, Massachusetts); Richard Burkert, executive director, Johnstown Area Heritage Association; August Carlino, executive director, Rivers of Steel Heritage Area; Sandra Carowick, former director, Quiet Valley Living Historical Farm; Terri Dennison, executive director, PA Route 6 Heritage Corridor; Eugene DiOrio, vice president and director, and Scott Huston, president, Graystone Society (Coatesville) and the proposed National Iron and Steel Heritage Museum; Janis (Jan) Dofner, communications director, Rivers of Steel Heritage Area; Steve Donches, former vice president of Bethlehem Steel and current executive director of the proposed National Museum of Industrial History; David Dunn, former director, Railroad Museum of Pennsylvania; Harold ("Kip") Hagan, superintendent, Steamtown National Historic Site; Olga Herbert, executive director, Lincoln Highway Heritage Corridor; Donna Holdorf, executive director, National Road Heritage Corridor; Sarah Hopkins, chief, Division of Environmental Education, Pennsylvania DCNR; Dan Ingram, curator, Johnstown Flood Museum; Chester Kulesa, historic site administrator, Pennsylvania Anthracite Heritage Museum and Scranton Iron Furnaces; Andy Masich, executive president, CEO, and director of John Heinz Regional History Center; Steve Miller, former director, Landis Valley Museum, and current director, Bureau of Historic Sites and Museums, PHMC; Dan Perry, chief operating officer, Lackawanna Heritage Valley Authority; Mark Platts, president, Lancaster-York Heritage Region (now Susquehanna Gateway Heritage Area); Norma Ryan, managing director, Brownsville Area Revitalization Corporation; Allen Sachse, executive director, Delaware and Lehigh Valley National Heritage Corridor; Edie Shean-Hammond, superintendent, Hopewell Iron Furnace National Historic Site; Lenwood Sloan, director of cultural and heritage tourism, Pennsylvania Tourism Office; Steve

Somers, director, Cornwall Iron Furnace; Phil Swank, executive director, Endless Mountains Heritage Region; Kenneth Wolensky, historian, Bureau for Historic Preservation, PHMC; Barbara Zolli, director, Drake Well Museum; and Kurt Zwikl, executive director, Schuylkill River Heritage Area. Other public history and tourism professionals who helped me with this research include Pamela Seighman, curator, Coal and Coke Heritage Center; Kirsten Stauffer, projects and outreach director, Lancaster-York Heritage Region; and Janet Wall, vice president for communications, Lancaster County Visitors Bureau.

I also would like to thank museum, site, park, and event directors and staffers whom I met on site during my travels and who spoke with me then in person or later by e-mail. They include Lori Arnold and Karen Popernack at the Quecreek rescue site; Carol Blair at the Petersburg Toll House on the National Road; Paul Fagley, environmental education specialist at Greenwood Furnace State Park; Raymond Grabowski Jr., president, Lake Shore Railway Historical Society (and my guide there, Jim); Sis Hause of the Danville Iron Heritage Festival; Glenn Kerr and Ted Ott at the Seldom Seen Mine; Nancy Kingsley of the Pumping Jack Museum and Oil Heritage Region Visitors Center; Ed Pany of the Atlas Cement Museum; Dan Rapak of the Harris Tower Restoration; Al Smith of the New Freedom Railroad Station; my mother's good friend Edith Umholtz at the Williamstown Historical Society; and Cindy Wooden of the Center for Anti-Slavery Studies.

I am grateful to my editor at Penn State University Press, Eleanor Goodman, for believing in this idea, as well as for her patience in awaiting its fruition. I also appreciate the work of Steve Kress, Amanda Kirsten, Laura Reed-Morrisson, Patricia Mitchell, Jennifer Burton, and Jennifer Norton, as well as the close attention and incredibly helpful suggestions of the anonymous reviewers of the manuscript.

As I explain in the introduction, a number of roads led me to this topic, but I especially thank a fictional character from a century ago, a woman in white named Phoebe Snow, for getting me started. Today she is only a ghost in a film about railroad heritage, but once she connected the two great industries in which my grandparents and great-grandparents worked. They are the other ghosts in this book. It is because they were coal miners and railroaders that I grew up in Pennsylvania. Despite its academic nature, this book has been, for me, a labor of love, a personal as well as professional—and a literal as well as philosophical—journey through my home state. To paraphrase the dedication inscription on one memorial to coal miners in the anthracite region, I owe Pennsylvania much.

National Register

1889 ↗
Historic District

PROUD TO BE A PART OF THE
Path of Progress
NEXT RIGHT

INTRODUCTION

Public Memory and the Legacies of Labor

Braddock, Pa.—As Americans wonder just how horrible the economy will become, this tiny steel town offers a perverse message of hope: Things cannot possibly get any worse than they are here. . . . In an earlier era, Braddock was a famed wellspring of industrial might. . . . Immigrants came to work in the mill, and through ceaseless agitation won union representation that enabled their children—helped by the [Carnegie] library on the hill—to achieve a better life. . . . [It is] a town whose story has evolved from building America to making Americans to eating Americans for dinner.

—*New York Times*, February 1, 2009

This portrait appeared on the front page of the nation's leading newspaper on the day the Pittsburgh Steelers won their sixth Super Bowl championship. The team's first four victories were achieved in the mid- to late 1970s, as the steel industry was beginning to topple; its other two, ending the 2005 and 2008 seasons, occurred amid the city's recent revitalization. By their victory in 2009—completing a "six pack"—the team was credited with having preserved the identity of the men in the mills. Over these three decades, "town and team have been forever forged into one," claimed a reporter for the *Patriot-News* in the state capital of Harrisburg. "Out of adversity came a resilient and ever-enduring pride. . . . As mills shut down, former steelworkers donned hard hats at Steelers games, rooting on a team that had adopted the town's tough, no-nonsense work ethic."[1]

Downtown Pittsburgh itself is now clean and "bustling," the article noted. But the collapse of Big Steel in this area three decades ago decimated so much of this region, even towns like Braddock where steelmaking actually continues.

As the American recession worsened in the opening decade of the twenty-first century, journalists frequently used Pittsburgh as a symbol of the nation. In 2008, when the *Pittsburgh Post-Gazette* ran a series of features on the personal impact of the current recession, some of their interview subjects shared hardship tales that stretched back to the 1980s.[2] Later that year, as the presidential election neared, the *New York Times* chose Aliquippa, a town northeast of Pittsburgh that once was home to steel giant Jones and Laughlin, as a barometer of just how desperate working-class white Democrats were in an economic downtown: "Voting for the black man does not come easy to Nick Piroli. . . . To the sound of bowling balls smacking pins, as the bartender in the Fallout Shelter queues up more Buds, this retired steelworker wrestles with this election and his choice."[3] Out-of-work coal miners rallied around the campaign of Republican John McCain, chanting, "We've got coal!" in response to his support for "clean coal" technology.[4] Democratic contenders Hillary Clinton and Joe Biden both claimed family ties to Scranton.

Scranton, too, is a media symbol of American deindustrialization, though it is used more comically. When an American version of the British television comedy *The Office* debuted in 2005, its producers located the U.S. counterpart of its "dreary branch office of a fictional paper company," Dunder Mifflin, in Scranton, a city "whose name never seemed to appear in print without the words 'hardscrabble former coal-mining town,'" wrote one television critic.[5] In a skit re-creating the 2008 vice presidential candidates' debate, *Saturday Night Live* comedian Jason Sudeikis, playing Biden, lampooned his working-class-roots rhetoric: "I come from Scranton, Pennsylvania, and that's as hardscrabble a place as you're going to find. . . . Nobody, and I mean nobody, but me has ever come out of that place. . . . So don't be telling me that I'm part of the Washington elite, because I come from the absolute worst place on Earth."[6] Biden himself walked the streets of Scranton, recalling his childhood, for national television news cameras, and Clinton spoke at the local high school about her childhood visits to her father's family in the area. Her appearance there on the campaign trail, wrote a *Times* reporter, was meant "to link the values of this gritty region—where her grandfather, descended from Welsh coal miners, raised his family—to her character and especially her perseverance. 'She's tough,' Christopher Doherty, Scranton's mayor, said in an interview. 'That's a real Scranton trait. That's an anthracite trait.'"[7]

The entire state of Pennsylvania was a favorite with television news reporters as they sought to "take the pulse" of ordinary people during that election year. Traveling aboard vintage Pennsylvania Railroad cars, *Good Morning America* reporter Robin Roberts remarked, "We saw two Americas from our train windows: the beautiful, ever-changing landscape, and the harsh reality facing the people living in towns along the tracks."[8] Critics have been concerned with the uneven economic consequences of deindustrialization for decades, and the 2008 election brought this issue again to the forefront of the popular-culture stage as well as the conventional political stage. Touring during and after the election year, including ten concerts in Pennsylvania, Bruce Springsteen resurrected songs about working-class disillusionment from his 1978 album *Darkness on the Edge of Town* and closed his shows with "American Land," a rollickingly angry song about the dashed hopes and poor treatment of nineteenth-century immigrants who came to "the valley of red-hot steel and fire."[9] On this tour, Springsteen also performed "Hard Times Come Again No More," a song by nineteenth-century American composer and Pittsburgh native Stephen Collins Foster. As Springsteen implied, hard times have indeed returned to industrial valleys, whose present-day residents feel embittered by broken promises.

Out of these ashes have risen the kinds of heritage sites (and stories) that are the subject of this book, a range of local history and tourism initiatives that are meant to restore local pride and create a new kind of revenue in struggling towns and cities. Frequently the subject of journalism, advertising, and film, these projects are public statements about identity and region. While they are very respectful of former residents, they are more than merely tributes—they are determined attempts to make the past useful in the present and future.

The public and critical reception of such efforts has been mixed. While some people are anxious to acknowledge their parents' lives and their childhood neighborhoods, others object to what they perceive as the marketing of personal tragedy. Plans to tell "the workers' story" are hailed by some as long overdue and by others as premature in a time of continuing unemployment and municipal decay. In some industries and regions, the latter feeling poses a special problem for public memory: how is it possible to consign to history (let alone to celebrate) industries that have disappeared so recently that their scars on the land—and in families and communities—are still visible? Conversely, in other regions, large-scale industry is so long gone that it is *in*visible, and public historians struggle to paint an epic picture that is impossible to imagine in present-day settings.

This book is an attempt to explore these issues through a literal as well as rhetorical survey of Pennsylvania's industrial and postindustrial landscape in the early twenty-first century. Its goal is to contribute to an ongoing conversation about what should be remembered of a lost way of life, how it should be recalled, in what settings, by whom and for whom, and at what temporal distance. More broadly, this is a study of the lasting meaning of industrial work, from yesterday as well as long ago, in public expressions of local and national identity. It is a scholarly and a personal journey through the vestiges of the past that circulate in the present.

The Surge in Public and Scholarly Interest in "Heritage"

While the problem is ongoing, U.S. deindustrialization began in earnest during the 1970s and 1980s. These economic losses coincided with a growing interest among the general public in genealogy and local history, sparked in part by the American Bicentennial in 1976, and with a rise in uses of nostalgia in American public communication and popular culture. Assessing the "values" expressed in the country's leading news magazines and television news programs during the 1970s, Herbert J. Gans detected a pervasive preference for "small-town pastoralism," an idealization of rural, simpler life presumably lost in the modern world.[10] Television shows such as *The Waltons* and *Little House on the Prairie* invoked folksy, rural nostalgia; magazines called *Memories* and *Reminisce* were launched; advertising campaigns hailed the timeless authenticity of mass-manufactured leisure products (Coca-Cola, for instance, was "the real thing").[11]

As Susan Davis has noted, the prevalence of nostalgic rhetoric in popular and political culture during the Reagan era coincided with the federal "defunding" of history (as well as arts) projects, a change ensuring that Americans were increasingly likely to learn about history less from museums than from tourism and mass media.[12] By 1990, the striking success of Ken Burns's PBS documentary *The Civil War* had opened the door to a spate of epic media presentations of history. Later in that decade, films such as Steven Spielberg's *Saving Private Ryan* would confirm the appeal of this media treatment of the past. Meanwhile, the landscape of industrial cities had changed in an interesting way. As academics and community organizers were just beginning to debate how to publicly recall workers' experiences, the buildings in which they once labored were transformed into hotels, brewpubs, antique malls, and office complexes. Young urban professionals bought riverside, loft-style condominiums in former factory buildings. Passenger train stations, absent significant passenger rail travel in the United States, became restaurants and art studios. As industrial work itself departed, industrial architecture became trendy and, paradoxically, more visible.

The later decades of the twentieth century inspired new kinds of interest in the past from politicians as well as the general public. The 1960s and '70s brought federal legislation fostering not only environmental conservation but also preservation of historic buildings and American folk traditions.[13] There was a corresponding groundswell of academic interest in social history, a "bottom-up" approach that focused on ordinary people and spurred funding for studies of local history, labor history, ethnic history, women's history, and (across all of those categories) oral history. That work raised questions about the relationship between local and national identity, the representational aspects of heritage industries, the changing nature of public history, and the cultural meanings of place. These subjects also became of interest to cultural geographers, urban studies scholars, and communication researchers. Collectively, these scholars have attributed the phenomenon of industrial heritage to factors well beyond deindustrialization itself, including baby boom nostalgia, increased ethnic pride, post-Vietnam disillusionment, and a resurgence of nationalism in the face of globalization. Related research has considered the political implications of tourism in a postcolonial world: about authority in representation, the question of who may "speak for" the experiences of particular cultural groups; about the implications of globalization and recent political change, throughout the world, for national identity and memory; and about the nature, forms, and practices of museums, which have increasingly incorporated media and interactive technology in an effort to entertain and as well as inform.[14]

Like the heritage industries themselves, academic literature about them took root first in the United Kingdom, where scholarly views of this phenomenon have been dim. Among the most critical has been Robert Hewison, who has called heritage culture "bogus history" and "a commodity which nobody seems able to define, but which everybody is eager to sell" to a public "hypnotized by images of the past."[15] He writes, "Heritage is gradually effacing history, by substituting an image of the past for its reality."[16] Kevin Walsh similarly condemns heritage sites as "a spurious simulacrum," declaring that "such places are literally on a road to nowhere."[17] John Corner and Sylvia Harvey contend that heritage sites that claim to "either 'bring the past back to life' or allow visitors to 'step back into it'" encourage only "sentimentalism and whimsy."[18] Concerned about "the heritage crusades," David Lowenthal writes that heritage "replaces past realities with feel-good history."[19]

Some American scholars have taken up this cry. Michael Wallace worries that the past has become just "a comestible to be consumed, digested, and excreted"; because of our fascination with heritage, he claims, Americans have disengaged from history, becoming "a historicidal culture."[20] Wallace is concerned with the problem of history getting into the wrong hands, especially those of media producers.[21] Wilbur Zelinsky adds antiquing, ethnic festivals, and historical pageants to the commercial culture capitalizing on "the magnetism of a comforting past."[22] Writing about tourism in Gettysburg, Jim Weeks argues that "a key feature of heritage over history is the substitution of image for reality that turns illusions into authenticity."[23]

Other analysts are somewhat more optimistic. Proponents of oral history, while cautious about the difference between personal memory and "correct" history, laud some heritage projects for bringing previously untold stories into the historical record, thus contradicting or contextualizing mainstream ideas about the past. The new scholarly deference to ordinary people also has reminded academic historians that vernacular narratives deserve to be taken seriously and that, as Linda Shopes explains, there is a "difference in the information the two groups think is historically important."[24] Other authors challenge the assumption that audiences are duped by commercial heritage presentations. "Just like an audience at a play, visitors are reflexively aware that what they see has been 'staged,'" write Chris Rojek and John Urry of heritage tourism sites.[25] Noting how little research there is on the audiences of public history, Michael Frisch and Dwight Pitcaithley contend that "both audience and presenters bring active interpretive processes to their onsite meeting" at heritage venues and that audiences have "general expectations" about and "a sense of what is appropriate in" presentations of history.[26] Jo Blatti, who *has* studied heritage site visitors, makes this point more strongly, writing, "Many of us are preoccupied by 'deficiencies' of public understanding rather than the astonishing and the miraculous imaginative capabilities shared by program producers and audiences."[27]

Addressing criticisms that imaginative stories about the past "purvey misinformation," some writers, building on the well-known contention of Hayden White, argue that the past is inevitably recorded in narrative form.[28] In their study of Colonial Williamsburg, Richard Handler and Eric Gable claim, "The dream of authenticity is a present-day myth. We cannot recreate, reconstruct, or recapture the past. We can only tell stories about the past in a present-day language."[29] At the same time, the past invoked by heritage narratives is not fiction but rather has a "connection to the real past," notes Tok Thompson, who cautions us "not to dismiss this link as 'inauthentic' or 'invented.' The past may be contestable, and changeable, but it is not vacuous. . . . The past really did happen."[30]

When I embarked on this project, I was theoretically somewhere in the middle of the continuum between celebration and criticism of heritage culture. Not surprisingly, because I teach in a communications school and once worked in the magazine industry, I am not a believer of the critical gospel that mediated or otherwise commercial historical projects are inevitably uninformed or ideologically oppressive. Nor, especially *after* doing this research, do I buy the academic claim that "amateur historians" are ill equipped to handle the past. People of all sorts, with diverse institutional and social positions, make their own sense of the past in ways that help them understand their own lives in the present. It is true, though, that this sense-making process can result in a wishful vision of the past that is markedly different from the material realities of the past. It is also true that certain kinds of people in certain kinds of circumstances are better able to shape and tell the stories that become shared memory.

These are the issues at the heart of memory studies, which over the past thirty years—the same time period as the boom in heritage culture—have emerged across a range of disciplines in the humanities and social sciences. The concept of memory has become a popular lens through which to see how the past is understood retrospectively and how social groups use ideas about history in order to make sense of their identity in the present. These processes occur over time, as memory is reshaped again and again. In his foundational writing on this phenomenon nearly a century ago, Maurice Halbwachs compared this series of transformations to the retouching of a painting, so that "new images overlay the old."[31]

Scholars use several terms to describe this kind of memory, which is shared rather than individual and takes public shape. Halbwachs called it collective memory; others call it social memory. In this book, I will use the term *public memory* to describe what I am studying, for three reasons. First, my primary interest is in how and what the general public learns about the meanings of the industrial past. Second, once they are out of school (and even while they are in school) most people tend to learn about history through a variety of kinds of public communication, including museums, tourism, special events, memorials and signage on the landscape, and mass media, including journalism, advertising, television, and film. Finally, people help shape and interpret the history tales they tell and pass on: memory narratives emerge from a circular kind of communication in which the line between the "producers" and the "audiences" is blurred. The history that results—while sometimes quite different, in form as well as content, from that told in academic history books—is nevertheless legitimate in the very fact that it is, indeed, a public statement. As David Glassberg explains:

> Public historical imagery is an essential element of our culture, contributing to how we define our sense of identity and direction. It locates us in time, as we learn about our place in a succession of past and future generations, as well as in space, as we learn the story of our locale. Images of a "common" history provide a focus for group loyalties, as well as plots to structure our individual memories and a larger context within which to interpret our new experiences. Ultimately, historical imagery supplies an orientation toward our future action . . . delineating . . . what we think is timeless and what we think can be changed, what we consider inevitable and what we term accidental, what we dismiss as strange and what we know is mere common sense. Public historical imagery, by giving recognition to various group and individual histories, also suggests categories for our understanding the scale of our social relations and the relative position of groups in our society.[32]

Here is a near-perfect articulation of the role of public memory in postindustrial (or still deindustrializing) communities. In such places, the question of what to publicly remember is a debate about survival as well as loss, transformation as well as memorial, and future as well as past; it is a process of crafting a useful story about local history and claiming an ongoing role in that story. The present-day orientation of such public memory gives rise to other debates about who should tell the story and how it should be told. It also raises questions about the nature of historical truth.

Public Memory as "Provocation" and Imagination

Among the earliest statements of goals for public history—and definitions of the difference between academic and popular history—were Freeman Tilden's 1957 "principles of interpretation," written for the National Park Service. These principles included, among other points: "Any interpretation that does not somehow relate what is being displayed or described to something within the personality or experience of the visitor will be sterile"; "The chief aim of interpretation is not instruction, but provocation"; and "Interpretation should aim to present a whole rather than a part, and must address itself to the whole man." Decades before academics began to talk about memory, let alone to bemoan heritage, Tilden encouraged public historians to make the past "a living reality" that is "peopled" with characters who inspire empathy from the modern public, to engage in a kind of interpretation that would "provoke in the mind of the hearer the questions, 'What would *I* have done under similar circumstances? What would have been *my* fate?'"[33]

This is what Robert Archibald calls "historical imagination" and what David Glassberg calls a "sense of history," an "intersection of the intimate and the historical."[34] As Glassberg explains, "The personal and experiential take precedence over the global and the abstract. . . . An orientation to the history of one's place, to one's family, to one's region perhaps constitutes the greatest difference between the history that Americans live and experience and the history practiced by professional historians." Through public history, he writes, "we invite ancestors whom we never met to enter our lives imaginatively through stories and pictures."[35] It is worth noting that those people "we never met" are nevertheless often known to us, not merely figments of our imagination, and our connection to them often is based on geographic or genealogical realities. Especially in the case of local museums or historical events, the typical "visitor" either is what Bella Dicks describes as "an interested journeyer through a family past" or is inspired by a feeling of "place memory."[36]

These imaginative connections are enhanced, not diminished, by the local nature of the site and by interpretation provided by local people, even though they are not likely to be professional historians. When Roy Rosenzweig and David Thelen polled eight hundred Americans about what history means to them, respondents said that they were most inspired by—and tended to most believe as *true*—knowledge of the past gained either through their own personal experiences or recounted to them by eyewitnesses who are family or community members.[37] Many of the places I visited in researching this book were staffed largely, or sometimes entirely, by volunteers, who also constitute the great majority of reenactors, or "living history interpreters," at special events. Several directors of sites with state or even federal funding told me that they nevertheless could not exist without volunteers. Moreover, one said, "The volunteers are our most important visitors."[38]

The sensory experience of place contributes to local people's perception of historical truth. Harold "Kip" Hagan, superintendent of the Steamtown National Historic Site in Scranton (a railroad museum), remembers what he observed on one tour group: "An old man was choking up and said to his wife, 'I haven't smelled those smells in forty years.' Ours is a live backshop. . . . For some of these older folks to come back and witness that, it's really moving for them, and to be able to tell their kids, 'Hey, this is the way it was,' that really matters."[39]

This anecdote offers one answer to the questions raised by Ronald Grele three decades ago in his essay titled "Whose Public? Whose History? What Is the Goal of a Public Historian?" His own answer, at the time, was that the goal "should be to help members of the public do their own history," becoming "a new group of historical workers interpreting the past of heretofore ignored classes of people."[40] A similar sentiment was embraced by the participants in a 1990 conference at the American Folklife Center, which addressed what was then perceived as a need for heritage projects "away from a top-down, prescriptive approach to heritage planning toward an approach more open and responsive to grass-roots cultural concerns."[41]

In their privileging of public memory and the lived experiences of local people, writes Amy Levin, local historic sites and museums "may ultimately tell scholars more about contemporary life than all the branches of the Smithsonian put together."[42] Local historians usually are well aware of the differences between their interpretation and that of history textbooks, and they are open about their intent. Many of the people I met in the state's many small historical sites are local historians who are overtly proud of their town and emotionally connected to the departed industry they either mourn or celebrate (or sometimes both). The work they do, usually unpaid, illustrates historian Carol Kammen's reminder that "the word 'amateur' comes . . . from the Latin *amator*, meaning 'to love.' An amateur historian is one who loves history."[43] While these people often possess a wealth of knowledge about the local past, they do not pretend to be objective, and their definitions of historical truth often depart from those of academics.

The website of the Southwestern Pennsylvania Heritage Preservation Commission explains that there are two kinds of stories about the past: one kind is "the stories of historians," made up of facts "selected to preserve the important details"; the other kind "draw[s] from our memories. They are preserved not by historians, but by us. The stories that we decide are important enough to pass down through the generations make up our heritage."[44] A local history video sold during the Iron Heritage Festival in Danville, Pennsylvania, where the first "T-rail" railroad tracks were made in the mid-nineteenth century, explains, "History records facts. It preserves dates and events, people and places. . . . However, it is our heritage that explains why we have become the people we are today."[45]

Danville native Sis Hause gives bus tours of her town's iron-making history, even though there are hardly any visible reminders of it. "I do three tours each year, and they all have been sold out, which amazes me," she says. When I took one of these tours during the festival in the summer of 2007, I was struck by how often other passengers interrupted her with stories of their own. One passenger, she recalls, "remembered a poem that a grandmother recited about one of the bosses at the 'Big Mill.' I often hear stories that are personal and not really information for the history books, but give me a feeling for the thoughts of those who lived in a company town. I sometimes think that maybe some do come to have the opportunity to tell the stories that have been handed down through their families." When the festival began in 1999, she says, most young people knew little of the town's history, and

> the oldest generation . . . who remembered a time when Danville was an iron town were few and far between; we were able to visit with most of them to listen to their stories. The next generation, myself included, remembered remnants of that time. There were still visible signs, such as slag piles, abandoned railroad trestles that led to the mills, foundations of old buildings, and a few of the original mills in my youth. I grew up in an area of town where many of the mineworkers and their families lived after the decline in the industry, so I had the opportunity to listen to them reminiscing about their days in the mines and mills.[46]

Steamtown's Kip Hagan makes the same point, recalling a program his museum had about a 1955 flood in the Scranton area: "People kept standing up and telling their memories of the flood. There are a lot of common threads that are out there. It's like a moth to a light. People want to tell their stories."[47]

This urge to "tell stories" is not merely a matter of reminiscence. In places where industrial structures do remain, strong local feelings can produce a complex memory. Writing about their oral history research with former textile mill workers in Manchester, New Hampshire, Tamara Hareven and Randolph Langenbach explain, "They were willing, and at times eager, to recall the bitter times along with the good. Memories of struggle with poverty, daily two-mile walks to the factory, unemployment and strikes, illness and death were all part of that story, and were intimately linked to the buildings." When sites of industry are still present in otherwise deindustrialized areas, they write, the buildings themselves gain a "symbolic value," standing "as silent witnesses" to "the way of life and the sense of continuity" that has been lost.[48] To those who do not personally remember a region's history, the buildings are powerful in a different way, write John Jakle and David Wilson. "Nothing strikes a sense of pathos more than the ruined factory. . . . Massive walls and towering stacks . . . speak of technical and organizational sophistication. To see them derelict is to see failed dreams."[49]

The Special Circumstances of Industrial Heritage

At the same time that they stand as testimonies to failure and loss, postindustrial landscapes also hold out the hope of heritage, redevelopment projects that may yield social as well as economic transformation. "Dying economies stage their own rebirth as displays of what they once were, sometimes before the body is cold," writes Barbara Kirschenblatt-Gimblett, who contends that heritage projects give industrial towns "a second life as exhibits of themselves."[50] Studying the evolution of former coal-mining regions, Richard Francaviglia identifies this outcome as one alternative (the other being decay and death) for "the last phase of a mining district." Francaviglia attributes the development of industrial heritage tourism to "a growing appreciation of history" among the general public but also writes, "Mining country provides powerful visual settings in which 'technostalgia'—the romanticizing of the industrial past—can thrive. . . . Before mining landscapes could be valued . . . a romanticized vision of their place in history and nature had to be developed."[51]

In 1996, the New York Times published an article titled "Unemployment: The Theme Park" about a new federally funded project to be created in southwestern Pennsylvania called the "Path of Progress," a group of tourism sites about industry connected by a driving route. The reporter described "a program that trains displaced steelworkers and coal miners to become guides in the very places where they once labored" in and around Johnstown, as part of "this city's curious and quietly radical passage from a place that makes things to a place that remembers," and explained, "Heritage tourism retails the often unhappy narratives of unlucky places, and is clearly a growth industry . . . betting that the factories where cannons were forged can be as compelling as the battlefields where they were fired, that the stories of ordinary working people can be as absorbing as those of the exalted and wealthy."[52]

This article raises a number of the issues that separate many academic and cultural critics (including journalists) from local historians and tourism promoters in their assessment of such sites. The article's title suggests the cynicism with which some critics have regarded the presumably sad fate of former industrial workers reduced to being mere tour guides, agreeing to perform for visitors seeking an authentically gritty, if imagined, experience. Writing about the initial local reaction to the planned redevelopment of the U.S. Steel site in Homestead, William Serrin accused developers, and potential future tourists, of "working-class voyeurism."[53] Another frequent thread in criticism is that heritage projects are driven by the greed of insensitive businessmen seeking to profit from the misfortunes of ordinary people. Yet, as Marilyn Halter notes, "The relationship is a much more dialectical give-and-take between culture and commerce. People interested in showcasing their own culture can draw on corporate funding to make that happen and, in many cases, are able to have definitive input into the process as well."[54]

While public history of all kinds is continually shaped by debates among producers and sponsors with conflicting interests, industrial heritage projects seem especially controversial. Michael Frisch offers this explanation:

> Imagine five broad armies marching towards what quickly becomes dramatically contested terrain. . . . First, in a moral as well as temporal sense, are the displaced workers, unions, and communities themselves, the ones whose lives and industrial livelihood have involuntarily become heritage and only heritage. . . . Second is a ragtag army of historical caretakers— those whose primary commitment and interest is to history as such . . . scholars, archivists, preservationists both lay and professional, vernacular history buffs, public historians from grassroots to major professional institutions. Third is an economic development community that comes to see, in industrial heritage, a possible resource for confronting deindustrial catastrophe. . . . Fourth are a diverse range of social change activists . . . who hope through industrial heritage projects focused on the stories, experiences, values, and ideals of working people to generate narratives or struggle and resistance. . . . Finally . . . is the state—the public sector from the local agency . . . to the National Park Service.[55]

In part *because* they are "dramatically contested terrain," industrial heritage projects seem to have a certain kind of credibility that has, so far, largely spared them from the general academic contempt for heritage culture. The vested interest of local people in telling their own industrial stories adds to the authenticity (if not always the factual accuracy) of the history they present.[56] From her observations of the visitor experience at British coal-mining heritage sites,

Bella Dicks concluded that, while the "public stage" on which heritage is reenacted may be paid for by professionals (or governments), it is very often occupied by amateurs, former workers, and others "attempting to represent their own history and identities."[57] The audiences for the stories they tell are also active participants with a vested interest. "Many visitors to industrial sites are making personal pilgrimages into family history," writes Diane Barthel. "Some have grandparents or great grandparents who worked in factories or collieries. These descendants come to reclaim the past and to pay respect."[58]

In her study of the creation of a federal historic site re-creating the lives of textile mill workers in Lowell, Massachusetts, Cathy Stanton calls its outcome a combination of "vernacular, 'traditional,' and commercial uses of history with professional and scholarly ones," a "cultural performance" controlled as much by the audience as by experts. Its planning process, which began in 1978, challenged "the idea that we can make any clean distinction between history and heritage," she writes.[59] As Robert Weible has noted, the Lowell project was the model for industrial heritage projects in the United States.[60] The coalition of partners and perspectives its success required—and the blurring of history and heritage—have characterized American industrial heritage projects through the present day. Academic researchers often are a part, rather than merely critics, of such coalitions. The extensive planning process in Lowell yielded not only a national historic site that is popular with tourists but also several academic conferences and books.[61] University-affiliated scholars also have had input into the discussions of how the collapse of steelmaking in Pittsburgh, Johnstown, and Bethlehem should be remembered.

It is hard to accuse promoters of industrial heritage tourism of profiting by preying on the misfortunes of ordinary people. Without question, such enterprises are driven by economics. In most cases, however, that need is quite real and is felt most sharply by local people, the very "natives" whose past is on display and who often are the performers and promoters of that past. Few such projects make a profit on their own; instead, they attract visitors into regions and towns where they spend money in shops, restaurants, and hotels. The historic site is "not going to be an economic developer itself—you're never going to make it at the gate," says August Carlino, executive director of the Rivers of Steel Heritage Area, which coordinates industrial heritage projects around Pittsburgh. Carlino sees the involvement of former steelworkers in historical interpretation not as sad but as a key factor in whether or not local residents buy into heritage redevelopment, a process of "tapping into the pride of individuals . . . with an ambassador role to spearhead a whole different attitude within the community. If they start talking it about themselves," Carlino says, then displaced workers may gain a sense of ownership of enterprise that otherwise could be distrusted as government and corporate interference.[62]

Why Study Pennsylvania?

Public history about steelmaking, the subject of chapter 7, is among the most recent offerings in a growing array of industrial heritage projects and sites across Pennsylvania. Just as the state was the "keystone" of the original thirteen colonies and a keystone of American industry, it also has been a keystone of heritage enterprise for more than a century. Thanks to the dominance and reach of the Pennsylvania Railroad during the nineteenth and early twentieth centuries, the state was a pioneer in mass-market tourism, and from the start it has told a national memory story with a variety of themes, beginning with the American Revolution. Today one of those themes is an invitation to "visit the birthplace of the American Industrial Revolution."[63]

In 1991, writing about plans for this new kind of heritage in western Pennsylvania, an Associated Press reporter predicted, "If industrial history does become a tourist lure, Pennsylvania will be its Florida."[64] Two decades later, the phenomenon has indeed spread across this state, perhaps more than any other. Even so, at present, industrial themes remain a small part of the state's heritage tourism, which remains driven by the popularity of a handful of destinations whose historic interpretations focus on the War of Independence (Philadelphia), the Civil War (Gettysburg), and the Amish (Lancaster County). Responding to a major survey done in the late 1990s, only 5 percent of "heritage-minded" visitors to Pennsylvania sites said that they were interested in the industrial past; about half of those people mentioned coal-mining history sites and just a handful mentioned steel. The survey also indicated that heritage "tourists" are very often local, or relatively local, people: 39 percent were Pennsylvanians, and another 33 percent came from adjacent states.[65] A 2008 survey of eight Pennsylvania heritage areas underscored this finding even more strongly, revealing that 68 percent of visitors were state residents.[66] Studies done specifically at industrial history sites similarly have found that between two-thirds and three-quarters of visitors are Pennsylvanians.[67]

In sum, even though the state is a leader in the phenomenon, "industrial heritage tourism" is still a small business whose customers often encounter it simply because it is in their own backyards or because they are visiting places for other reasons. When I asked a tour guide at an iron furnace site in central Pennsylvania how visitors became interested in learning about such history, she replied, "They trip over it." It is hard to know what visitors think of industrial heritage presentations or even heritage culture in general; most surveys done so far have focused, instead, on what they spend.[68] Except on site-specific surveys (some of which are discussed in the following chapters), market researchers have not asked people what they learn.

Moreover, as I also realized during my travels, industrial history is not told separately but rather is mixed in with presentations of a town's or region's broader past. Portraits of particular people, companies, neighborhoods, and events are painted on a vast canvas of the town's life, one that recalls high school football championships and military service as well as industrial output and accidents. This is a fiercely proud and fiercely local kind of story, more affirmative than commercial. It was by far the most common kind of historic presentation I encountered.

Less common but more visible are sites and projects that do market industrial history, similarly intertwining it with general history, as part of commercially successful tourism. In those presentations, labor is narratively situated within a rosy but hazy picture of a general national past. The following is just one recent example of such language from a state tourism brochure: "As seen on postcards. Railroad towns. Boroughs that sprang up near natural springs. Or small cities that popped up during the oil boom—yes, we started that, too. In Pennsylvania you'll find the America you've always pictured in your mind. Right down to the wrap-around porches. . . . Have you ever awakened in a century-old stone farm house . . . and opened the window to a seemingly endless sea of cornfields? In Pennsylvania, you can. You can even help milk the cows."[69]

As saccharine as this passage is, it is not really untrue. You *can* milk the cows, thanks to the development of "agritourism," and in some areas, the cornfields do seem endless. The state's northern tier is dotted with charming Victorian towns, such as Meadville and Emlenton, which are visible evidence of the nation's first oil boom a century and a half ago. Pennsylvania has dozens of railroad history sites, and it has a strong claim to industrial history in general. Anyone scanning a state map will find abundant clues in towns named Minersville, Coalport, Coaldale, Steelton, Ironton, Mechanicsburg, Slatington, Lumberville, and Oil City. "Pennsylvania's workers have been at the heart of American labor history for over two centuries," write Howard Harris and Mark McCollough, who declare, "The story of Pennsylvania's wage earners is representative of the history of all working people in the United States."[70]

This book is based on the same premise. The story I hope to tell here is not merely a regional one. Because of the state's actual industrial history *and* its emergence as an early promoter of public history about industry, Pennsylvania is an ideal laboratory in which to study a national and international phenomenon.

How This Book Came to Be

I am a journalism professor whose research has been, mainly, about the roles of media in history (media of the past) and memory (how the past is discussed in media of the present). These interests have led me to a wide range of topics, and some of them led to this book. I collected news coverage of the rescue of the Quecreek miners in 2002 and then the deaths of the Sago miners in 2006 because I was fascinated by the nostalgic tribute journalists paid to coal miners, as if they were figures from the past rather than the present. In between, I spent a month as a "scholar in residence" at the Railroad Museum of Pennsylvania studying an early twentieth-century tourism advertising campaign for the Lackawanna Railroad featuring a woman in white named Phoebe Snow. It took a while for me to realize that these topics were related.

I began this project still within my own academic territory, thinking that I would study how memory about the industrial past emerges as themes in journalism and in tourism promotion. The boundaries of Pennsylvania would create a literal and historic frame for my study, for reasons discussed above. In addition to reading these media of the present, I searched for past examples, as well, in archives and libraries. I figured it would make sense for me to go to these tourism sites myself and see how history was presented there. My university granted me a research leave of one semester, which I was sure would be plenty of time to see the museums and other interpretive sites having to do with industrial history in just one state.

After I had made several driving trips, I needed to better understand what I had seen at particular sites or on highway signs telling me that I was in the Oil Heritage Region or on the "Path of Progress." So I began doing interviews, in person, on the phone, and by e-mail, with tourism officials, regional planners, state and local historians, and other people I had happened to meet. They answered my official questions about how they did their historic interpretation and what kinds of visitors they had and how they marketed their sites. Then, in most cases, they just started talking. Having explained what they did, they then told me *why,* a question I hadn't asked. The answer most often had to do with their families and their childhoods and their memories of the land around them. These conversations led me to more people, who offered similar memories as well as assignments of additional sites I needed to visit.

The more people I talked to, the more I realized I did not know. Part of what I've needed to learn has had to do with industrial (labor, science, technology, business, and social) history itself, with facts of the past; part has had to do with feelings of the present. I have been amazed to discover how many people, in our supposedly rootless, postmodern era, have a strong sense of ownership of public memory about certain industries and certain towns. In addition to long and enthusiastic answers from my interview subjects, I have received a steady stream of unsolicited and often insistent advice. This project became a frequent topic of conversation with all sorts of people. I have talked about it with not only other academics and students but also relatives, neighbors, friends, the mailman, doctors, my pharmacist, car mechanics, and people sitting next to me on trains and airplanes. Nearly every person has begun with the initial reaction of my journalism department colleagues: "Um, you're doing *what?*" And then each one proceeded to tell me about a particular place—a train station, an old mill, a memorial, a particular neighborhood, the still-standing factory building where a father or grandfather once worked—that I *simply must see.* I learned that I had blundered into a subject on which nearly everyone has something to say and to which nearly everyone feels some kind of emotional connection. Often that feeling was quite strong, and I was told not only what to see but also what to think about it.

This level of personal investment, combined with what I experienced at so many industrial heritage sites once I went to them, resulted in a significant shift in the goals of my project. I came to realize that most of what I was studying was not really tourism, even if it was overtly described as such in journalism and promotional materials. The majority of the historic sites that have emerged (or are still emerging) to tell the story of coal mining or oil drilling or steelmaking or railroading are marketed in language addressed to "visitors," and often they are funded through economic development programs whose expressed mission is to bring in the tourist dollar. But in most of the places I visited, I was the only out-of-towner. Several people expressed astonishment that I had come at all. As one regional tourism official told me, "Not everybody wants tourists— some people just want their story to be told and preserved for their families." At least so far, most industrial history sites do indeed tell very local stories, albeit ones that stake a claim to national values and progress. What I was studying, it turned out, were public expressions of "inherited" local identity, statements made more for the sake of civic pride than for the commercial consumption of tourists.

I started my travels with a six-month research plan and a list of about twenty historic sites and tours that I was pretty sure represented the phenomenon I thought I was studying. Three years later, I was still making "one last trip." By the time I finished my overdue manuscript, I had been to 224 sites or events, all of them in Pennsylvania. In addition to visiting 104 museums, I toured 5 coal mines, took 27 "factory tours" (which are not all actually factory tours, but that's a matter for another chapter), attended 18 heritage festivals with industrial themes, located 28 worker memorials and 16 iron furnace remains, and rode 18 tourist trains or trolleys. I realize that I did not finish the job. I missed several industrially themed heritage festivals and many historical society exhibits that include industrial displays. I failed to talk to all of the people who have something to say about this topic. I apologize to the people and the places I have left out.

What I did do, I hope, was to visit enough sites, talk to enough people, and read or view enough media to gain some sense of patterns in tourism, museum interpretation, memorials, and other forms of public memory of past industry. This book recounts the stories and imagery that I heard and saw repeatedly across the state and across industries. Those overlapping narratives provide the thematic structure for the chapters that follow. Collectively, they tell a bigger American story of pioneers and immigrants whose courage in the face of dangerous but glorious labor built the nation, whose fidelity to cultural tradition left a rich legacy ripe for reclaiming, and whose sacrifice gave us our modern world.

"ALMOST A NATION"
The History of Industrial Heritage in Pennsylvania

To tell the story of Pennsylvania's industries would be to parallel the history of the marvelous development of the modern world. "Industrial Pennsylvania" is so indelibly stamped in the brain of the human race that it stands out as a "trade mark" among the century's greatest achievements. It was built on a foundation of iron and steel, coal and timber, agriculture and stock-raising, and has risen to a superstructure of supreme heights, unfolding in the mind a vista of boundless possibilities.

—*Pennsylvania Highways* brochure, 1930

From the dawn of middle-class American tourism, its promotional language has been full of hyperbole, and Pennsylvania sightseeing literature has been no exception. Within the state's borders one could experience the full range of American life, proclaimed this and other early travel guides, which had titles such as "All in Pennsylvania" and "Pennsylvania Has Everything."[1] "Pennsylvania Presents Them All!" began one 1940 guidebook, which promised, "Rugged mountains or peaceful valleys . . . streamlined industry or historic shrines. . . . There is a world of interest within an easy drive of wherever you are in Pennsylvania."[2]

Industrialization was part of this glorious mix. The "heavy industries"—notably coal, steel, and railroading—were celebrated as part of the state's public identity while they were at their peak. At the same time, there were the first glimmers of nostalgia for other industries, notably oil and lumber, whose peak had passed. The ways in which all of these industries were described in early tourism literature would set the stage for the industrial heritage projects of the late twentieth and early twenty-first centuries.

"Industrial Titan" or "Sylvan Paradise"? Early Tensions in the Tourism Mix

The origins of Pennsylvania industrial tourism—while not yet industrial *heritage* tourism—date to the 1870s and lie in the charming town of Mauch Chunk, an early resort because of its industrial wealth (gained through the anthracite coal-mining and railroad industries) and its location in the Pocono Mountains, close to New York and Philadelphia. There, tourists could take a thrilling, high-speed ride on the Gravity Railroad, along the steep tracks on which coal cars had descended from Summit Hill into the Lehigh Valley (prior to the building of a tunnel, which freed the tracks for tourists). This adventure's appeal was moral as well as novel, writes John Sears. "Mauch Chunk confirmed the values of many Americans in the nineteenth century—the faith in progress, the pride in America's growing power and wealth—and reconciled the underlying contradictions between their fascination with technology and their love of grand and picturesque scenery."[3] A ride on the switchback presumably engendered the sentimental pastoralism that a number of scholars date to the late nineteenth century—a time when, for affluent Americans, a trip through nature was not an arduous journey but an escape from urban industrial reality.[4]

By the early twentieth century, tourism was taking shape as a modern industry that catered not just to the upper classes but also to the middle and, to a limited extent, working classes. Tour packagers, hotels, railroads, chambers of commerce, and, increasingly, highway associations and motoring clubs urged these travelers to "see America first." The new tourism combined commercial enterprise with Progressive-era ideas about the value of fresh air and self-improvement through education, and it coincided with growing public and academic interest in preserving American historical sites.

Toward the latter end, the Pennsylvania Historical Commission was established in 1915. Its first report contained this statement: "History, like charity, should begin at home. It should not end there. There are many people who have visited the historic localities of Europe, but have never been to more interesting localities at their very doors. . . . The young people, and the older people, of this State should see and 'know Pennsylvania first.'" Referring to the role of the state in the French and Indian War, the American Revolution, and the Civil War, this report acknowledged industrialization but characterized it as a *distraction* from understandings of the state's great past:

Cut out of American history what these events stand for, and the part played in them by Pennsylvania, and one loses the real plot of the entire drama of American history. Pennsylvania historians have been too modest, or too much fascinated by the mere glitter of the wonderful industrial development of the State, to give just credit to the tremendous moral force which the State and its people have exercised in the development of the American Nation. We must call attention to the facts in our history. We must make known these facts by monuments and markers, as well as by books and essays.

An appendix to this document listed "Sites Suggested to be Marked." Of the 114 sites proposed, only five were industrial history sites, and their inclusion was justified with references to the American Revolution—for instance, "The old charcoal furnace and cannon foundry at Cornwall (1742), used during the Revolutionary War to furnish government supplies. . . . "The old tunnel of the Union Canal (cir. 1796) . . . reputed to be the first tunnel in the United States, the canal in which General Washington was interested as the connecting gateway between the Susquehanna River and Lake Erie on the one side and the Schuylkill River and the Atlantic Ocean on the other. . . . "Mary Ann Furnace, owned by George Ross, the Signer."[5]

A year later, the commission acquired Old Economy Village, the intact site of a religious community that had established textile mills, a sawmill, a flour mill, and other industries north of Pittsburgh in the early nineteenth century. It opened to the public in 1921, "ahead of Williamsburg by five years," a historical account notes.[6] While this certainly was a site of industrial history, its buildings are colonial style, and its grounds emphasize gardens—in this, the state's first historical venture, a story of industry long past was told in a lovely setting. Yet this property overlooks the Ohio River, lined at the time by roaring steel mills.[7]

Early tourism promoters were not quite sure how to address the state's very visible industrialization within their tributes to its beauty and its history. A 1919 travel book offering eight routes for tourists to take by car or train through Pennsylvania, including the Lincoln Highway (Route 30) and the National Road (Route 40), made no reference to steelmaking, even though these roads run just under Johnstown and Pittsburgh. The author did note that some of the best views could be seen from railroads that functioned mainly as "coal carriers, with little provision being made for passenger traffic; yet they lead through some of the most delightful sections of the state."[8] (This scenic aspect of short-line coal railroads would turn them into the present-day tourist trains discussed in chapter 2.) On a 1925 map of Pennsylvania pinpointing 122 "main points of historic interest," only three were industrial sites: the Cornwall Iron Mines, the Pioneer Furnace in Pottsville ("the first used to smelt iron with anthracite coal"), and Honesdale, "location of first railroad in America on which a locomotive was run."[9]

That same year, the State Publicity Bureau published an automobile tour booklet whose foreword indicated the tension between the state's pride in its industrial dominance and its desire to attract tourism. This statement would be repeated, in similar terms, in Pennsylvania tourism materials throughout the rest of the twentieth century: "The Keystone State enjoys a world-wide reputation as an 'Industrial Titan.' Of this her citizens are justly proud, but her brilliant record in the Nation's history and the compelling lure of her great out-of-doors merit a greater degree of attention than has hitherto been accorded." A photograph of a steel mill operating at night (captioned "Pittsburgh's roaring steel furnaces at night cast lurid reflection in the sky—fascinating and spectacular") was followed by nature scenes titled "A Sylvan Paradise." In the end, industrial pride won out. "Industrial Titan" was the title of a two-page spread containing thirty-six small photographs of various industrial sites, quantifying the state's coal output, listing twenty-six product categories in which the state either led national production or had the largest production plants, and declaring, "Pennsylvania leads every other state in capital and horsepower engaged in manufacture, producing one-eighth of all manufacture in America."[10]

In 1926, the year of the nation's sesquicentennial, the tourism industry sought to convince visitors attending the main celebration in Philadelphia to explore other parts of the state as well, taking driving routes that were promoted by name: the Lincoln Highway, the Lackawanna Trail, the William Penn Highway, the Lakes to Sea Highway, the Roosevelt Highway, the National Pike, the Baltimore Pike.[11] One tourism publication that year included among its "Points of Interest in Pennsylvania" sections titled "The Oil and Gas Country" and "Coal Mines"; of the latter, it said, "In the hard coal regions the huge banks of culm, the coal breakers, the deep shafts, are all very interesting."[12] Another booklet contained an advertisement for a coal-mine tour in Scranton.[13]

Yet there were already some public hints that coal mining was becoming a subject of nostalgia as well as pride. George Korson, then a reporter for the *Pottsville Republican,* started collecting folk songs of Pennsylvania coal miners, publishing *Songs and Ballads of the Anthracite Miner* in 1927 (as well as a second collection, *Coal Dust on the Fiddle,* sixteen years later).[14] Twenty miles away in

Hegins, a new event called the Hegins Pigeon Shoot began in 1934 as part of that town's "homecoming" days—an event suggesting that "the heyday of the region, based on a coal and agricultural economy, had already passed, and . . . that many young people were leaving the area for better opportunities in the cities," writes Simon Bronner. He adds, "A pigeon shooting contest . . . drew on memories of a better day for the region" and "encapsulated the pioneer cultural heritage of the region symbolized by hunting and shooting."[15]

Reclaiming the "Wilderness Trail": Nature and Folk Symbolism During the Great Depression

The Pennsylvania Historical Commission also focused on a pioneer story, though one with less bloodshed. In another article about driving routes published during the sesquicentennial year, the commission's chairman, Henry Shoemaker, gushed, "One can go about, and about, and again about, always over new roads, and seeing new sights, receiving fresh and more vivid historical impressions, for such is the endless kaleidoscope of wonder and charm that has been and is always PENNSYLVANIA."[16] Shoemaker, who later became the official state folklorist, was determined to recover and promote a distinctly preindustrial vision. "Shoemaker's campaign for conservation of folklore, history, and nature advanced America as a unified nation based on the principles of its founding in the wilderness," writes Bronner. In books and newspaper articles, Shoemaker told stories "imbued with a romantic regionalism that expressed the glory of the frontier and its common, hardy folk."[17]

David Glassberg explains that, during this period, "popular history in America . . . maintained a vision of the place as the hero," with an emphasis on "folk symbolism" meant to act as "a bulwark against a standardized national culture."[18] When Henry Shoemaker did write about workers, he situated them within an idyllic place from the past. He organized "Raftsman Reunions," according to Bronner, who quotes from newspaper coverage of one such event in 1929: "The rhythm and beat of old time tunes in the thin but rollicking strains of the accordion, just as rivermen in lumber camps stamped and swayed to them 40 years ago, tales of heroism and hairbreadth escapes 'on the river' and the enthusiastic reunion of the survivors of those heroic days, marked the annual gathering of the lumbermen and raftsmen."[19]

This salute to woodsmen came at a time when their work had greatly diminished, following more than half a century of what Joseph Speakman calls "the reckless clearing of Pennsylvania's forests."[20] Throughout the nineteenth century, the iron industry, which used great quantities of wood to make the charcoal that fueled its furnaces, and then the rapidly growing lumber industry itself stripped vast stretches of northern Pennsylvania bare. "Formerly our woodlands were so vast and the out-of-doors so boundless that we gave little attention to them," explained a booklet published by the Pennsylvania Department of Forests and Waters in 1925. "With the rapid progress of forest devastation and the equally rapid increase of population we have been brought face to face with a serious situation that affects the physical, mental, social, and moral life of all the citizens." As this passage suggests, the impetus for reforestation was not just a matter of environmental concern during an era of increasing urbanization and its attendant problems of poor sanitation, overcrowding, crime, and a presumably growing assortment of "vices." In the lingering rhetoric of the Progressive era, this publication called for a "proper handling of the State Forests for wise recreational use" and declared, "It is as imperative to see that our citizens have a proper place to play as it is that they have good working conditions. . . . There is no better place for tired bodies, weary minds, and depressed souls than a sylvan retreat with a gala garment of green. There one finds quiet and rest. There the heart is lightened, the mind eased, the vitality restored. The out of doors lifts us up and casts away our burdens."[21]

Another state booklet for motorists, published in 1926, closed with a similar sentiment, claiming: "The spirit of the woods makes us happier and stronger. It points the way to a happier and healthier life. It lifts us upward and onward."[22] A decade later, the Pennsylvania Forestry Association marked its fiftieth anniversary with a special issue of its magazine, *Forest Leaves,* that praised the "inspirational values" and "silent, restful beauty" of the forests "unspoiled" by modernity, and the author vowed that they should stay that way: "Let us have good auto roads to get us to the edge of the woods; but, when we get there let us abandon our cars, shut out the honk of the horn and the smell of the gas, and follow the wilderness trail on foot or horse."[23]

This was a new experience rather than an old one. Previously it was unlikely, as well as difficult, for an ordinary person to spend a weekend "following the wilderness trail." But at the turn of the century, the state had purchased more than one hundred thousand acres of former forestland with a plan to revive them as sites for leisure rather than future industry.[24] Between 1899 and 1946, more than seventy million new trees were planted in these areas, many of which became Pennsylvania State Forests.[25] This reforestation is credited in part to Pennsylvanian Gifford Pinchot, who as head of the new National Forest Service during the century's first decade spearheaded forestry programs nationwide, and it was taken up in earnest during the 1930s by the Civilian Conservation Corps. Called "Roosevelt's Tree Army," conservation corps workers planted trees, erected forest-fire lookout towers, and built the roads, bridges, dams, lakes, and cabins that would transform these lands into outdoor recreation and vacation destinations.[26]

Other New Deal agencies, notably the Works Progress Administration (WPA) and the Farm Security Administration (FSA), funded projects that added to public knowledge of the cultural meaning of Pennsylvania regions. Some of this work made reference to the state's industries. Hundreds of the nearly three thousand images taken in Pennsylvania by FSA photographers depicted steelmaking and coal-mining workers and towns; one of the best known is Walker Evans's image of a cemetery cross on a hill above the smokestacks of the Bethlehem Steel plant.[27] The WPA funded artists to create murals in post offices across the country, and those in Pennsylvania included scenes of coal mining, steelmaking, lumbering, cement making, glassmaking, slate mining, textile mills, locative repair yards, and agriculture.[28] In both art and photography, however, these New Deal projects emphasized the worker—the ordinary man—over the work, not contradicting but complementing the era's folkloric imagery.

Another WPA program, the Federal Writers' Project, created guidebooks for every state. Their *Guide to the Keystone State* was meant to boost local pride as well as appeal to potential visitors. In its foreword, State Historian S. K. Stevens hailed the volume as "a contribution to better citizenship through making Pennsylvanians conscious of their traditions and backgrounds. In these troubled times such a work may well aid in the preservation of those fundamental values so essential to the maintenance of our democracy." Following this was a preface that called the state's residents "the descendants of the first pioneers, together with those of later immigrants."[29]

Only through the lens of immigration—a story of "the people"—was industry seen favorably in this 1940 book. Calling Pennsylvania "America's great and original melting pot," writers credited "the mining and steel districts" with drawing "immigrants from virtually every country of Europe . . . inevitably bringing with them much that is distinctive of their homelands to add rich chords to the State's great social symphony." The book also noted that "the hardihood of the Pennsylvania miner" had "brought into existence one of the most powerful labor unions in the country—the United Mine Workers of America." Its descriptions of industry itself, however, were unflattering. Pittsburgh was described as "packed with smoke-grimed buildings," and in Scranton coal mining had "blackened the beautiful Lackawanna, scarred the mountain sides, made artificial hills of unsightly coal refuse, and undermined the city itself." The guide urged readers to think of Pennsylvania not as "an industrial commonwealth, with belching blast furnaces" and a "congested anthracite district," but as a land of "fertile farm lands, with the quiet rural homesteads of Quaker and Pennsylvania Dutch."[30]

Some FSA photography promoted the latter view, constructing imagery of a kind of long-ago rural life that later would become the lynchpin of Pennsylvania tourism. Steven D. Reschly and Katherine Jellison attribute the early tourism marketing of the Amish to photography commissioned by both the Farm Security Administration and the Federal Writers' Project, aided by what was then called the Vacation and Travel Development Bureau of the state's commerce department.[31]

Privately funded museums celebrating preindustrial life also emerged during the peak period of industrialization. During the opening decades of the twentieth century, the wealthy and eccentric Henry Chapman Mercer had become convinced of the value of collecting artifacts from pre- (and early) industrial eras. Mercer's own factory in Doylestown made decorative tiles (which today still line the floor of the State Capitol Building in Harrisburg) not far from Philadelphia's massive industrial landscape. In 1916, he opened a museum in a seven-story, concrete tower filled with some forty thousand objects representing blacksmithing, cigar-making, cider presses, milling, butter- and cheesemaking, glassblowing, and basket- , barrel- , and broom-making; to these he added emblematic pioneer objects, including a Conestoga wagon, a whaling boat, and the reconstructed classroom of a one-room schoolhouse.[32]

Born just after the Civil War, brothers George and Henry Landis were troubled by the changes that both industrialization and eastern European immigration were bringing to Pennsylvania, and they set out to collect and preserve the rural, Protestant "Pennsylvania German culture that was beginning to fade." In the 1920s they opened a museum to showcase their collection of preindustrial tools and Pennsylvania German artifacts, and after their death, the Landis Valley Museum became a state-run museum about farm life.[33] The establishment of this open-air museum coincided with the beginnings of tourism promotion of the surrounding "Amish Country," with language such as this: "Here is a happy valley which has not retrogressed from simpler times; where you'll find some of the Nation's most productive farms, where the loudest sounds are those of birds, a man calling to his plow horse, the laughter of barefooted children wading in a brook, and the steady clack of an old-fashioned hand loom where a woman is weaving."[34]

In adjacent Berks County, a preindustrial story was being told at Hopewell Furnace, where some four hundred Civilian Conservation Corps workers were reconstructing an iron-making village that once had supplied weapons and ammunition for the Revolutionary War. Its early promotional materials promised a heritage story "not of a single historical event, but rather of a broad sweep of American growth and productive effort . . . an American Saga."[35] Here, pastoral ideals were incorporated into an increasingly patriotic rhetoric in American public culture, one that would help reconcile the contradictions of industry and nature. Speaking today about the creation of Hopewell Village as a national historic site, Superintendent Edie Shean-Hammond observes that it reveals as much about the 1930s and '40s as it does about the colonial era: "This is a product of the Great Depression, a product of hope, that industry and nature can live in harmony, that the American dream can work."[36]

Promoting the "Path of Glory": Cold War Industrial Boosterism and Highway Tourism

The declaration that "industry and nature can live in harmony" is most convincingly made in a rural site from which industry has departed (a phenomenon that is the theme of chapter 3). During the middle decades of the twentieth century, it was not possible to believe such a message in Pennsylvania's cities where massive industrial production was spurred first by World War II and then by Cold War–era competition for global technological and economic dominance. The strong postwar economy that this production created led to a rise in leisure time and tourism, especially family tourism, across the United States. A 1947 research report issued by The Pennsylvania State College Bureau of Business Research predicted enormous growth of the travel industry in the postwar period.[37] In Pennsylvania, the language of that tourism industry began to tout, rather than camouflage, the state's industrial might.

World War II enabled this thematic shift in the focus of state pride to occur fairly smoothly. A 1941 promotional booklet, issued to the public by the Lehigh Coal and Navigation Company on its 150th anniversary, noted that coal had been discovered nearby when George Washington was president and that the company's own history "falls little short of spanning the history of the United States. The nation has been transformed from a small agricultural community to a vast and mighty industrial nation and a great world power." Just as elsewhere in the United States, the publication vowed, "The present national emergency has aroused the patriotic feelings of the people. They and the Old Company stand ready to meet any demand that may be made upon them in the cause of national defense."[38] At the thirty-sixth annual National Conference of Governors, held in 1944 in Hershey, attendees received a book providing a "pictorial record of Pennsylvania's greatness" and expressing this effusive wish: "We cannot hope to induce all Americans to visit the 17,000 manufacturing plants of our State, but if we could take the folk of our Country at midnight to the hills above Pittsburgh, where the broad reaches of its twin rivers are illuminated to the brightness of day by the soaring sparks of Bessemers and the glow of incandescent blooms dumped endlessly from our open hearths, they would see better than words can ever tell the dynamic energy of our people and the fervor of their devotion to the great cause of National victory."[39]

After the war, tourism publications were filled with boasting claims about and photographs of coal breakers, steel mills, and railroad yards. Introducing one 1946 publication, Governor Edward Martin referred to "the romance of our industry" and declared the state to be a place "where 'the best is yet to be.'"[40] Another state tourism booklet included a color, nighttime photograph of flames shooting out of the top of a Pittsburgh steel mill, their brightness glancing off the river below, with the caption, "Reflections of the mighty steel industry tell story of Pennsylvania's industrial supremacy."[41] In a third publication, a section titled "The Pocono Mountains Paradise" noted that "the gigantic mines and collieries of another part of this area, which produces all of America's true anthracite, also provide interest for the visitor." Its section on western Pennsylvania explained, "Besides the roar and flame of the 'Valley of Steel' that stretches out from Pittsburgh, and the giant industrial plants that send products to every corner of the globe, you'll find a surprisingly busy waterfront. Pittsburgh's annual shipping tonnage matches that of the Panama Canal in normal years."[42]

The Pennsylvania Historical and Museum Commission (PHMC), as the Pennsylvania Historical Commission was renamed in 1945, published tourism guides to its museums at Drake Well, birthplace of the oil industry in Titusville, and at the Cornwall Iron Furnace near Lebanon.[43] In 1946 the PHMC began a state marker program, placing more than one thousand of them during its first five years. These site-specific signs provided information about canal and railroad systems and about the iron, oil, and coal industries, although only one or two mentioned lumber, and steel was noted only tangentially in a single marker titled "Pittsburgh."[44] The marker system coincided with the postwar boom in highway travel, and drivers could request guides by mail or pick them up at tollbooths on the Pennsylvania Turnpike.[45]

This era also saw a rise in civic boosterism and promotion of local commerce, resulting in rhetoric that praised contemporary and historic achievements for a local rather than tourist audience. Beginning in 1946 the state Department of Commerce created "Pennsylvania Week," described as "a toast to the Commonwealth's glorious past and to her bright future," a series of local school programs, newspaper articles, radio programming, and displays in stores, banks, hotels, museums, and churches. "Let everyone from Bank President to Boy Scout play some part," exhorted the manual.[46] Promotional literature explained the two "prongs" of its mission in one of the earliest explicit statements about postindustrial economic development: "One is to re-emphasize the greatness of the past and the achievements of the present, both in the State and in the community. The other is to *use* that knowledge as the starting point in developing the many opportunities for economic, cultural and recreational betterment." The 1948 brochure noted that certain industries such as coal mining were declining and that other industries, including tourism, had to be encouraged to grow in the state: "Like an individual, Pennsylvania must move forward or stagnate."[47] That year's event featured "industrial expositions and plant open houses," appearances by Miss Pennsylvania 1948 Ruth Douglas and actor Jimmy Stewart, and a four-day, statewide tour by business executives riding "a shiny new train—manufactured entirely in Pennsylvania."[48]

The following year, Governor Edward Martin went so far as to declare, in a promotional book, "Pennsylvania is America."[49] In 1949, marking ninety years since Edwin Drake struck oil in Titusville, a booklet issued by Esso gas stations (the name "Esso" came from the initials of their owner, Standard Oil) reflected on "the most turbulent era in history" and pondered ominously, "What lies ahead no one, of course, can foretell. As we enter the last decade of the first century since oil has been added to the list of known resources, the two great questions seem to be whether democracy or tyranny shall prevail, and whether man will make science his servant or allow it to become his master."[50] When the PHMC assessed its first five years in 1950, it justified its work in domestic language and with a Cold War rationale, emphasizing historic preservation as "the first duty of citizenship":

> The danger of being deprived of the cherished institutions that constitute the American way of life is very real and imminent. Understanding must rest upon a greater diffusion of popular knowledge about our history and

the historic roots of our development and progress. The best place to develop this knowledge of our history is at home. . . . A deeper love of our
country and appreciation of our heritage should rest upon the firm bed-
rock of love of state and community. This naturally translates itself into
love of country and understanding of all our national ideals and aspira-
tions as Americans.[51]

Such patriotic declarations blended with continuing hyperbole in travel promotion. A 1952 article in *Better Homes and Gardens* proclaimed, "Pennsylvania
is more than a name—it's almost a nation."[52] During that decade, the PHMC
used similar language when it launched a project called "Operation Heritage,"
a campaign to increase heritage tourism by linking its various properties: "The
Pennsylvania Trail of History is truly a path of glory marked by historical
monuments, museums, and markers which serve as a constant reminder of the
people and the events which shaped the destiny not only of Pennsylvania but
of the United States." It went on to propose "dramatic living museums," one of
which would "recreate . . . a frontier oil village of the 1860's" at Drake Well.[53]

Although that plan did not come to fruition, the celebration of Drake Well's
centennial in 1959 was a pageant of American industrial boosterism, small-
town pride, and Cold War rhetoric. Once again, Esso issued a publication, an
annotated driving map, promoting the site. One part of it, titled "1859–1959:
100 Years of Progress," noted the importance of asphalt, made in part from oil
products, declaring, "It will surface many miles of the new National System of
Interstate and Defense Highways. Our road builders are doing a magnificent
job on this system, and asphalt is helping them speed the program to provide
more miles of better highways for even greater progress."[54] The magazine of the
Gulf Oil company described the centennial day itself:

> The thousands of people who attended the celebration were treated to a
> live telecast, the "shooting" of a newly-drilled well, the sealing of a time
> capsule, the dedication of a commemorative postage stamp, addresses by
> prominent oil industry and government officials, band concerts, a barbe-
> cue, and—ending the day in the "blaze of glory"—a spectacular fireworks
> display. Early risers throughout the nation had a chance to witness a part
> of the festivities on television. NBC's "Today" TV show originated live
> from Drake Well Memorial Park on the morning of August 27. Dave Gar-
> roway, Jack Lescoulie, and Charles Van Doren were all on hand for the
> two-hour telecast.[55]

Other activities included an "exhibit of Oil Americana" at Titusville High School, the "arrival of wax figure of Colonel Drake by Helicopter," "barber shop quartet, harmonica and old-time fiddler contests," a "pageant-drama" titled "100 Years Ago" at a local theater, Youth Day featuring athletic contests, a Grand Parade of Oil with "floats depicting oil history" amid marching bands, a drum and bugle competition, and an Oil Centennial Ball "with the music of the Tommy Dorsey Orchestra" in the high school gymnasium.[56]

Celebrations of industrial might continued through the 1960s and into the 1970s. When the town of Oil City marked its own centennial in 1971, its ten-day celebration took a similar form and tone as the Titusville extravaganza, including a Young America (youth) Day, a Belles (women's) Day, an Industry Day when tours were given of area business including two oil refineries, the crowning of a Centennial Queen, the burying of a time capsule, a Centennial Square Dance, a Century of Progress Parade, and "The Story of Oil City," a theatrical event that was held on the high school football field and described as a "Mammoth Historical Spectacle," a "thrilling, fast moving theatrical production re-enacting the stirring history of the Oil City Area. . . . Cast of over 250 of your friends."[57]

Yet during the century's middle decades, public rhetoric about industry also was changing, as the anthracite coal industry began to shut down, as new concerns about the environmental impact of industry arose, and as urban decay spread and middle-class Americans fled to suburbs. In Philadelphia—once proudly touted as the "Workshop of the World"—the landscape was transformed forcibly. Charlene Mires recalls the public ceremony that began a demolition project enabling the creation of Independence Mall State Park in the 1950s: "By starting the demolition process with ceremony, the promoters of expanded parks around Independence Hall defined the destruction of the nineteenth-century urban landscape as an act of triumph. . . . When the nineteenth-century buildings were in place, the varying states of structural deterioration in the blocks near Independence Hall offered unmistakable evidence that the nation had changed considerably since 1776, not necessarily for the better. Without the nineteenth-century buildings, an illusion of eighteenth-century stability and continuity could be sustained." Downtown Philadelphia's makeover created "an architectural impression that the significant events of the nation's history occurred during the era of the American Revolution, a time defined by crisply maintained, stately buildings, ornamental plazas, and carefully tended lawns" rather than the warehouses that for a century had grown up around the building where the Declaration of Independence had been signed.[58]

"Discover the New Pennsylvania" invited the title of a 1964 guidebook in which Governor William Scranton bragged, "Our cities and towns are putting on new faces and scrubbing up the old." The same publication included "The Miracle of the Anthracite Area," an article celebrating Scranton's rebirth as a home to "industrial parks" through which a variety of smaller industries were replacing the coal industry. "Scranton is the first town in the world built on a single natural resource which has managed to outlive the vanishing of that resource," it claimed. "Now it has been followed by the other hard-coal towns, and a Commonwealth program based on their work is helping communities throughout the state do the same thing."[59]

Something less cheery was in fact going on in the anthracite coal region during the 1960s, as Thomas Dublin and Walter Licht have documented.[60] Even where mining already had ended, the landscape bore the industry's scars. One Philadelphia reporter's trip to the anthracite region in 1969 caused her to ask: "Good grief. Where am I? What happened here?" She described the landscape of strip-mining: "All around you is black, churned earth, cavernous holes in the ground, looming spoil piles . . . total desolation."[61]

Labor History as "Your Own Special Journey": The Personalization of a Postindustrial State

The U.S. bicentennial in 1976 was a transitional moment in public history and in public ideas about industrial heritage. Though this event was ostensibly about the nation, its celebration played out primarily on small-town stages, as John Bodnar has noted.[62] In Pennsylvania, many such observations simultaneously saluted America's industries and memorialized their loss or impending departure. The state's public identity as an industrial powerhouse was explained in both the present and past tenses, and it was increasingly personalized to appeal to the imagination of local residents as well as visitors.

For major manufacturers, this milestone was an opportunity to continue their midcentury bragging, taking credit not just for their own past but for American history itself. That summer the State Museum in Harrisburg hosted a traveling exhibition titled "Steel in the History of America," funded by Bethlehem Steel and "featuring nearly 500 photographs and drawings depicting historical events and persons who played key roles in the nation's history," a local newspaper explained. Its themes included "the discovery of America by

Europeans, the first iron casting made in this country, the Colonial period, the first pioneers and the Westward movement. . . . the Civil War, the development of Bessemer steel, the founding of the Bethlehem steel Corp. and World War I . . . the 1920s and 1930s, World War II, the postwar period, and steel today." On display "in communities in which the corporation has operations," this exhibit was meant to instill local worker pride as well as to garner admiration from the general public.[63]

Elsewhere, the language of the public industrial story was shifting, in some cases from progress to memorial and in other cases from corporate pride back to a more individualized and folkloric vision of work. Many towns observed the bicentennial by erecting monuments and memorials in their public parks to the historic achievements of townspeople. That year several worker memorials were dedicated in the anthracite coal region, from which major industry was, by then, largely gone. The language of their dedication connected local industry with national history by characterizing workers as patriots whose job was done (a theme of chapter 5).

Bicentennial activities also included tributes to long-ago industrial and transportation history. In Codorus State Park, the Daughters of the American Revolution (DAR) rededicated a marker (initially put there in the patriotic flurry of local history that took place just after World War II) on the site of Mary Ann Furnace, which had supplied cannonballs for George Washington's army.[64] In 1976, when the first annual National Road Festival was held in southwestern Pennsylvania, area residents donned buckskin and gingham and drove covered wagons across this route, already dotted with DAR projects (including roadside milestones, two restored 1830s toll houses, and a pioneer "Madonna of the Trail" statue).[65]

Amid such traditional patriotic gestures, much bicentennial tourism had a new, personal tone. "Come to Pennsylvania," invited one state tourism pamphlet. "You'll get to know America. And maybe you'll get to know yourself." Among the fifteen destinations it promoted were Pittsburgh, described as a "Renaissance City" that had been "reborn"; Hershey Chocolate, where a new attraction called Chocolate World recently had replaced the tour of the actual factory with a ride through a simulated production process and a large retail store; and the region that quickly was becoming one of the state's top tourism draws, "Pennsylvania Dutch Country."[66]

Public history sites and heritage tourism emerging during this era in Lancaster County interpreted a very real, continuing industry through a nostalgic prism. This new lens on agriculture revealed not only a distant past but also 1970s ideas about "basic" living and the land. A 1979 feature published in a Lancaster newspaper began with this scene:

> The young man in the patched linen work shirt reined in his team of horses, looked up from his hand plow and turned his gaze toward the source of distance traffic noise. Wiping perspiration from his brow with a rough-woven handkerchief, he spoke softly, . . . "Somewhere along the line, we lost contact with the self-sufficient lifestyle. We've become too dependent on non-renewable resources. The most satisfying part of my job is demonstrating how to be responsible for one's own needs, to be here to talk about it when people slow down enough to reflect on the basics of life." Steve Miller's job is that of farm interpreter at the Pennsylvania Farm Museum at Landis Valley. [67]

A tourism map described the surrounding area as a land of "well-kept farms with hex sign-decorated barns. And folk festivals that celebrate food, friends, and life as it used to be. . . . quiet, small towns such as Bird-in-Hand, Lititz, and Paradise, where faithfully restored colonial shops and villages show you what life was like in the good old days."[68]

Rural settings for heritage tourism helped counter the growing concern of tourism officials over "misperceptions," as a 1987 state task force report on tourism and travel complained, "that the state is heavily industrialized and 'run down'; that there are not tremendous natural and rural attributes; that some Pennsylvania tourist attractions are 'worn out'; that the major urban centers are polluted and dull. Advertising, public relations and promotional efforts must address these misperceptions and create a focused image for the state as a travel destination."[69] That goal posed a special challenge in light of the growing interest of localities in preserving their own industrial history. A 1989 newspaper article describing local tourism efforts to promote Scranton as a "nostalgic destination" was nevertheless proudly titled "Memories of Coal, Rail Eras Still Much Alive in Scranton."[70]

Some industrial heritage interpretation began to presume that that the actual industrial past was gone from memory and therefore could be reconstructed. A travel feature in the *New York Times* was titled "Two Pennsylvania Towns Recall Days When Coal Was King" but then explained that Eckley Miners Village offered visitors "a window on the lives of . . . immigrants" through which "visitors can relive that past."[71] Here, "recollection" was not individual memory but an imaginative process through which visitors could "relive" something both far beyond and long before their own lives. Regardless of the visitors' own class or occupation, this connection was to be made to the industry's workers, a common-man focus much in line with the longing for "the basics of life" in agricultural heritage interpretation. A 1989 state tourism guide celebrating industry (oil, coal, and railroads) and "ingenuity" (the Conestoga Wagon, first radio station, the Slinky) emphasized the contributions of ordinary people:

> With coal from the Earth and the railroads that carried it, towns like Scranton and Wilkes-Barre, Allentown and Altoona stoked the engine that drove America's industrial might. Pennsylvania cities like Pittsburgh and Johnstown—and the diversity of people who came there to work—helped us produce more steel and iron than any other state. . . . A trip through Pennsylvania will show you that history isn't made just by famous people in big cities, but by generations of hard-working people from every corner of the Commonwealth. . . . The traditions of America's past . . . maintain a flourishing heritage in the Pennsylvania of today. It's a long and proud history, one rich with the courage of patriots and the culture of immigrants from across the globe. We welcome you and your family to share it. And we invite you to start your own special journey here, in Pennsylvania.[72]

Here in this text is the fully formed language of modern industrial heritage tourism: the proud, celebratory tone of Cold War–era tourism (except for a change in tense, reassigning industry to the past); the situating of industrial history in smaller cities rather than the bigger cities where ongoing industry is still quite visible; the starring role of the common man as the country's backbone, aligned with the "patriot" in historical importance; an understanding of immigration as a story of "hard-working" people who were inexorably drawn to a special place; and general references to "culture," "tradition," and "heritage" that presumably we all (expressed as *you*) have inherited. The experience of industrial heritage tourism, then, is all of these things mixed together—but, mostly, it is "your own special journey."

In 1991 Scranton's Anthracite Heritage Museum held a "Family Heritage Day," featuring "the special ethnic heritage of Northeastern Pennsylvanians. Watch master artisans recreate crafts and music of past generations. Join a Civil War unit as it prepares for battle. Get tips on tracing your genealogy in special family history workshops. See your family history come alive." In addition to the genealogy workshops, activities included demonstrations of hat-making, quilting, and weaving; the Northeastern Pennsylvania Folklore Society performed; and Civil War reenactors demonstrated a "Drill and Firing of Weapons." None of these activities was specific to coal-mining history. Yet this event also was not tourism; it was a collective imagination of regional identity and assertion of its place in national identity.[73] Many historic sites began to regularly offer heritage events that, while showcasing their own specific themes, included a little something for everyone. In 1994 the Landis Valley Museum held a fair featuring not only agricultural demonstrations but also "a snake exhibit, magic show, . . . cow-chip bingo, pie-eating contests, cake walks, family sing-alongs, sack races, old-time board games, spelling bees and 1890s school lessons" as well as "a variety of Civil War-era people."[74]

It was within this cultural context, in which "heritage" was personalized and thematically very flexible, that much of today's public interpretations of industrial history were created. More than half of all markers about "Ethnicity/Immigration" and more than two-thirds of all markers about "Labor/Working People" were installed during the 1990s.[75] In 1990 the Pennsylvania Bureau of Travel Marketing, part of the Department of Commerce, offered a "Travel Package" of promotional materials highlighting industrial heritage sites across the state, including the industry-related PHMC sites, attractions around Scranton, and a collection of southwestern Pennsylvania sites that recently had been organized as "America's Industrial Heritage Project" (which, at the time, included tours of the still-operating Bethlehem Steel plant in Johnstown).[76] During the same year, the Pennsylvania Department of Conservation and Natural Resources (DCNR) began its Heritage Areas program to preserve the "legacy" of industrialization, noting, "The stories of the challenges and triumphs, trials and tribulations of the people and places instrumental in making America an industrial giant are a source of great pride to our citizenry."[77]

The emerging rhetoric of industrial heritage paralleled the evolution of the state's tourism (and license plate) motto during the closing decades of the twentieth century. During the 1970s Pennsylvania was "The Bicentennial State." In the early 1980s visitors were greeted with the conversational "You've Got a Friend in Pennsylvania." By that decade's end, the motto was far more national and grand: "America Starts Here" (a billboard announcement that came as a surprise to drivers passing through the tollbooths from New Jersey). Today its echo can be heard in the mission of the DCNR Heritage Areas program, which claims, "America's industrial heritage started here." That report dates "industry" to an era when the state was "both bread basket and iron forge to the colonies" and identifies "Industrial Heritage Themes" including iron and steel, coal, textile, machine and foundry, transportation, lumber, oil, and agriculture.[78]

Such a conceptualization leaves room for a broad range of interpretation, and its thematic flexibility is evident in the nature and promotion of the state's current twelve heritage areas. That ongoing enterprise, which also has offered new definitions of regional identity, has helped shape the current cultural geography of Pennsylvania tourism and public history—the subject of the following chapter.

"A JOURNEY THAT WILL INSPIRE"
Regions, Routes, and Rails

Since the beginning of time, the river has been a magnet—a natural force, drawing people to its banks: explorers, travelers, merchants, industrialists, and those just passing through. In modern times, the river still beckons: to adventure seekers, nature lovers, trailblazers, outdoor enthusiasts, and those "just passing through." The Delaware Lehigh National Heritage Corridor is more than a series of connecting waterways and rails—it connects you to more than you ever imagined. Come, take a journey that will inspire, invigorate, and invoke a deep appreciation of the past and a renewed vitality for the future. The river is calling.

—Delaware and Lehigh National Heritage Corridor booklet, 2007

The subject of this heritage text is the Delaware River, which runs along Pennsylvania's eastern border. Those "just passing through" its region today are, as the quotation marks suggest, addressed as leisure travelers rather than pioneers, industrialists, or merchants. Yet those earlier characters are the stars of the historical story told here and in similarly conceived areas. Whether designated as such by the state or federal government, heritage areas are the result of coalition building among museums, historical societies, tourism promoters, building developers, environmental groups, business owners, town and county governments, and sometimes other interests, all of whom hope to tell stories about the past in order to enhance their present-day surroundings.[1] Their interpretation is thus, often, thematically very mixed. The process of qualifying for heritage area status is complicated and lengthy, taking as long as fifteen years.[2]

In deindustrialized regions, this phenomenon is "based on the idea 'Let's use these old industries to bring economic rejuvenation to this area—we can make an industry of it,'" explains Mark Platts, president of the Susquehanna Gateway

Heritage Area, which combines York and Lancaster Counties. Heritage areas—or regions, corridors, or routes—map a leisure experience for travelers while reminding local residents what is on their doorsteps. "Our website is a network of 200 sites and attractions, and it helps you create an itinerary, and then it will print out a map showing driving directions and where everything is," says Platts.[3] The processes of naming and publicizing a heritage area also reframe local identity for the people who live in it, create a rhetorical bridge between regional character and nationality, and often situate the industrial past within grand, even mythological, ideas about landscape.

From "Ingenuity" to "Bounty": Telling a "Connective" Story About the Land

In 1988, the Delaware and Lehigh National Heritage Corridor became the first region in Pennsylvania to gain national heritage area status. It began with a plan to build a trail along the Lehigh Canal. Since then it has come to emphasize industrial history, with a narrative that features Bethlehem Steel as well as anthracite coal miners and with the tagline "Where America Was Built."[4] Executive Director Allen Sachse explains its evolution:

> The DL story started out as being about the DL canal and then it was the coal fields. We realized that if we were going to tell the story, it should be about the whole industrial system that was built to move and market coal. . . . Even the majority of people who live in the area don't clearly understand the connections between the industries. Here was a region of the country where mining took place, which spurred community growth, and it was all transported to industries in the Lehigh Valley and in Philadelphia and New York and worldwide.[5]

This heritage region produced a regional touring guide called *The Stone Coal Way* ("stone coal" was a term for anthracite coal, which is hard) containing photographs and historic information about local towns and their industrial pasts.[6] Some of these are called "Market Towns," while others, along the Delaware River and closer to Philadelphia, are "Landmark Towns." The idea is to encourage "connectivity" through a regional sense of heritage, says Sachse; otherwise, "many of those areas would not be looking at their neighbors. . . . Most interpretive sites focus on their site but not as part of the landscape, and historically they haven't looked at the larger scale."[7] The Delaware and Lehigh Heritage Corridor has state as well as national heritage area status. The state heritage area program was launched in 1990 with the explicit aim to "tell the story of Pennsylvania's industrial history," explains Brenda Barrett, the Director of the Bureau of Recreation and Conservation in the state's Department of Conservation and Natural Resources (DCNR), which administers the program.[8]

The first region to receive state heritage area status was the Lackawanna Heritage Valley Authority, based in Scranton, a natural site for industrial heritage interpretation. It, too, focuses on heritage themes of coal mining and transportation—in its case, railroading—as well as iron-making and the "support industries" of silk and lacemaking. Among its projects are a forty-mile rail trail, a greenway along the Lackawanna River, and an effort to reclaim remaining acid-mine outfalls in this valley. Such environmental projects are under way in physical surroundings that reveal little of the past that produced the need for them. Chief Operating Officer Dan Perry says, "Right now one of the greatest challenges in interpreting coal is how little visible industry remains. In 1900 there were at least 100 coal breakers in this area. Today there are none at all."[9]

In areas with an even less evident past, "industrial history" has been broadly defined, especially as heritage areas have grown in number, today totaling twelve across the state. "Now we would say that we're focusing on important Pennsylvania stories," says Barrett. By joining together thematically, a group of towns or areas can brand themselves in a way that provides a public declaration of the meaning of the land—and the meaning of the past in the present. While that branding is unquestionably meant to boost area businesses, it is directed as much toward residents as it is toward outsiders. The required theme of industrial history, therefore, effectively invokes local memory even in visibly deindustrialized areas. "This is different from tourism," Barrett says, echoing Sachse's point. "It's about local identity."[10]

Not all of the state heritage areas are geographically compact, and so "local identity" sometimes is defined in terms of some condition that is shared by people living in disparate places. Perhaps the best example is the Schuylkill River Heritage Area (both a national and a state heritage area), which links the metropolis of Philadelphia with the former coal-mining town of Pottsville, one hundred miles away. As the group's title suggests, these otherwise very different places are connected by a river. Like the Delaware and Lehigh National Heritage Corridor, the Schuylkill River Heritage Area grew out of a trail-building project called the Schuylkill River Greenway Association, and the waterway for which it is named (and its parallel canal) once carried coal out of the mountains and down to the big city and beyond. On the wall of its visitor center, in a restored building of the former Phoenixville Iron Foundry, is a map titled "The Schuylkill River: Scenes from its Industrial Past," with photos or illustrations showing other now-gone industries: a coal breaker in Tamaqua, a silk mill and a steel mill in Pottsville, woolen mills in Conshohocken and Valley Forge, a coal yard in Philadelphia, and even the Lubin Silent Film Studio in Betzwood. "Tourism is only one element" of what the group is trying to do, explains Executive Director Kurt Zwikl. "We're as much about restoring a local community's pride."[11]

Due to its unusual composition (this heritage area includes Valley Forge National Park and Independence Hall as well as a major former coal region), the Schuylkill River Heritage Area is able to present a very ambitious national narrative through local lenses. "We tell the story of three revolutions: the American Revolution, the Industrial Revolution, and the environmental revolution," says Zwikl.[12] "The Schuylkill River Heritage Area is the birthplace of the movements that shaped the nation, fueled its growth, and reclaimed its future," the group's website proclaims. "America's past and its future start here."[13]

Similarly broad themes—including "ingenuity," "freedom," and "bounty"—structure the promotional language of the Susquehanna Gateway Heritage Area, previously called the Lancaster-York Heritage Region. This is an area with much general American history (the American Revolution, the Civil War, the Underground Railroad), much industrial heritage (iron-making, transportation, agriculture), much tourism (related to the Amish)—and yet no geographic reason for being thought of as a "region" except for the fact that the two counties comprising it are on either side of the Susquehanna River. So that waterway has become its thematic focus, with projects including a Susquehanna River Water Trail of twenty-one interpretive panels (waysides), a guide and website promoting local food markets, and the construction of riverside wildlife and recreational facilities.[14] The river is central to the story visitors hear and see in a film shown at visitor centers in the two counties. As the film's aerial views reveal this region's lush farmland and picturesque small towns, its narration calls the river "the thread that ties this region together, in some areas shallow and placid, in others, deep and strong."[15]

The upper branch of the Susquehanna River snakes through the Endless Mountains Heritage Region in the state's north, which gained heritage area status in 1998 because of its agriculture and lumber history. In truth, explains Executive Director Phil Swank, "Our theme is quite broad. It's really anything related to the earth." Today, "the driving force is stewardship of the river," he

says, explaining that recent projects have included a river-trail greenway project, a "sojourn" for canoers and kayakers, and maps for boaters and campers
that include information about area wildlife, such as the locations of eagles'
nests—all meant "to help communities feel connected to the river."[16] Surely few
people would suspect that such offerings are part of an industrial heritage program. In fact, this group's vision statement echoes the anti-industrial rhetoric of
Progressive Era tourism literature, reading, in part, "The Endless Mountains region is a haven for the spirit. It is a place where we enjoy peace, quiet, and safety,
and the thousand stars of the night sky. We live in harmony with our natural
and cultural heritage, enjoying a beautiful countryside and healthy settlements
that reflect our history."[17]

Artisan Trails and the "Path of Progress": Driving into History

Also running across the state's northern tier, spanning eleven counties, is the
longest and newest state heritage area, the PA Route 6 Heritage Corridor. Previously just a scenic drive across the mountains, U.S. Highway 6 was reconceived
in 2005 as an industrial history route, thanks to its passage through three other
heritage areas home to, collectively, railroading, iron, coal, agriculture, lumber,
and oil history. The road connects these thematically different areas not just to
one another but also to national mythology. Driving across Route 6 is a chance
for travelers, according to a tourism brochure, to "retrace the historic trails
traveled by pioneers," an experience "like seeing the progression of America
itself" in areas "settled by patriots and forged by immigrants."[18] Somewhat tau-
tologically, the main industrial theme that garnered heritage area status for this
region is transportation. That theme includes the road's own history as "one of
the first transcontinental highways," notes Executive Director Terri Dennison,
who adds, "We connect coal to farming to lumber to oil. The story of Route 6 is
really the story of the growth of a nation as the nation moved west. It's the story
of how these industries helped build America."[19]

Such language has fueled Pennsylvania tourism for nearly a century. In
1920, two new organizations, the American Automobile Association and the
National Highways Association, heralded the new Lincoln Highway in historic
terms. Calling the road "a channel for the 'westward movement,'" this early
driving guide noted that cities along its route, including Philadelphia, Gettysburg, and Pittsburgh, were sites "of transcendent importance, in the sense
that they have influenced all subsequent history on this continent." The author

wrote, "If the principal events of American history, east of the Ohio River, were to be reproduced as a system of moving pictures, localities along the Lincoln Highway in Pennsylvania would . . . form a background for them."[20] One year later, in October 1921, the road was filled by the Good Roads Jubilee Pageant, described as "the world's largest parade," involving thirty thousand people and six thousand cars, including "George Washington's coach from Valley Forge."

Travelers today learn those facts from a wayside along the road near Chambersburg, next to the ruins of Caledonia Iron Furnace, a site within what is now the Lincoln Highway Heritage Corridor.[21] Executive Director Olga Herbert describes a "200-mile Lincoln Highway Roadside Museum" that includes "12 amazing murals, 65 interpretive waysides, and 23 reproduction vintage gasoline pumps painted by professional artists."[22] This thoroughfare is dotted by modern metal signs showing the face of Lincoln, a large "L," and the road's name, augmenting the few surviving stone mile markers that were erected by Boy Scouts in 1928. In the town of New Oxford, another wayside reveals that the heritage group's work is in fact a reinscription of the name on the road, explaining that "by the end of the 1920s, the federal highway system changed names of early routes to a system of standardized numbering . . . and the Lincoln Highway was renamed U.S. Route 30."[23] That change never really took hold for this particular road, and proof is visible just above this historic tablet: an ordinary intersection signpost, clearly not new, reading "Lincolnway." Abraham Lincoln remains closely connected to the identity of this road, which passes through Gettysburg, has inspired several travel books, and remains a popular tourist driving route across the state.[24]

Like the other heritage area directors, however, Herbert is as much interested in its meaning for locals as for tourists. "Local residents did the research for the text that is on the 65 interpretive exhibits and provided some of the images," she notes. "Local historical societies verified the context of each exhibit for accuracy. A local committee worked with me in selecting the content of each mural. . . . When they have visitors they are sure to 'show off' the mural in their town, or to take them to see some of the pumps."[25]

Cultural geographer John Brinckerhoff Jackson preferred the word "way" to "road" in describing the social meanings of such routes. "*Way* signifies not only path, but also direction and by extension, intent and manner," he wrote. "We 'have our way,' we 'do things in a new way,' we follow 'a way of life.' The phrase 'ways and means' suggests that the word can indicate resources at our disposal for attaining an end."[26] When driving routes are conceived as journeys through (or into) the past, they become "ways" of culture and commerce as well as concourse. Several state highways are now promoted as—to use another cultural geographic word—"trails" to and through a cultural experience of "traditions" as well as history. The PHMC organizes its twenty-four sites into four "Trails of History," one of which is an "Industrial Heritage Trail."[27] Both Route 6 and the Lincoln Highway are marketed in state tourism as "artisan trails," the latter offering travelers goods that are "handmade along the Highway," such as blown glass and paper-cutting art, created by "outstanding old world artisans."[28] Running north and south in the center of the state is a highway labeled "Route 15 by Way of the Arts" because of the artists' studios and antique stores along this highway that passes through Lewisburg and Williamsport.[29] The area between York and Philadelphia is touted in regional tourism as "The Pennsylvania Arts Experience," with this explanation: "For centuries, artists and artisans have been attracted by the area's sublime landscape—the broad Susquehanna, dramatic river bluffs, gentle hills, and fertile farmland—as well as the distinctive architecture of its historic cities and towns. . . . Today, renowned artists continue the region's artistic tradition working in unique studios tucked away in renovated barns or restored spaces. . . . Overnight visitors can retire to a quaint BB or to the Lancaster Arts Hotel, a sophisticated hostelry housed in a renovated tobacco warehouse."[30]

All of these appeals are ostensibly about industry, or "craftsmanship," that "recaptures" a sense of both the local and national past. In such a conceptualization, travel (or, for locals, weekend activity) is less about destination than about atmosphere, and different types of culture—as well as different time periods of history—blend together into an experience. Route 45, which runs for about one hundred miles between Lewisburg and State College, is marketed as "an artisan paradise" (one advertising campaign claims that "Art Thrives on 45"); it also is called "The Purple Heart Highway" since it leads to the Pennsylvania Military Museum in Boalsburg and "the nearby monument commemorating the first Memorial Day celebration," notes the author of a regional magazine travel article. The author concludes, "PA-45 and the towns it passes through offer an automobile travel experience that feels more like 1957 than 2007."[31] Here, tourism itself is offered as a nostalgic experience, creating the same feeling you might have had when you rode down this highway in the back seat, rather than at the wheel.

Other driving routes promise a connection to a much more distant past. One example is a U.S. Route 40, known as the "National Road," a portion of which cuts through the southwestern corner of Pennsylvania. As a main route used by settlers during the decades after the American Revolution, it "carried the dreamers and their dreams from the Eastern seaboard to the expanding western frontier," notes a promotional brochure.[32] Today it is watched over by an enormous stone woman, bonneted and fierce-faced, clutching her small children as she gazes toward the future. Called the "Madonna of the Trail," she is one of twelve such statues placed along this interstate highway in 1928 by the Daughters of the American Revolution to honor "the pioneer mothers of covered wagon days."[33]

Every May for the past thirty-five years, area residents have reenacted her journey during the "National Road Festival." Wearing buckskin coats and coonskin caps, they drive Conestoga wagons along this "Road That Built the Nation," passing two 1830s toll houses (also restored by the DAR) and Fort Necessity, a French and Indian War battlefield run by the National Park Service, where the National Road Heritage Corridor has a visitor center. "A lot of people find their way here because they love the history of it," says Executive Director Donna Holdorf.[34] Yet while the festival seems to tell a historically specific story, its events range "from a period fashion show or a watermelon-seed-spitting contest to a Native American festival or old-fashioned baseball games," considerably broadening the definition of pioneers.[35] While pioneer reenactment ostensibly tells a preindustrial story, in recent years it has served as an occasion to promote several industrial heritage sites in the area as well.

The Petersburg Toll House, just inside the Maryland border on the National Road, is described as being "in essentially the same condition as when the great mass of immigration passed by—headed for a possible better life with their possessions."[36] At the repurposed Flatiron Building in Brownsville, also on the National Road, a museum expands on this idea. Its "Making of America" exhibit tells "the story of the two significant eras of Brownsville's history . . . the Westward Expansion, also known as the National Road Era (1809–1859) and the Industrial Era, also known as the Coal, Coke, and Railroad Era (circa 1890–mid 1950s)," a period that brought another great wave of newcomers to this area.[37] Museum staff members have done oral history interviews with residents who remember that second pioneer experience. "People talked about how they felt when they got here, what they thought," says Brownsville Area Revitalization Corporation Director Norma Ryan, who believes that in both eras the region's challenges drew a certain kind of traveler. "It's the hard-working who came here," she says. "Why are the Steelers so tough? This is a tough area. They worked hard and are tough people."[38]

The conflation of pioneering and immigration connects the rural, antebellum period of this region's past with the rapid rise of heavy industry. Understood as a single period of time, the preindustrial and industrial eras become a story of progress—first, literal progress westward, then cultural progress through the assimilation of immigrations, and finally economic progress in those residents' upward mobility amid the booming local industries of coke, railroading, iron, and steel. In fact, the National Road intersects with the "Path of Progress," a marked driving route connecting historic sites around Johnstown and Altoona and initially funded as part of a federal redevelopment initiative called "America's Industrial Heritage Project." A reporter for the *Washington Post* enthusiastically endorsed the idea when it was unveiled in 1995: "The Path is a new and estimable tourist creation that links a variety of historical sites celebrating America's pioneer industries, among them coal mining, iron making, farming, road building and railroading. . . . Though the Path is historic by design, it could just as well be designated a scenic route. . . . I drove beside tumbling streams; skirted tidy farm yards, where cattle, sheep, horses and even buffalo grazed; and meandered through dense woodlands."[39]

This prose echoes early promotion of the Lincoln Highway, celebrating American achievement within a nostalgic tribute to nature and landscape. Although federal funding for this tourism project is now largely gone, some five hundred miles of roadway are still punctuated by signs. Driving through this sparsely populated region, you come to feel that you are almost always on the Path of Progress, even if you're not quite sure what it is.

No More the "Road of Anthracite": Railroad Nostalgia and Tourist Trains

The most visited site along the Path of Progress is Horseshoe Curve, a national historic site that is key to the story of westward movement and to transportation and industrial history. Until the middle of the nineteenth century, the National Road was one main route for the "dreamers" attempting to go west by traveling around Pennsylvania's formidable Allegheny Mountains; another option was the Portage Railroad, on which, from 1834 to 1854, canal boats were pulled by a steam engine up one side of the mountains and then let down the other side. But in 1854 a new passageway opened, thanks to clever engineering and difficult labor that laid a winding, gradually inclined path of train tracks through the Alleghenies. Its central feature was a stretch called Horseshoe Curve, just above Altoona. Today, Amtrak and freight trains still run through it, passing a historic site overseen by the National Park Service. I remember going there as a little girl with my Uncle Sam, who was a conductor on the Pennsylvania Railroad, and marveling as we were encircled by seemingly endless chains of freight cars. The feeling is much the same more than forty years later, except that the trains come along less frequently.

Railroad history is the most appealing kind of industrial history in Pennsylvania, combining the adventure of travel with what Diane Barthel calls "the romance of power."[40] Its "rolling stock"—great Baldwin steam locomotives, elegant Pullman sleeping and dining cars, charming cabooses—make the Railroad Museum of Pennsylvania the most popular of all the state-run historical sites and one of the top railroad museums in the country.[41] Staff members at railroad historic sites and much promotional literature describe the trains, especially steam engines, as if they were alive, "living and breathing, right here in front of me," as one museum director said to me.[42] The physical size and restored interiors of these trains invite historical imagination of a past world that is simultaneously romantic and heroic.

Such imagination is encouraged at the state's other two major railroad museums as well. An exhibit titled "American Heroes" in Altoona's Railroaders Memorial Museum laments a modern world in which "physical bravery is less in demand" and declares of past railroaders, "These men were the prototypes of manhood in America."[43] Steamtown, a national historic site in Scranton visited by as many as one hundred thousand people a year, shows a short film called *Steel and Steam* that tells a more wistful story: Dressed for the early 1900s, a little boy in a western Pennsylvania farming community watches the train come through his small town and sees livestock and farm machinery loaded on to it. He vows to have a career on the railroad, and does, becoming a conductor; the industry gives him economic as well as geographic mobility. His story is told from his own memory, as he recalls his childhood wonder, the beauty and power of the trains, and a misty, ghostlike woman in white.[44]

That woman, though not named in the film, is Phoebe Snow, and she is an interesting study in both the nostalgia and the amnesia of railroad heritage today. She began life in 1901 as an illustrated character who appeared in advertisements for the Lackawanna Railroad, alongside rhyming verses whose rhythm was meant to mimic that of the train.[45] Phoebe promised the cleanliness of travel on this particular railroad, which used cleaner-burning anthracite (rather than dirtier bituminous coal) to fuel its steam engines.[46] Today her face and verses appear on posters and postcards sold in the gift shops of coal-mining and railroad museums, some of which also recall a streamlined passenger train later named for her; the sides of some freight train cars still in operation bear the legend "The Route of Phoebe Snow"; and visitors to the Poconos (one of the destinations that rhymed with her name) might notice a gravel incline off a state highway signposted as Phoebe Snow Road.[47] But few people could tell you who she once was. Her function as a symbol of *industry*—and, in particular, of the vital link between coal and railroading on "the Road of Anthracite"—has been lost to nostalgia. Indeed, very much railroad heritage today is unmoored from its historical context.[48]

It is important for me to pause here and acknowledge that the specifics of railroad history are *very* well retained by the many railroad preservation societies throughout Pennsylvania (and elsewhere). They have painstakingly restored train cars, cabooses, lookout towers, and passenger stations, and some have established small museums that remember railroading's industrial past as well as local industries such as coal, iron, agriculture, and textiles. Among these are the Harris Switch Tower in Harrisburg, the New Freedom Station in New Freedom, and the Lake Shore Railway Museum in the Erie-area town of North East, where staffers, most of them volunteers, spent hours showing and explaining to me what they had restored and collected.[49] This kind of devotion is singular among the heritage phenomena I encountered in researching this book. These railroading fans are not, however, the general public, and the general public is relatively unlikely to encounter them (and their sites) unless they actively seek them out, as I did.

More people are likely to encounter architectural references to railroading's past. All across the state, former train stations have been saved, renovated, and converted into libraries, tourist information centers, art galleries, offices, community museums, and private homes.[50] The magnificent 1908 Lackawanna train station in Scranton is now a Radisson hotel with a fine restaurant in its arched, glass-ceilinged waiting room. The former headquarters of the Pittsburgh and Lake Erie Railroad is now "Station Square," a dining and retail complex in Pittsburgh. Former passenger stations from Tarentum to Tamaqua have been turned into restaurants, the latter serving fare with names such as the King Coal Filet, Flagman's Stuffed Flounder, and Conductors Choice.[51] At the Front Street Station, a "railroad eatery" in the central Pennsylvania town of Northumberland, sandwiches are named the Club Car, the Caboose, the Chesapeake Express, the New York Limited, and the Rail Splitter. As its menu promises diners, "The Front Street Station dining experience will take you back to the days of waiting to board the Pittsburgh Flyer of the Washington Express, relaxing and watching the steamboats on the river . . . and feeling the steamy blasts of the locomotives trackside. We welcome you to our memories."[52] Collectively these spaces conjure the romance of travel more than the history of industry.

So do the many tourist trains and trolleys that take vacationers into "yes-teryear" during the summertime.[53] Except for a handful of excursions, they do not run far—usually a few miles in each direction—and these short strings of restored cars tend to end up where they started. Most of them run on narrow-gauge tracks on which cars once hauled freight, especially lumber and coal, from remote areas to main lines. Most of them, in other words, were never passenger routes. Yet it is the presumed romance of long-ago passenger travel that they invoke. Writing of this same tourism (and industrial history) phe-nomenon in Wales, J. Geraint Jenkins notes this irony—"the main purpose . . . was to bring the products out of the mountains"—while explaining their ap-peal: "Nothing evokes more nostalgia than the age of steam. Steam engines, traveling at a snail-like pace through the countryside for a mile or two, drawing passenger-laden coaches, provide a romantic picture of 'the good old days.'"[54]

Most of the beautifully designed and restored passenger cars on Pennsyl-vania's tourist railroads were manufactured between the 1910s and the 1930s, and some of them are pulled by great, pulsing Baldwin Locomotives made in Philadelphia before the First World War. These dates are usually provided in the narration. Beyond that information, these trips' presentation of the past is a hazy one. The "vintage" advertisements displayed above the windows in the cars' interiors promote products ranging from washing powders of the 1880s to automobiles of the 1950s. Promotional materials and onboard guides use the same kinds of general phrasing, such as "all aboard for a journey into the past" or "leave your cares behind as you journey into history."[55] Most rides include music, sometimes recorded and sometimes performed by costumed "conduc-tors," with songs ranging from Civil War tunes to "The City of New Orleans."

Very many of these routes pass through beautiful land that belies its own history. The Tioga Central Railroad travels along the shores of Lake Hammond, through the mountains north of Wellsboro, reforested after the decline of the lumber industry. The Lehigh Gorge Scenic Railway runs parallel to a river pre-viously filled with coal dust but now full of kayakers and whitewater rafters. Farmland is the setting for the Wanamaker, Kempton, and Southern Railroad, which runs between Kempton and Wanamaker in a region once dotted with coal-mine breakers and textile mills.[56] The feeling these train rides invoke is serenity amid nature, rather than memory of industry.

When tourism and excursion trains do embrace historic themes, they have little to do with industry. On certain weekends, reenactors restage Civil War battles on fields beside both the Oil Creek and Titusville Railroad (an-other beautiful route) and the Middletown and Hummelstown Railroad. "The soldiers are right outside the train," the guide on the latter promised during my summertime ride. "Join us for this live history lesson."[57] For its thirtieth anniversary in 2005, the Railroad Museum of Pennsylvania and the Strasburg Railroad (which is directly across the street) jointly held a "Trains and Troops" weekend with this description: "Greet our guys and gals in uniform, experience many splendid railroad and military archival displays, enjoy patriotic music and learn the significant role railroads played time and again in the defense of our nation. . . . Ride the troop trains on the Strasburg Rail Road with living history reenactors."[58]

The usual narration on the Strasburg Railroad focuses on the Lancaster County farmland through which it travels, a "journey . . . through gently rolling hills and across immaculate farms in the heart of the Pennsylvania Amish country . . . where daily life is a reflection of a more humble time."[59] The live narrator marvels that the Amish live much as they did when they arrived in America two centuries ago. Out the window, riders can see backyard clotheslines strung with dark trousers and dresses, farmers guiding horse-drawn plows, and families driving buggies down Route 741—which, the narrator notes, began in 1711 as the Conestoga Trail, a route traveled by the famous wagons made right here in Lancaster County. This long-ago vision is described on a ride called the "Road to Paradise." Ironically, its only unscenic moment occurs *in* the town of Paradise, when the little train stops (to switch its engine and reverse direction) alongside the distinctly industrial tracks used by operating freight and passenger trains.[60]

Even that modern-day railroad employs the same bucolic imagery. A recent Amtrak brochure describes the scenery along the route of "The Pennsylvanian," which passes along those main tracks through Paradise on its journey from New York to Pittsburgh: "time appears to stand still as you take in wooden bridges, horse-drawn buggies, and the simple traditional clothing of the farmers as they work their patchwork quilts of land dotted with rustic barns."[61] Relatively few people travel by train on any regular basis anymore, and, in our driving society, train travel is thought of as something from the past. The state Department of Transportation offers a car license plate featuring a picture of a speeding Baldwin locomotive under the injunction "Preserve Our Heritage."[62] Generally oblivious to the many freight trains still crossing the landscape around us, we seek instead a ride into the past aboard "authentically" reconstructed fantasy vehicles. Those railroads are a form of nostalgic entertainment disconnected from industry; our enjoyment on board comes from letting go of history rather than holding onto it.

In a way, then, tourist railroads provide an ironic counterweight to the goals of heritage areas and driving routes, which attempt to reinscribe departed industry onto the landscape, to relink towns and regions to one another and to the specifics of their past. Tourist railroads loosen that link, generalizing history through a scenic and pleasant journey to nowhere in particular. The hazy nostalgia they invoke—their definition of the past as an unspecific moment of "yesteryear"—is not limited to railroad heritage. It is common as well in memory of rural life, a "simpler" time of determined pioneers taming the wilderness and yeoman farmers living on the land. Their story is told in the following chapter.

PENN-BRAD HISTORICAL
OIL WELL
PARK

SPONSORED BY
BRADFORD DISTRICT PENNA.
OIL PRODUCERS ASSOCIATION
AND
DESK AND DERRICK
CLUB OF BRADFORD

"OVERCOMIN' WHAT NATURE PUT IN YOUR WAY"
Rural Heritage and Pioneer Mythology

Every year, visitors journey to the Lancaster-York Heritage Region for a glimpse at our neat rows of corn and rolling green fields. The scenes remind them of times when life was simple and deals were sealed with a handshake. Look closely and awaken your sense to the gifts of the land. . . . Reach back and touch a time when people were on a first-name basis with the farmer. Embrace the soothing sounds of nature while visiting one of our rustic wineries, mills, or farm museums where the hustle and bustle of city life seems a million miles away.

—"Growing Traditions: Lancaster-York Heritage Region Discovery Guide"

These bucolic stereotypes appear in a regional tourism brochure that actually has a rather progressive purpose: to promote the purchasing of locally, and in many cases organically, produced food. Its appeal to the twenty-first-century tourist is simultaneously modern and nostalgic, drawing on long-held ideas about the cultural meanings of farming. Writing about "the American quest for a secular paradise," Wilbur Zelinsky has explained, "The self-sufficient single-family farm tilled by virtuous Jeffersonian yeomen has been the physical embodiment of this ideal. And a persistent reverence for this rural Eden and the only slightly less idyllic small town still lingers in the folk memory."[1] Zelinsky wrote this nearly four decades ago. Today, such an ideal not only still lingers but permeates far more than "the folk memory"—it dominates modern tourism imagery of Pennsylvania.

In Pennsylvania, there is a special kind of "folk" at the heart of this phenomenon: the Amish, who are not unique to this state but are showcased here as nowhere else. Amish tourism has received considerable attention from scholars and critics, and so I will not dwell on it. It is enough to say that for more than half a century,[2] Lancaster County has aggressively marketed its most reticent citizens, inviting tourists to "travel beyond the main roads. . . . and wave as you pass the occasional buggy, children on scooters heading to school, or the farmer leading his team of mules."[3] A writer for *Washington Monthly* magazine explained the appeal of this community: "They are, in the popular imagination, a peaceful people who spend their time going to church and making preserves, while the rest of us lost our spiritual way, got jobs moving paper around, became obsessed with buying stuff, and watched our families fall apart. . . . The Amish are the guardians of old-fashioned American values."[4] Here is the main message conveyed at farming heritage sites and living-history re-creations of rural life, including but extending beyond "Amish Country." As David Walbert notes, "Popular portrayals of the Amish have associated not only the Amish way of life but by extension rurality itself with innocence and, therefore, with the past." Moreover, he contends, "The equation of rurality with the past would seem to absolve Americans of the responsibility to take rural people and rural communities seriously."[5] In this nostalgic vision, farming itself seems "old-fashioned," more of a memory than a modern reality.

In fact, agriculture is Pennsylvania's number-one industry, and it literally surrounds the Amish tourism industry. "If Lancaster County were a state, it would be thirty-seventh in agriculture," says Steve Miller, once director at Landis Valley, the state-run farming museum near Lancaster, and now director of the PHMC Bureau of Historic Sites and Museums.[6] Yet farming here appears less industrial than it does in the Midwest. Pennsylvania agriculture is tourist friendly, partly because more than 80 percent of the state's farms are small "family farms" and partly because dairy is by far the largest type of agricultural production.[7] The more than half a million cows to whom Pennsylvania is home are prominently featured in what has come to be called agritourism.[8] "Grabbing hold of an udder is as tough as grasping for a wet bar of soap," a writer for the state tourism magazine *Pennsylvania Pursuits* reported after she and her family spent a weekend away from their "daily grind of city lights and noise" in order to "work" on a Mennonite-owned family farm in the Lancaster County town of Gordonville.[9] A newspaper article describing stays at one dairy farm listed chores that "range from grooming a calf to feeding goats to quilting a hot pad or digging potatoes and making (and eating) homemade ice cream," explaining that visitors "can help milk the cows at 7:30 A.M.," and adding, "for late risers, there's a similar afternoon option."[10]

Other farm owners provide "agritainment," the word used in promotion of the Cherry Crest Farm near Strasburg, an "adventure farm" where children may ride tractors, make their way through a five-acre corn maze, and watch baby chicks hatch.[11] An advertisement for another such site in Mercersburg featuring farm tours and a corn maze promises "Family Adventures" and "Country Fun" and invites visitors to "make a moo friend."[12] On the Kreider Farms Tour in Manheim, visitors are driven through the "cow palace" containing twelve hundred dairy cows and then are taken to see the "milking merry-go-round," whose fifty stalls rotate continuously as cows step on and off to be milked by machine; the cows then walk past a wall-mounted, rotating pad that gives them a massage. The fact that the cows know to go and do this, on their own, three times a day, personalizes (or cowizes) large-scale dairy farming.[13]

So does the Pennsylvania State Farm Show, where animals guided by teenagers compete for prizes every January in Harrisburg. While this agricultural trade show has been open to the general public since its start in 1917, only during the past decade has it been actively promoted as an entertaining outing for nonfarmers. Touted as the "largest indoor agricultural event in America," the weeklong event now attracts as many as half a million people.[14] Its events still include livestock judging, farming equipment demonstrations, a rodeo, sewing and baking contests, and scholarship presentations by the Future Farmers of America. But today the show also features wine tasting, Irish dancing, a cook-off in which restaurant chefs compete to be named "Best Chef of Pennsylvania," a "Celebrity Cow Milking Contest" (cows are milked by television reporters and state politicians), a singing competition called "Farm Show's Got Talent," and "tractor dancing," in which square-dancing maneuvers are done by people driving tractors. (Really. It's actually fantastic.)

These performances are covered daily on the front page of the Harrisburg *Patriot-News* and broadcast live on the Pennsylvania Cable Network. Such media attention has expanded public interest in the Farm Show and has given wide exposure to some longtime components of the show, such as the "sheep-to-shawl" competition in which teams of shearers, spinners, and weavers effect that transition in less than three hours. This takes place in an arena unfailingly packed with spectators and is followed by a televised shawl auction; in 2009, the winning shawl drew a record-breaking $3,400 bid. Media also feature the baby-chick slide and chick-hatching station, the sixty-year-old merry-go-round, and the butter sculpture, which in 2009 depicted a military family carved from nine hundred pounds of butter.[15]

Public celebrations of agriculture are enacted on a smaller scale at the three dozen town and county fairs that take place across Pennsylvania each summer, "offering visitors a glimpse of the nation's agrarian traditions, the aroma of everything from pigs to popcorn and the taste of everything from homemade ice cream to funnel cakes."[16] Such events celebrate and draw public attention to a current industry that in recent years has been, like other industries, undergoing economic crisis. At the same time, like the factory tours discussed in chapter 6, they portray work as fun, and they emphasize the aspects of this industry, such as regional foods and hand-weaving, that represent "craft traditions" from the past. The Farm Show's "Family Living" displays feature demonstrations of wool-weaving, wood-carving, blacksmithing, wheat-weaving, broom-making, and soap-making. While these activities are likely to be more interesting to the general public than swine judging and irrigation technology, collectively they paint an antimodern picture of farming. In this picture, present-day farmers seem to be people from the past—whom, occasionally, we can "reach back and touch."

"The Extraordinary Ordinary Past": Reenacting Rural Life

Public interpretation that endeavors to tell agricultural *history,* therefore, must reach even farther back in time; indeed, most of it skips over the past two centuries. An organization called the Rural History Confederation is actually a coalition of colonial house museums in the counties surrounding Philadelphia.[17] Other sites are antebellum "farmsteads" and historic mills, which dot the landscape and seem to be a favorite kind of preservation project. All across the state—from Haines Mill near Allentown to McConnell's Mill State Park near the Ohio border—visitors can, on special weekends or during the summer, watch while restored machinery groans into action as it did more than 150 or 200 years ago. At "The Mill at Anselma" in Chester Springs, built in 1747, I bought mixes for cornbread and muffins, wrapped in gingham cloth tied with twine. The more than 250-year-old Burnt Cabins Grist Mill, now the hub of a campground in south-central Pennsylvania, sells its flour, pancake mix, and muffin mix at the state Farm Show.[18] In Latrobe, the Saint Vincent Monastery still operates a gristmill, selling its flour in a store "with a viewing area where visitors may see Benedictine monks grind grain, much as they have done since 1854"; an adjacent museum displays old farming as well as milling equipment.[19]

Colonial and antebellum rural heritage sites provide an attractive backdrop for "living history" demonstrations. The Quiet Valley Living Historical Farm, near Stroudsburg, recalls the daily activities of the Depper family, who lived there for more than a century beginning in the 1760s. "Barefoot women spin yarn and cook over an open fire, and children play hoop and ball in the field beside the barn," a regional magazine profile explains. "Guests leaving the farm at the end of the day often feel as if they've walked through a time warp and back into a bustling world of cell phones and supermarkets."[20] This site is in fact quite close to the bustling world, near the New Jersey border, and its website promises that "150 years ago is just a short drive from anywhere!"[21] More remotely located are the Bradford County Farm Museum, along state's northern border in the town of Troy, and the Meadowcroft Museum of Rural Life, in the southwest near the Ohio border. Both are outdoor museums made up of nineteenth-century buildings moved there from surrounding areas, including (in both cases) a one-room schoolhouse, a two-story log cabin, a church, and a barn containing old carriages, wagons, and farming equipment. Like the more commercial Bedford Village, discussed below, these rural tourism sites are arranged and promoted in a way that invites visitors to, literally if temporarily, "step back in time" and walk through the past.[22]

The same invitation is issued, albeit with more complex historical context, by the two farming museums run by the PHMC. One, the Somerset Historical Center in western Pennsylvania, interprets "two and half centuries of rural life in southwestern Pennsylvania," beginning with Native Americans and continuing through the "influx of new residents" as first the National Road, then canals, and then railroads brought immigrants to work in the region's heavy industries of coal and steel. More recently, according to a film shown in the museum, have come two periods of "exodus" of young people away from farm life, first to work in industrial cities during the nineteenth century and then in pursuit of urban and suburban upward mobility after World War II.[23] Throughout the year, this museum offers classes in skills such as coopering (barrel-making) for maple sugar collection and making a "hand-crafted wooden hay rake."[24] Yet it also devotes significant attention to modern agriculture, acknowledging farming as an industry and expressing a sense of ongoing industrial loss similar to that found in small-town museums about the oil, coal, and steel industries.

In eastern Pennsylvania, the Landis Valley Museum tells a distinctly preindustrial story. The orientation film highlights its garden, which grows herbs, vegetables, and flowers from heirloom seeds (sold in the gift shop), and celebrates "craft traditions," including harness making, blacksmithing, cooperage, and textile weaving. Those crafts, along with tobacco making, candle- and soap-making, wood-carving, leatherworking, and broom- and pottery-making, are interpreted in the complex's sixteen buildings, which include a schoolhouse, a hotel, a tavern, and several houses and barns.[25] Throughout the year, the museum holds classes in Pennsylvania German arts and crafts such as *Scherenschnitte* (a paper-cutting art) and *Fraktur* (a drawing and printing technique once used for birth and marriage records), as well as blacksmithing, woodworking, tinsmithing, rug-hooking, and quilting.[26]

Most of these are, of course, forms of industry in the sense that they are acts of material production and that people once had an economic need for them and earned livings doing them. As PHMC's Steve Miller explains, "We try to be myth-busters . . . to show that life is difficult for people at all times. We try not to paint a romantic picture of the past, even if people come here seeking it."[27] Here and at several other historic sites, interpretation is explicit in conveying that these "craft traditions" once were the everyday, unavoidable tasks of common people. Yet that is their special value in the modern world. They conjure "the extraordinary ordinary past," in the words of a magazine article about the annual Mifflinburg Buggy Festival, which features "such craftworks as spinning, weaving, chair caning, and buggy painting" as well as carriage rides.[28] In the same region of central Pennsylvania, Lewisburg's annual Rural Heritage Days include demonstrations of threshing, stone carving, cow-milking, bean-shelling, cornhusk-mat making, and "clothes washing the Colonial way," while children compete in sack races and hoop rolling.[29] The thousands of people drawn every Labor Day weekend to the annual show of the Williams Grove Historical Steam Engine Association learn how hay is baled and wooden shingles are made as they wind their way through fields of antique tractors.[30]

The geographic locations of these events (Mifflinburg was, in fact, a coach-making center, just as Lancaster was home to *Fraktur* artists) and the participation of local people, as both reenactors of and witnesses to the past, create a sense of authenticity, even as these are openly acknowledged to be staged events. Moreover, "authenticity" is defined as its opposite: a step outside of our real lives into a staged past in which we presumably wish for "simple, physical labor" and admire—or join in with—those who perform it. Pennsylvania Deputy Secretary of Tourism J. Mickey Rowley calls this "an interesting paradox. In our urbanized world, where many of us are cut off from simple physical labor, we sometimes hunger for a sense of connection to that more natural way of life. And we seek it out on our vacations. We stay at farms, where we can see basic work being done and even, in some cases, help. We volunteer to go out and help with tapping maple trees and gathering sap to make maple syrup. We take courses in chainsaw carving or learn to make a quilt."[31]

Diane Barthel writes that such "nostalgic leisure experiences offer a liminal 'time-out' from contemporary society, a chance to play in the past. . . . Liminality is also found in the sense of play and escape they provide, as costumed characters enact the past, inviting visitors to imagine themselves part of the historical drama."[32] In this fantasy, labor is not an act but a lifestyle—"rural life" constructed holistically—and people of the past are not strangers but "our ancestors." The time in which they live is "a mythical utopia situated somewhere in the past . . . curiously located out of time," adds Barthel.[33]

Such interpretation obscures historical realities, as many heritage critics contend. John Corner and Sylvia Harvey claim that "the depiction of rural labour often elides specific social and economic relations altogether. Skilled craftsmen . . . are often appropriated for heritage by having their imposed toil displaced and naturalized as displays of individual resourcefulness and quiet fortitude."[34] Women's lives also are "appropriated for heritage," writes Patricia West, who notes that demonstrations of hearth-cooking and wool-spinning not only "convert a dull and backbreaking chore to an entertaining experience" but also "foster the elimination or distortion of servant labor."[35] Ian McKay is even more critical of "reassuring images of the Folk . . . celebrated . . . for their Good and Simple Lives"; in fact, he argues, "To rewrite the history of subaltern classes and groups in ways that ostensibly pay them homage, all the while draining their history of specificity, is one subtle and effective method of preserving their inferior position."[36]

Glamorized performances of work, rural utopian settings, and temporal vagueness have "the effect of installing the visitor in a twilight zone between the rural past and the fully industrialized present," argues Tony Bennett.[37] Ironically, that visitor's sense of connection to the past is enhanced by its open-ended conceptualization, its reenactment by seemingly timeless characters, and these sites' lack of didactic interpretation. David Lowenthal calls them "anti-museums. . . . not repositories of high culture . . . not places where children have to be kept in order, where things must not be touched."[38] Instead, as an advertisement for the Landis Valley Museum promises, "You touch the history. The history touches you."[39] Lowenthal further notes that rural history museums portray people of the past "as perpetually industrious—even their leisure was strenuous folk dancing. Blacksmithing, sheep shearing, wool dyeing, spinning, grain flailing, winnowing, weaving, shingle making, sawmilling, cooperage, cabinetmaking, log squaring are ceaseless at most pioneer villages."[40]

This performative remembrance process is at its height during the fall festivals held at the farm museums discussed above. Every September, the Troy

Farm Museum holds a Pennsylvania Heritage Festival and the Somerset Historical Center holds Mountain Craft Days; every October, the Quiet Valley Living Historic Farm has a Harvest Festival and the Landis Valley Museum celebrates Harvest Days. At all of these events, costumed volunteers reenact "craft traditions." During Quiet Valley's Harvest Days, reenactors invite visitors into buildings where, remaining in character, they explain what they just happen to be doing, whether it is making bread, stirring soup, or sewing clothing. I was especially struck by the willingness of teens to buy into these activities: boys dressed like Huckleberry Finn chopped wood, and one costumed girl, about age fifteen, gave me a long explanation, in tones suggesting that she was speaking in the nineteenth century, of how apple butter is made. Some rural life reenactors assume the identities of particular characters, becoming the town blacksmith or the preacher. At the Meadowcroft Museum of Rural Life in far-western Pennsylvania, a schoolteacher dressed for 1892 handed us *McGuffey's Readers* and showed us, on the blackboard, some lessons we would have learned in that year.[41] Other reenactors are just "residents." And, as I noticed from one site to the next, the great majority of them are dressed for the 1860s.

Indeed, "the past" is most often demonstrated in Pennsylvania as the Civil War, which was represented at the majority of the industrial heritage festivals I attended, no matter what industry was being remembered. Attending the Oil 150 celebration in Titusville (the sesquicentennial of the discovery of oil there in 1859) were reenactors representing the Bucktail Regiment, lumberjacks and oilmen who fought in the Civil War wearing deer tails on their caps.[42] At the opposite end of the state, Union soldiers play a role in annual festivals held at two iron furnace sites located just five miles apart in southeastern Pennsylvania. At Hopewell Furnace, reenactors demonstrate their weapons as costumed women weave wheat, bake pies in outdoor ovens, spin wool, and teach children how to roll wooden hoops.[43] During the Hay Creek Festival, which draws thousands of people to the former site of Joanna Furnace, Civil War reenactors camp alongside not only costumed women making kettle-cooked soups and "Schnitz und Knepp (apples and ham)" but also a Revolutionary fife and drum corps.[44]

The American Revolution was in fact fought near Joanna Furnace, which made ammunition for that war. The Civil War was not fought there, though, and—with the notable exception of Gettysburg and a few surrounding towns close to the Mason–Dixon Line for two weeks in 1863—it was not fought anywhere in Pennsylvania.[45] Yet Civil War cannons are fired every summer at Eckley Miners Village in the state's northeast and at the Pennsylvania Heritage

Festival in Troy, just fifteen miles away from New York State border.[46] Battle is a recurring weekend activity at southwestern Pennsylvania's Old Bedford Village, which hosts reenactments of the French and Indian War, a "Napoleonic Reenactment," and a weekend in June when more than a thousand spectators come to watch some eight hundred reenactors, with horses and cannons, refight the War Between the States.[47]

"This Army of Pioneers": Boom Rats and Woodhicks Settling the Wilderness

Outdoor rural life museums are likely sites for military reenactment for several reasons. They have open land. Their living history demonstrators tend to be volunteers and therefore history enthusiasts. The battle reenactors also presumably visit the museum, bolstering attendance figures at these remotely located attractions. Even so, it is odd that so much fake blood is shed at sites purporting to re-create a "simpler time" of trusted neighbors.

During the weekdays, Old Bedford Village is not a battleground but a collection of mid-eighteenth- to late nineteenth-century houses that have been moved to this site to create a "village" where crafts are reenacted as they are at other rural life museums.[48] Its website's language is clear about the interpretive premise: "The early American artisan formed the industrial base of our great nation. Nearly every pioneer brought a particular skill to the new world. At Old Bedford Village, these skills are demonstrated in an authentic fashion. . . . They include coopering, quilting, candle making, blacksmithing, weaving and spinning, and basket making."[49]

Battle and blacksmithing make sense together when they are understood as elements of a nation-building story, a tale of pioneers who did whatever was necessary to forge their way through the wilderness and found a democracy. Portraying past Pennsylvanians as brave settlers elevates them to heroic status at the same time that it invites us to imagine ourselves in their shoes, to dream that, if challenged, we too could face dangers and overcome obstacles as they did. "Pioneer museums," writes Lowenthal, "seek to purvey an American founding myth" emphasizing "presumed pioneer traits—self-reliance, manliness, faith in progress." Such sites "stress pioneers' unfailing zest for life and confidence in achievement. The accompanying hardship and loneliness were endurable through faith that efforts would be rewarded, that nature tamed would be bountiful, that setbacks were temporary, and that the way on lay ever upward. And the pioneers' fortunes became those of all America, made strong and prosperous by their cumulative efforts."[50]

This is a good summary of the progress narrative common to historic interpretation of the iron, oil, and lumber industries, at sites across the northern tier of Pennsylvania, and throughout its state forests and state parks. In this heritage story, adventurous and determined men—ambitious on behalf of the country as well as their own fortunes—braved the wilderness to harvest its riches and build (or fuel) America. Within that story is a recurring subplot of nature's recuperative and restorative powers. Even though these industries still exist here (indeed, Pennsylvania is the nation's leading producer of hardwood lumber[51]), they are publicly remembered as long gone, so far in the past that their origin stories are told as legends.

Williamsport once was home to more sawmills than anywhere else in the country and was the site of the "Susquehanna Boom," where logs were corralled in the river before being sent downstream to the Chesapeake Bay. Now it is better known as the home of the Little League World Series every August, but lumber history is told in its tourism, including rides on the *Hiawatha Paddlewheeler*. As this riverboat travels along a beautiful, sparkling, tree-lined stretch of the west branch of the Susquehanna River, passengers hear a recorded narration that explains the term "boom rats" (men who scrambled across the boom to secure or release logs) and "woodhicks" (lumberjacks) and that lists the various jobs in the logging industry, such as choppers, fellers, sawyers, scalers, and haulers. Over fiddle music, the narration then tells the story of a folkloric character—"the Susquehanna Valley's own Paul Bunyan"—named Cherry Tree Joe McCreary, a man from Muncy so strong that he was able to break up a seven-mile logjam by himself.[52]

Here and elsewhere in the north of Pennsylvania, the lives and work of lumbermen are interpreted as a masculine adventure in the wilderness. This presumably lost manliness is reenacted and reclaimed at annual summer events that are close cousins to the rural heritage festival: lumberjack shows. The Woodsmen's Show in Galeton is an athletic event in which men compete in log-rolling, ax-throwing, tree-felling, and chainsaw-wood-carving contests.[53] At the Bark Peelers' Convention, a festival held in the same region every July at the Lumber Museum of Pennsylvania, volunteers become nineteenth-century woodhicks who guide teams of horses pulling huge tree trunks across the land and who operate a sawmill that splits, saws, and sands the wood. Here, too, men reclaim nineteenth-century skills in a birling contest and a "greased-pole-climbing" event. Nonathletes may participate in the legend as well, as contestants in tobacco-spitting, frog-jumping, and fiddling contests, and as consumers of maple candy and kettle corn.[54] Parker Dam State Park closes its summer season with woodhick games as well as logging and blacksmithing demonstrations over Labor Day weekend.[55]

The Woolrich Company, which for 180 years has manufactured outdoor clothing, makes the most of woodhick mythology in its material promoting its company store, also in this region. Even as they tap into myth, its historical claims are quite legitimate. Woolrich began in the northern Pennsylvania woods in 1830 to outfit lumbermen, railroad workers, and settlers—to meet "the demands of America's pioneers," product tags explain. "From these humble beginnings, a legend was born." The company still operates in a town that is "as it always has been. . . . This village has the simplicity that most Americans yearn for in their own over-scheduled, stress filled lives."[56] Once a workmen's clothing supplier, Woolrich now markets to a leisure market of hunters, campers, rafters, and hikers. (Promotional material notes that the front pockets of its "railroad vest," originally designed to hold "the universal railroad watch" and "tickets and other items," are ideal for carrying items from "GPS units to iPods."[57])

Woolrich's transformation represents not only a profound shift in the cultural meanings of nature but also the long and difficult relationship between northern Pennsylvania's big industries and its abundant forests. This complicated history is acknowledged at several historic sites located on or near forestland. Despite the current (and original) peaceful beauty of its woodland setting, the town of Woolrich was once named Factoryville because it was full of woolen mills in the mid-nineteenth century.[58] Much of the subsequent replanting of trees was spearheaded by Gifford Pinchot, whose family mansion in Milford, named Grey Towers, is now a National Forest Service site. *Pennsylvania Magazine* called it the "birthplace of the conservation movement" in an article spotlighting Envirofest, an environmental film festival held there each fall.[59] Grey Towers also hosts an annual Festival of Wood primarily for children, with activities such as "bluebird box building" and appearances by Smokey the Bear.[60] On the mansion tours, rangers show turn-of-the-century photographs of the stark, treeless landscape that surrounded the home when Pinchot began his forestry mission, work that continued on a much broader scale through the Civilian Conservation Corps (CCC) during the Great Depression.[61]

The contributions of Pennsylvania's nearly two hundred thousand CCC workers are documented in a "memorial" cabin and display at the state Lumber Museum and in CCC museums located in Parker Dam State Park in north-central Pennsylvania, Laurel Hill State Park in the state's southwest, and Promised Land State Park in the state's northeast corner.[62] Visitors can see displays of uniforms, bugles, mess kits, and other equipment and watch newsreels about the logging industry as well as the work of the CCC. Several state parks hold annual CCC worker reunions, and at some of these, attendees—now in their nineties—have offered their memories in filmed oral histories that are shown in the museums. Like the lumberjacks who cut down the forests, these once-young men who built them up again are remembered as "pioneers." One interpretive panel in the Parker Dam museum contains this quote from a former worker, Donald B. Miller: "We shall be proud to have been members of this army of pioneers, as our forefathers were proud of being the forerunners of a nation."[63] Workers are memorialized with statues in several state parks as well. Labeled a "monument," the one in southwestern Pennsylvania's Laurel Hill State Park—where more than two hundred CCC-built structures remain, the most in a single park—is situated grandly on a pedestal beneath tall poles bearing the American and Pennsylvania flags.[64]

CCC workers also restored historic sites within forests, including the stone foundations of iron furnaces that had crumbled after the more productive steel industry displaced most iron companies beginning in the 1870s. Thus much of iron industry history is interpreted by state park rangers and told on waysides written by the Pennsylvania Department of Conservation and Natural Resources. In one case, a national historic site resulted from the CCC's rebuilding of an entire ironmaking town, Hopewell Village, which Superintendent Edie Shean-Hammond calls "the Williamsburg of Pennsylvania."[65]

"Then and Now": The Triumph of Nature and the Failure of Imagination

Hopewell is a major site, visited by some sixty thousand people a year. In general, though, neither tourists nor Pennsylvanians are likely to be aware of the industrial history lessons contained in state parks. One problem is the increasingly limited state funding for staffing. I was lucky to see the small but terrific CCC museum in Parker Dam State Park, given that it is open only two hours every Sunday during the summer. A second issue, of course, is that state forests and parks attract visitors for other reasons. "People come to our sites for recreation," says Sarah Hopkins, chief of the Division of Environmental Education in the Department of Conservation and Natural Resources (DCNR). They learn about history, she says, only if "they stumble on it."[66]

With waysides and publications, that state agency has made an effort to interpret the past for those who do stumble on it. Bicyclers who travel the Pine Creek Rail Trail, which snakes for sixty-two miles through Pine Creek Gorge in north-central Pennsylvania, get a state-produced map that also provides this history lesson: "By 1840, 145 sawmills had been in operation in the Pine Creek watershed. . . . By 1920, hardly a marketable tree was left standing. The majestic pines had become ship masts, the bark of massive hemlocks fed the leather tanning industry, and the hardwood helped fuel the Industrial Revolution, thereby expanding the American frontier."[67] Visitors are sure to notice the beautiful iron furnace remains, which look like the shells of stone churches, in Greenwood Furnace, Pine Grove Furnace, and Caledonia State Parks.[68] Hikers through the woodland paths of Canoe Creek State Park are likely to stop and marvel at the stately, tomblike remains of kilns that once supplied lime for Pittsburgh steelmaking.[69] Nearby, in Keystone State Park, a wayside describes the coke-making industry of the site's former owner, the Keystone Coal and Coke Company, which also supplied the Pittsburgh mills, and its text reminds visitors, "When visiting the tranquil forests, fields and lake, remember that Keystone State Park was born of the fires and noise of the steel mills."[70]

Yet these settings—their natural beauty, their remote locations, their peace and quiet—make it very hard to remember what they were born of. Today, as Bob West has noted about English industrial heritage locations, they "have become ruralized . . . so that the industrial past appears aesthetically or 'organically' tied to the countryside."[71] Even as lumber history sites stress the massive deforestation that occurred a century ago, even as I grasped this fact intellectually, I simply could not picture acres and acres of bare land as I drove across the beautiful and aptly named Endless Mountains region of northern Pennsylvania. Even when interpretation encourages it (and the visitor tries *hard*), imagination fails.

At most such sites, museum and wayside interpretation is perfectly clear about historical realities, and some of it nearly implores visitors to do their best to ignore what's around them. In Marietta, along the Susquehanna River in south-central Pennsylvania, a historic marker titled "A Buried Story" notes that, despite the town's current charming appearance, "from 1845 to 1900, the riverbank between Marietta and Columbia was a beehive of industrial activity," including eight anthracite iron furnaces plus constant river barge and railroad traffic bringing in coal and exporting iron. "Today," the sign says, "the vegetation of a peaceful county park conceals most of the remains of the formerly vibrant industrial complex."[72] In Canoe Creek State Park, one sign reminds

visitors that what they see are only the bases of the lime kilns ("Try to visual-
ize the eight-story-high exhaust stacks and steel cylinder furnaces"); another
invites people to "walk this trail, and you'll take a walk back to 1900. You'll find
not a quiet and serene park, but the center of a booming limestone industry.
Listen for explosions from the quarry and the rumbling of rock-laden dinghies
on the tracks. Feel the heat from the kilns burning limestone to lime. Use your
imagination to discover the sights and sounds of Canoe Creek's past."[73]

But it's impossible. As I stood there reading this sign, alone in the warm sunshine, all I could hear were birds calling out from the trees and water trickling
through a nearby stream. The kiln bases looked perfectly clean, their honed
whiteness set off by bright-green grass and a deep-blue, midsummer sky. This
was one of the loveliest places I've been in Pennsylvania. It was almost as beautiful as Oil Creek State Park.

Along that park's main road is a boardwalk flanked by waysides whose texts
describe Petroleum Centre, the town that grew up instantly around the oil
boom in the 1860s. Its roads were full of mud; its creeks were slick with oil;
its hills were bare, the trees cut down to build derricks and houses; the din of
building and pumping was ceaseless as men worked around the clock. We learn
all of this from signs that sit, neatly lined up in two rows, on land crisscrossed
by streams and biking trails, amid quiet disrupted only by the breeze through
the trees. In Pithole, another PHMC-run site a few miles away, a lone building
sits on a remote hill, telling the story of the boom town that existed for just two
years during the 1860s. Except for this little museum, nothing is there now but
fields and woods and silence.[74]

The Drake Well Museum, also in Oil Creek State Park, tells the story of oil
as a story of heroically determined people. The museum still shows a 1954 short
movie called *Born in Freedom,* starring Vincent Price as Colonel Edwin Drake,
who came here in the mid-nineteenth century determined to establish a commercial oil well. This delightful Cold War–era western (*"We done it, Colonel, we
struck it! No one will laugh at you now!"*) concludes with narration telling us that
the oil industry was "created by American ingenuity, freedom, independence.
America is deeply indebted to Drake, the man of vision, and to all men like
him. May our country's future be enriched by all who follow in his footsteps."[75]
Beginning in the sesquicentennial year, a new film—*The Valley That Changed
the World,* produced by Pittsburgh PBS affiliate WQED—is also shown in the
museum, and while it is considerably more modern and polished, it has much
the same conclusion. As it ends, we hear the voices of expert sources mixed

with that of the narrator: "The oil industry is a story of people. It's not so much what comes out of the ground, but who had the will to put that bit down in the ground to get that oil. . . . Drake's perseverance and ingenuity . . . reflects the spirit of the people of the valley that changed the world. . . . It was more to them than just making money . . . they were making the world a better place."[76]

Elsewhere, the story of oil is told as a story of *nature's* triumph, a comparison between "Then and Now," the title of a display inside the Venango Museum of Art and Science in nearby Oil City. A large wall panel there has been cut into angled sides (looking like half-open vertical blinds), so that if you stand on one side you see a black-and-white photograph of the oil region during the 1860s boom and if you stand on the other side you see a color (mainly green) photograph of the natural beauty of the area today.[77] *A Contrast in Time* is the title of the Oil Creek State Park Visitor Center's orientation video, which features alternating black-and-white and color landscape photographs (old and ugly versus new and lush) and this narration, in part: "Where forests of oil derricks once covered the hillsides and valley floor, now leaves of oak, maple, and pine shade the landscape. . . . What changed the Oil Creek Valley for a short decade in the 1860s is gone, and the healing powers of the natural world have returned."[78]

A similar message—*look what nature has put back*—is delivered by both the narration and the route of the Oil Creek Titusville Railroad, which makes three-hour trips through the park. Its path is one of the most scenic of all the tourist trains I rode while researching this book. This ride's recorded narration concludes, "As you heard our story, were you able to imagine the valley as it once was, filled with thriving boom towns, flowing wells, and colorful characters, and everything, everywhere, covered with oil?"[79] The answer, frankly, is *no*. As in the several heritage areas that were originally conceived to tell industrial history but now focus on environmental projects, the present landscape hides its past, obscuring comprehension of the words of the historical narrative.

Nature is increasingly the thematic focus of industrial heritage. Among the special activities held in the oil region during the anniversary summer of 2009 was a series of weekend "excursions" along the Allegheny River, on which canoers and kayakers could "travel back in time" and "camp on the same islands where oil bargemen once slept." Despite its unfortunate title, Rivers of Oil, this event is typical of the merging of industrial history and outdoor recreation.[80] In 2010, an Appalachian Trail Museum opened inside a restored gristmill on the site of the former Pine Grove Iron Furnace, which is at the midway point on that hiking route and is set within a leafy state park.[81] Throughout the state, what once were railroad beds, canal towpaths, and logging trails now are hiking and biking trails, reclaimed through the national Rails to Trails program, the Pennsylvania DCNR, the various state heritage areas, and local environmental groups. These include the sixty-mile Delaware Canal towpath from Easton to Bristol on the state's eastern border, and more than one thousand miles of rail trails all across the state. Like mills and iron furnace sites, such pathways are the focus of special events such as the Towpath Trot, a 6K run during the Walnutport Canal Festival. The *New York Times* has pronounced the 132-mile Great Allegheny Passage, which runs along a former coal railroad route from Pittsburgh into Maryland, "a world-class biking destination," describing the experience as "part industrial history lesson, part nature excursion and part fun house."[82]

Also in western Pennsylvania, a Canal History by Bicycle tour is offered along the former route of the Allegheny Portage Railroad, a series of inclined tracks over which canal boats were pulled up and then let down the Allegheny Mountains from the 1830s to the 1850s. Now a national historic site, its sits in a beautiful forest through which visitors hike to see the recreated steam engine room and the restored inn where travelers including Charles Dickens and Jenny Lind stopped. The Portage Railroad was an engineering feat that also required hard labor on a large scale, resulting in "a system of inclined planes and a 900-foot tunnel carved through solid rock by Welsh coal miners."[83] The film shown in the visitor center tells a story of inevitable American progress through the wilderness. It is narrated by a costumed, loveable-geezer character who speaks directly to the viewer as he stands amid lovely nature and remembers his youth as a canal-boat mule boy who, when he was seventeen, signed on to build the Portage Railroad in 1830. His ruminations begin and end with these two passages:

> That's life. You grow up. You work hard. You tumble back into the earth. But by gosh we had our day, didn't we? . . . Talk about overcomin' what nature put in your way. Well, look out! You can't block progress, especially when you got a whole country of people chompin' at the bit, wantin' to go west or send a boatload of supplies in that direction. . . .
>
> Seems there's always a better way to cross a mountain. Well, for a long time, we *were* the better way. . . . We were some kind of solution to some kind of problem, we were. See, back then, this country never had very far to look for an original idea. Well, I don't suppose that's ever really changed. Nah, probably never will. No, I don't suppose there's any problem us folks can't solve, even if it's as big as a mountain.[84]

A New Battle Against Nature: Present Uses of Heritage Themes

This folksy dissertation includes most of the themes of heritage interpretations of agriculture, lumber, and oil in Pennsylvania. Their common narrative recounts industrial history as a process of pioneers conquering the wilderness while demonstrating the same resolve and ingenuity that we—"us folks"—still possess today. Costumed performances bolster the connection between all of us living in the present and our pioneer forebears from the past. The choices those forebears made in order to "overcome" nature are understood, in hindsight, as inevitable ("You can't block progress"). After the settlers did what they had to do, nature healed itself, giving us this beautiful land on which to recall and reenact history. It is as if we can *visit* history in such bucolic settings, where the past seems to be intact—despite interpretive reminders that the land looked very different during the actual past.

To make this imaginative connection, we must manage to ignore the realities of the present as well as those of the past. Agriculture is the best example of this phenomenon, as interpreters demonstrate hand-threshing at tourism sites surrounded by fields full of modern combines. Nostalgic stories of woodhicks and oilmen obscure the continuing presence of the lumber and oil industries in Pennsylvania as well. There are charming, small-scale reminders, such as the handmade wooden furniture sold in shops and at festivals in the state's northern tier, and the pumping jack—over an actual oil well that has been in operation for 130 years—encircled by the drive-through lane of the McDonald's in Bradford.[85] And there are less-charming large-scale reminders, such as the crude-oil refineries that rise up along the roadside in Bradford and Warren.[86] Generally, though, these current industries are not part of the heritage story. When they occasionally creep into it, the pleasant tone of that story changes.

Much of the public history interpretation discussed in this chapter describes natural beauty as the fortunate outcome of industry. Yet the pioneer theme so often found in these heritage narratives also allows the opposite: a recasting of nature as the villain, the obstacle to be overcome and conquered. This second plot has resurfaced in public rhetoric about the current Pennsylvania oil and natural gas industries, especially as production has increased recently. In early 2008, the *Wall Street Journal* published an article about the rising fortunes of independent drillers in the state's northwest due to the skyrocketing cost of oil, and the moratorium on drilling in Pennsylvania state forests was lifted (prompting another newspaper to use the headline "Oil Wells Drain Beauty from State Forests").[87] That summer, I was reminded of these changes during a talk given to a group of visitors at the Penn-Brad Oil Museum, a site near Bradford funded by the local Oil Producers Association. The staffer's historical account of the region's "pioneer" independent oil producers segued into a criticism of today's "big government," which, she said, certainly should allow more drilling now that we have plenty of environmental laws.[88]

That claim was staked more forcefully by former U.S. Representative John Peterson a year later, during Drake Well's 150th-anniversary celebration. On the grounds outside the museum, storytellers costumed for the 1860s slapped their thighs as they traded tall tales of Herculean oilmen, death-defying coon dogs, and exploding outhouses. Inside the museum, a very different tale was being told. There, industry representatives discussed the Marcellus shale, a field of natural gas that runs throughout the northern and western regions of Pennsylvania and that is now being drilled, potentially creating as many as forty-eight thousand new jobs. During this explanation, one industry executive showed pictures of wind turbines exploding in flames and said of the need for domestic oil production, "We all remember September 11th." Then came Peterson, a Republican who during his ten years in Congress was a vocal proponent of the resumption of offshore drilling. Indignantly he predicted that "China and India are planning to take every job that we have left" while environmentalists continue to "control our lives" by denying free industry. "The government owns 40 percent of our land," he complained, referring in part to the nearby Allegheny National Forest, where the U.S. Forest Service has expressed concern about the more than two thousand new oil wells that have been drilled there since 2007.[89]

Here, in the form of environmental activists and federal environmental protection policies, was nature as the enemy of progress. Once again, pioneers in the wilderness would need to fight against it in order to get to the future. From his podium in Titusville, the retired politician sounded much like the blustering narrator in the Allegheny Portage Railroad film: *Talk about overcomin' what nature put in your way. Well, look out! You can't block progress, especially when you got a whole country of people chompin' at the bit. . . .*[90] On August 27, 2009, a century and a half after Edwin Drake struck oil, John Peterson's polemic was met with the local audience's energetic applause inside the Drake Well Museum. Outside, a Model T tooted its horn as it carried visitors around the grounds, a carousel organ played snare drum waltzes, and the soldiers of the Bucktail Regiment cleaned their weapons.

KUTZTOWN
Fire Co.

Welsh Kann Boi
(Corn Pie)

Brotwascht Dambe
(Sausage Stew)

Gnoddelsupp
(Riwwel Soup)

Pierogies

**Uffgamauld Rinsfleasch
Uff En Bunn**
(Hamburgers)

**Uffgamauld Rinsfleasch
Mit Kase Uff En Bunn**
(Cheeseburgers)

Hees Hund
(Hot Dogs)

**G'Broda Siess Sackwascht
Sandwich**
(Grilled Sweet Bologna Sandwich)

Sode – (Soda)
Weiss Millich
(White Milk)

Schocklaad Millich
(Chocolate Milk)

Kaffi – (Coffee)
Eis Tee – (Ice Tea)

"WHERE I CAME FROM, HOW I GOT HERE"
Ethnic Diversity, Cultural Tourism, and the Memory of Immigration

They built the American Dream . . . coal miners, steelworkers. . . . They were immigrants to the United States, who came here to build a better life for themselves and their families. In addition, they built the bridges, railroads, and skyscrapers that transformed America into a modern nation. . . . Faced with harsh conditions . . . they kept their traditions and values alive, enriching the life and culture of a changing nation. They changed what it means to be an "American."

—Frank and Sylvia Pasquerilla Heritage Discovery Center promotional pamphlet (2007)

Thus begins the explanation that greets visitors to the newest major museum in Johnstown. The deindustrialization of this steelmaking city was the narrative backdrop for the 1977 movie *Slapshot,* about the fictional, struggling "Charlestown" Chiefs minor league hockey team. Between 1973 and 1982, the number of workers at the once-massive Cambria Steel Company shrank from nearly twelve thousand to just over two thousand; ten years later, they were out of work entirely when the plant closed.[1]

Along the Conemaugh River—which flooded in 1977 as well as, more famously, in 1889—the former industrial site has attained both brownfield status and a designation as a national historic landmark. While its buildings await redevelopment, its workers' stories are told in the nearby Heritage Discovery Center. Richard Burkert, executive director of the Johnstown Area Heritage Association, describes the Discovery Center's main exhibit, titled "America: Through Immigrant Eyes," as "almost a successor to Ellis Island. That's a gateway experience, but where did these people go?"[2] The exhibit's promotional materials promise, "The setting is Johnstown, but the stories will be familiar to all Americans."[3]

"Honor Thy Father and Thy Mother": Ethnicity as Inheritance

When you enter this museum, you're given a choice of cards, each one containing the (real) name and picture of (an actor playing) a particular immigrant; as you walk through the exhibit, you then learn what happens to "your" immigrant. My choices were Katerina, Stefan, Prokop, Moshe, Anna, Andrej, and Maria, and Josef, all of them symbolic of the large waves of eastern European immigration to this area around the turn of the twentieth century. Josef, "a 12-year-old Polish orphan," is the main visual symbol of the exhibit and the organization's website.[4]

Here, the working-class past is almost entirely personalized, though the interpretation emphasizes the hardships these people faced, including their ill treatment by more established ethnic groups who had the better jobs in the mills and mines. It also stresses the dangers of work in the iron, steel, and coal industries, especially for these most recent immigrants in this nonunion, company town that had a clear worker hierarchy, within which workers were segregated by nationality, language, religion, and neighborhood. But, as wall text tells us as we leave the historical part of the exhibit, "That was then. . . . This is now."

"Now" is presented in an area where visitors may sit and watch, on video, current Johnstowners talking about their grandparents and about growing up in those segregated cultures during difficult times. Their reminiscences are proud ones, laced with fond memories of food and dancing and social clubs, of close friendship and family within tight-knit communities.[5] These narrators are the inheritors of ethnic legacies but are themselves fully assimilated within Johnstown and within America, now that the old industries are gone. In the meantime, a nearby display explains, Johnstown has welcomed newer immigrants, mainly Asian, who have come to work in the new industries of technology and health care. This part of the museum also contains a set of computer kiosks, called "Our Stories," where visitors may make a video recording of their own recollections or comments and listen to those of other visitors.

At the very end, we learn about "our" immigrant's descendants, who assure us that, ultimately, their hardship was worthwhile. A touchscreen display asks you to cast your vote in a single-question poll: Should America allow more immigration? Then you get the cumulative poll results. The last time I was there, in

July 2009, the vote was:48,038 for "Yes!" and 19,453 for "No!" In a conservative region of a largely conservative state—and in a twenty-first-century national climate of rising intolerance of immigrants—this is a somewhat surprising result. Its decisiveness suggests that the presumably depoliticizing technique of personalization may repoliticize as well, by repositioning immigrants as future "ancestors."

That shift in status surely is aided by the fact that, as many tourism and public history professionals acknowledged to me in interviews, the typical visitor to the state's museums and historic sites is not really a tourist but rather a local person, often with "visiting friends and family."[6] Scholars have found this to be true of heritage tourism far beyond Pennsylvania. In his observations of heritage destinations in Ireland, Tok Thompson notes that "at least half of the people attending have been Irish citizens." Thus, he concludes, "Heritage is clearly important . . . not just as something to sell the foreign tourists, but also for providing meaning and identity for our own lives."[7] Bella Dicks discovered much the same phenomenon in her study of Welsh coal-mining heritage sites, which provide "a public platform for the past self," she writes. "To see heritage purely as a means of marketing the vernacular past is to miss . . . its local belonging and its use as self-representation."[8] A large part of that self-representation is tribute, a kind of celebratory memorial that draws on either family lineage or a more general idea of community in order to connect people of the present with a past we cannot really imagine.

August Carlino, director of the Rivers of Steel Heritage Area around Pittsburgh, makes this point in general terms: "Our mission is a lasting respect to those past workers, and to their descendants who continue to honor and preserve their stories and memories."[9] The Senator John Heinz History Center in Pittsburgh, which occupies a former warehouse, urges donors to "Honor Thy Father and Mother" by paying to have their names engraved on "a handsome tile made of stainless steel, aluminum, or iron" in the museum's floor.[10] Elsewhere in the state as well, individual steelworkers' and coal miners' names are etched onto memorials. Workers' names are engraved on gold plaques in the "Railroaders' Hall" at the Railroad Museum of Pennsylvania in Strasburg and inside bronze horseshoes at the Horseshoe Curve National Historic Site in Altoona; in the latter town's Railroaders Memorial Museum, an exhibit titled "Are You a Railroader?" invites visitors to type their last names into a computer database of Pennsylvania Railroad employees.[11] Hundreds of cement workers' names are listed alphabetically, thus emphasizing family and ethnic connections, at the Atlas Cement Company Memorial Museum in the eastern Pennsylvania town of Northampton. Honoring the now-defunct company that supplied cement for, among other major sites, Ellis Island, this museum emphasizes immigration in a wall mural showing people in various eras of dress; one is the Austrian father of museum founder Ed Pany, a former high school teacher who has devoted the past decade to running this local tribute to the "melting pot" of workers who settled the area in the early twentieth century.[12]

Ethnic identity is the interpretive key for historical understanding at industrial history sites where the local workforce was strongly associated with a particular nationality. In Jim Thorpe, the town formerly known as Mauch Chunk, the story of the Molly Maguires, coal miners who were executed (and arguably framed) for their part in labor violence, is recounted at the Old Jail as a tale of Irish heroism, and the gift shop sells Celtic crafts and Irish music.[13] An Irish wedding is reenacted regularly in the restored church in Eckley Miners Village, a living-history site near Hazleton.[14] Not far away, in the town of Bangor, named for Bangor, Wales, the Slate Belt Heritage Center welcomes visitors under a red, white, and green flag bearing the slogan "The Little Welsh Place: Y Lle Cymru Bach."[15] Slate heritage is also told in Delta, located at the bottom of the state near towns called West Bangor and (just across the Maryland border) Cardiff. Here, workers are renovating two 1850s stone houses, the Jones Cottage and the Williams Cottage, along Slateville Road off Pendyrus Street, which are, a brochure explains, "identical to houses found in the slate quarrying region of North Wales. . . . The Jones Cottage will be restored to the early immigrant-era status, which will enable visitors to learn about the family life of our early Welsh slate splitters."[16]

"Wales in America" was the title of a recent exhibit at the Pennsylvania Anthracite Heritage Museum in Scranton, though this site's permanent exhibit—titled "Anthracite People: Immigration Ethnicity in Pennsylvania's Hard Coal Region"—interprets ethnicity more broadly. Its orientation film uses iconic Ellis Island photographs, and we see the *Lehigh Valley Black Diamond*, a train, as a voice says, "I took a train to Wilkes-Barre." The film's narrator concludes that although the coal industry "no longer attracts immigrants from other nations," immigration continues to occur in "the Anthracite Region." Displays throughout the museum expand on these themes, beginning with an Ellis Island section and ending with framed newspaper articles about recently arrived Mexicans in Scranton. In between are displays of cultural artifacts (crafts, clothing, religious objects, festival posters) of people from Poland, Lithuania, Hungary, Croatia, Wales, England, Ireland, Germany, and India, plus a section on African American coal miners that features a bust of George Washington sculpted from coal by African American artist C. Edgar Patience.

Collectively, this interpretation is explained in wall text: "The ethnic history of the anthracite region is one of change through time. Through conflict and cooperation each ethnic group has participated in that heritage. From their roots in a common industrial background, Anthracite People have formed a unique culture in the United States of America." But one leaves wondering, *What unique culture is that?* So many possibilities are represented here, in the name of coal.[17]

Sampling the "Social Goulash": Ethnicity as Food

The story of immigrant workers in the Pittsburgh area is a similarly multinational one. The narrator of a film sold at the Coal and Coke Heritage Center in Fayette calls them "an almost unprecedented, sustained mixing of peoples, call it a social goulash or a cultural mosaic." Then an interviewed woman, the daughter of a coke worker, sums up the same point this way: "Everybody eats pizza or pierogi or lasagna or halupkie. It's all good."[18] Pittsburgh markets itself as a city of neighborhoods, and although those neighborhoods tend to have been (and in many cases to still be) defined by ethnicity, race, and religion, they are publicly characterized in gastronomical terms. In a travel article marking the city's 250th anniversary in 2008, a *USA Today* reporter claimed that this city's "multicultural neighborhoods offer rich, one-of-a-kind flavor" and interviewed "Enrico Lagattuta, the owner of Enrico Biscotti Company."[19]

Food and foundries merge together in the narration of the "Babushkas and Hard Hats" bus tour given by the Rivers of Steel group. Communications Director Jan Dofner explains the chemical process of steelmaking, tells the story of the rise and fall of the industry, and recounts the 1892 Battle of Homestead, which pit striking workers against Pinkerton guards. But mixed into her substantive account of industrial and labor history are sweeter morsels. My group stopped at a cooking school, where we were given aprons and allowed to "make" (mix premeasured ingredients for) Polish cakes and take home the recipe. On the bus, Dofner passed out "Slovak" cookies that, she told us, represented "the single most important culinary tradition" of Pittsburgh: the "cookie table," a wedding reception tradition to which all women in the community would competitively contribute.

This memory device also explained her use of the term "cake eaters" to describe the mill owners and managers, whose Protestant wedding receptions, she explained, featured cake rather than cookies. The steelworkers—her own family and their neighbors—she called "Hunkies," using this word to refer to generally to all people of eastern European descent. Her narration of the landscape of the city's now-trendy South Side, once a string of working-class neighborhoods containing "more churches than anywhere else in the world except for Rome," was peppered with references to old-world food, as our little bus passed microbreweries, sushi bars, vegan cafés, and Starbucks outlets.[20] The Rivers of Steel headquarters is the Bost Building, a national historic landmark that once served as workers' union headquarters during the 1892 strike, and its contents offer tourists a mix of history and heritage. Upstairs, a changing exhibit tells steel history; downstairs in the gift shop, they sell, among other things, a cookbook whose recipes represent thirteen nationalities, organized by country, but opening with this toast: "Let's all lift a cup to our common humanity and break bread, no matter what our origin."[21]

In 2006, Pittsburgh's public television station, WQED, produced a program titled *What Makes Pittsburgh Pittsburgh?* The answer, it turns out, is food—although the food emerges from a narrative about ethnic pride. This documentary, which is sold in the Heinz History Center, explains, "People of similar backgrounds liked getting together, and obviously still do. Social clubs formed, dance groups . . . and maybe some culture from the old country got preserved, especially when it was served with goulash and other goodies." We see people singing at the (Welsh) St. David's Society while eating little liver patties called faggots. We see costumed children dancing at a Bulgarian cultural center in West Homestead that supports itself by making and selling soups. Standing over a pot of soup, a woman says, "I feel it's my legacy from my parents because they came over here and they struggled and they built a life for themselves but they never forgot their heritage." We visit a Hungarian restaurant, whose chef-owner says, "For me, to reenact my heritage every day is kind of important. . . . Once you've tasted my food, you become part of the family." Then an unidentified voice adds, "The best way to get somebody interested in your culture is through their stomachs."[22]

The same premise underlies many of the "Shunpiker's Guides" that appear in Pennsylvania newspapers and magazines. Offering accounts ostensibly written by weekend visitors to particular regions, these stories look like articles but are actually advertisements created by the state tourism office. In one, visitors to Scranton—"amid memorials to mineshaft disasters and about as many Catholic churches as there are saints"—search for the best slice of pizza. In Pittsburgh, the writers eat Cajun food and oysters before they drink Iron City Beer at a bar whose owner "worked the mill in '79, when the last pig iron was cast into Pittsburgh steel." The article/ad recounts his commentary: "'40,000 men worked these mills,' Demo's eyes close with memory. 'You could hear the roar across the river and up the slopes.'" Then our surrogates head up those very slopes of Mt. Washington, in search of hand-pulled pretzels and calamari.[23]

"It's the Story as Much as the Bread": Ethnicity as Consensual Tradition

"Shunpikers," as the term suggests, are travelers who "shun the turnpike and beaten path," who "like to get lost and find hidden gems," says Lenwood Sloan, the state's director of Cultural and Heritage Tourism. They are interested in the past less in terms of history than in terms of culture. Sloan distinguishes between two kinds of tourism: "Heritage tourism is place-based. . . . It almost always has a zip code. Cultural tourism is about the things that people leave, the foodways and folkways—language, dress, humor, artifacts, what defines people. Heritage tourism came out of preservation. Cultural tourism came out of arts councils and humanities groups. Culture has immediacy and consensus. Cultural communities are also 'crossroads' experiences—modern and old, international and local. Heritage communities tend to confirm and reconfirm identity and sense of place."[24]

In this definition, "cultural tourism" is a repositioning of ethnicity from fixed, occupational, and place-based identity to fluid and transferrable customs and artifacts ("the things that people leave") that may be shared and experienced by all kinds of people, regardless of their background. Herbert Gans uses the term "symbolic ethnicity" to describe the result of such a shift.[25] Marilyn Halter expands on his point: "Symbolic, or voluntary, ethnicity is, above all, comfortable and usually manifests as a form of leisure activity expressed in entertaining festivals and fairs; cultural spectacles of music, art, film, theater, and dance; and samplings of a smorgasbord of both traditional and nouvelle cuisines where diverse groups can coexist in harmony rather than put the focus on histories of social inequities, interethnic tensions, entrenched notions of cultural superiority, and anti-immigrant bias."[26]

Similarly, Barbara Kirschenblatt-Gimblett sees this phenomenon as evidence that we have entered "an era of historical identification by consent (and dissent), rather than descent."[27] Yet, as she suggests, Sloan's definition of cultural tourism taps into ongoing debates about public history and tensions between professional and vernacular uses of the past. His vision for the popular uses of the past aligns with Robert Archibald's goal of "useful storymaking based on fact." Archibald also writes, "History is about making useful narratives for the living. . . . History is a conversation . . . about who we are, what stories we will tell. It is a search for common ground between people with diverse interpretations and experiences."[28]

Local people—necessarily nonhistorians—are key to this conversation. One state tourism office project is the "Artisans Trails," seven driving routes that link sites where "traditional" foods and crafts are replicated, including glassblowing, iron forgery ("those first industries of Pennsylvania," Sloan calls them), hand-dipping of candy, specialty cheese-making, beer brewing, bread-making, and more. Central to their appeal are the on-site "artisans" who, in their interactions with visitors, convey the meaning of their labor in the present as well as the past. "Mass consumers are fascinated by the intimacy of these cottage industries," Sloan says. "We conceive of the people who own and work at the sites primarily as storytellers. It's the story as much as the bread. Lineage stories—where I came from, how I got here."[29]

Cultural approaches to tourism have grown over the past two decades alongside two other trends. In the academy, some historians have turned to oral history projects as a way to address contested histories (such as the histories of immigration and deindustrialization), acknowledging that people's memories, whether or not they are factually accurate, are nevertheless revealing and important; such researchers have tended to embrace public history scholar Michael Frisch's belief that historians and laypersons have a "shared authority" for making sense of the past.[30] And public history funders have increasingly favored programs that feature oral history and folk art—the memories, performances, and traditions of ordinary people, especially those experiences that can be understood as ethnic. Writing about the "Hunkies" or "Slavs" of northeastern Pennsylvania's anthracite region, Donald Miller and Richard Sharpless note that during the nineteenth century, "Slavs were heartily criticized for their ceremonies, which were not understood by outsiders, who often considered them demonstrations of a barbarous and corrupt culture."[31] In the twenty-first century the reenactment of such ceremonies is at the heart of heritage culture, eagerly sought by outsiders wishing to "experience" a lost authenticity.

The federal Department of the Interior partly sponsored the now-defunct America's Industrial History Project, which created public history programs for the area surrounding Altoona and Johnstown. One was the Path of Progress driving route discussed in chapter 2, and another was an oral history project yielding an audiotape that could be played during car trips around this region. That tape's unidentified narrator explains its premise in words echoing the views of Robert Archibald: "Heritage is a dialogue between past and present. . . . History is composed of many different perspectives. . . . The stories that you will hear relate past achievements and sorrows to the concerns of the present day. We need to ask ourselves what these stories mean to us, as we travel along roads and pass through towns built on the labor of generations of working people."[32] Most of the reminiscences on this tape are sad ones, about death and poverty, that are specific to steelworking, coal mining, and railroading but not specific to nationality.

The opposite is true of the Rivers of Steel Tradition Bearers project, which initially was based on a series of radio programs that aired on a Pittsburgh National Public Radio affiliate in 2005. Sponsored in part by the National Park Service, these programs mixed "mill worker memories" with features on the area's many ethnic communities. A companion website, still accessible in 2010, offers photographs and video of the participants. A video collection of "Millworker Memories" remains, and there is a segment in which artisans explain glassmaking and ironwork (though the former is described as "art" and the latter is described as a preindustrial "craft" that has been recovered from history). The other eleven segments are organized by culture, defined in nearly all cases in terms of race, ethnicity, or religion. One segment featuring food offers an optimistic take on the religious consequences of deindustrialization: "the 3 P's of Lent," *paska* (Easter bread with a crossed top), *paczki* (a kind of doughnut), and *pierogi* (filled dumplings), are discussed by Yugoslavian, Polish, and Hungarian women whose Catholic churches have been forced to merge. Segments on the other expected ethnicities of Pittsburgh (Italian, Croatian, and Slovenian) discuss music and lacemaking, while a segment on African Americans focuses on a church and hairdressing shop.

Fully half of the segments, however, feature the music, clothing, and arts of groups not traditionally associated with Pittsburgh or steelmaking: collectively, these performers and craftspeople represent fifteen countries from Asia, the Middle East, and Latin America, as well as Native Americans and American Jews (the latter identified by religion rather than nationality).[33] The organization serves as a clearinghouse for schools, churches, and other groups seeking "tradition bearer" speakers or performers who represent more than three dozen nationalities and demonstrate cultural traditions ranging from East Indian sand-painting and Scottish Highland piping.[34]

All of these people function as what Lenwood Sloan calls "ambassadors," representatives not only of places and communities but also of history, even though—or perhaps especially because—they live among us in the modern world. As bridges between the past and present, they call on a broader public of locals as well as tourists to "keep the past alive" through performance, narrative, and material culture. They direct our attention to ethnic symbols of an industrial past that we have somehow inherited and therefore have an obligation to preserve, even though the historical circumstances that produced such culture are often forgotten.

"A New Ethnic Consciousness": Diversity as Division in an Anti-Immigration Climate

Of all the heritage themes discussed in this book, the most pervasive is ethnicity. Ethnicity is the narrative device through which labor becomes patriotism, and through which specific experiences of the past become general ideals of the present. In heritage interpretation, industrial workers are understood as immigrants; immigration is understood as ethnicity; ethnicity is understood as cultural traditions; and cultural traditions are understood as legacy—*everybody's* legacy. Ethnicity is interpreted as "an *inheritance* which is rhetorically projected as 'common,'" write British heritage scholars John Corner and Sylvia Harvey, resulting in a narrative "strategic *indivisibility* . . . subsuming awkward differences within larger continuities."[35]

Yet just as awkward differences were real in the past, they remain real in the present. It requires a narrative sleight of hand to explain ethnicity and unity together. The heritage story told in Pennsylvania, especially its steelmaking regions in the west and coal-mining regions in the east, is not one of a shared struggle, but one of parallel struggles; it is a tale of "tight-knit" worker "communities" that were in fact divided from one another by ethnic segregation. Heritage nostalgia for such a past thus has a peculiar quality. Kenneth Wolensky, a historian for the PHMC Bureau for Historic Preservation, explains this phenomenon: "It's almost seeing the past like it was larger than life—the good old days, even though they weren't so good. . . . People are looking to reconnect with the working-class communities of the past; they're looking for substance, a sense of security, that life was simple, but comfortable, secure, safe—the church, work, family, the ethnic club. You didn't have to learn about the world . . . you could live in isolation and get by. Today, you can't count on that anymore."[36]

Wolensky made these comments during a conversation about Steelton, another town that bears the obvious scars of deindustrialization even while some steelmaking continues. The preservation of its cultural "inheritance" was part of the rationale offered by the Harrisburg *Patriot-News* in a 2009 editorial supporting funds for economic development there. The reason to save this town, the newspaper's editors wrote, is not steel history, but the ethnic history that has made it "such a special community": "Steelton once was home to half a dozen churches that related to a specific European region. . . . Now one of those churches is a mosque, and there are more recent Latino immigrants, as well."[37] While applauding the region's ongoing diversity, this passage also confirms a continuation of the segregation and social exclusiveness that John Bodnar found in his study of immigration patterns in Steelton during the early twentieth century, a time when immigrants "turned inward" so firmly that they "acquired a new ethnic consciousness which surpassed anything they had known in Europe."[38]

That this also was the case in western Pennsylvania is implied in the Rivers of Steel tour guide's reference to "more churches than anywhere else except for Rome,"[39] less a measure of religiosity than evidence of how many separate Catholic national identities were so long preserved in this "melting pot." Even in 1991, just a few years after the collapse of Big Steel in Pittsburgh, *National Geographic* published a positive portrait of the city in which the writer nevertheless noted that "each neighborhood has evolved as a separate community with its own ethnic flavor. . . . While you're visiting one neighborhood—Polish, Italian, Jewish, German, Slavic, Arab, or African-American—the others might as well not exist."[40] In 2009, six Catholic churches were forced to merge in Johnstown's "Cambria City" neighborhood, historically home to the city's immigrants and today home to the Heritage Discovery Center's proud presentation of ethnic heritage. Reporting this news, the local newspaper began its story with the blunt but optimistic lead, "There is strength in numbers and strength in tradition." Yet on the paper's website, a local resident posted a response that "if the bishop thinks for one moment that this will promote unity among the people, then he has rocks in his head."[41]

Part of the modern reverence for immigrant communities is a modern-day wish to be able to, as Wolensky puts it, "get by in isolation." This is nostalgia for ethnic segregation—or to put it in the kinder language of heritage, a wish to be among people who "knew who they were." It is subtly (and, occasionally, not so subtly) implied in celebrations of "neighborhoods" and "traditions." An exhibit at the Railroaders Memorial Museum, titled "Where Everybody Knows

Your Name," recalls a lost Altoona in which "the Bavarian Club served natives of that German region, Italians relaxed at the Christopher Columbus Club, and a separate black Elks Club chapter was organized by the African-American community."[42]

The thematic prevalence of this kind of sentiment elides the historical realities of segregation. One can hardly object to the marker in Hazleton that honors the victims of the Lattimer Massacre as having "made the supreme sacrifice." Yet how much do those who pass by that marker today—in this region full of summer coal-country festivals with ethnic themes—understand that those miners were shot *because* they were immigrants, or more specifically, because they were considered by locals to be the wrong kind of immigrants? While there are some notable exceptions, the relative lack of heritage interpretation about the very real ethnic divisions of the past deprive us of historical context that might illuminate the ethnic divisions of the present.[43]

In the anthracite region, an anti-immigrant movement has emerged in response to a rise in Mexican immigration to the area. A group called Voice of the People organized in support of Hazleton Mayor Lou Barletta's proposal to fine businesses that hire illegal immigrants and landlords who rent to them, legislation that attracted national press attention when it was passed in 2006. Two years later, the national spotlight was again on the presence of Mexican immigrants in this region. The headline of a *Philadelphia Daily News* article summed up the events that put the small town of Shenandoah into the news: "Town Torn Apart: Shenandoah's Ethnic Strife and Violence Bring America's Immigration Issue into Sharp Focus."[44] Within a two-month period, one Mexican man had been badly beaten, and another, an illegal immigrant engaged to a local white woman, had died after a fight with four white teenagers, former high school football players. Under the headline "Immigrant's Death Splits Blue-Collar Town," the *Chicago Tribune* painted a dramatic scene of this incident: "Ethnic slurs ricocheted in the night, echoing what many have muttered for years in this crumbling mountainside town that was once the thriving jewel of Pennsylvania's coal country. Then, fists flew. . . . This pocket of blue-collar America . . . is spinning in the ugly vortex of the nation's racially charged war over illegal immigration."[45] Despite these headlines' references to a "split" or "torn-apart" town, less than a year later an all-white jury acquitted the teenagers of all major charges.[46]

At the center of Shenandoah is the Pennsylvania Anthracite Miners Memorial, one of the state's largest such monuments, which are one subject of the following chapter. Its three-part wall bears miners' engraved names that collectively represent a "social goulash"—Greek, Polish, Czech, Irish, Italian, Hungarian, Welsh, and English. But mining itself is long gone from this area, and in its wake is a different kind of social goulash that led to the town's recent notoriety. A *New York Times* article provided a broader cultural view:

> After anthracite coal was discovered near the town in the late 1800s, immigrants poured in, mainly from Europe. The hamlet grew to a borough of 25,000 before the mines started to close. The immigrant groups largely got along, but they also felt the need to ethnically divide not just their churches—some of which are still considered "the Italian church" or "the Irish church"—but also the town's volunteer fire companies. The town's biggest festival every year is Heritage Days near the end of August, when the major ethnic groups, among them the Lithuanians, Irish, Italians, Greeks and, more recently, Mexicans, put floats in a parade and sell ethnic food from booths.[47]

The events in Shenandoah repoliticize the notions of ethnic heritage that are so blithely celebrated during the many small-town festivals that take place nearly every summer and fall weekend across the state. This recent violence provides a stark reminder that ethnicity has historically been linked with labor history and with territorial battles over employment in hard economic times. And it suggests that immigrant ethnicity is proudest when it is understood as part of the past—even as it remains quite evident in the present.

"DEEP VEINS OF LOSS"
Sacrifice and Heroism in Coal Country

John Seigenthaler (anchor): More than 100 years ago hundreds of thousands of miners toiled in the mines of Pennsylvania, and coal was king. Now the number has dwindled to about 8,000 miners in the state, but they still come from proud communities.

Virginia Cha (reporter): Quecreek, Pennsylvania, one of the small towns that make up Somerset Country, a close-knit coal mining community that supports its own when trouble strikes. . . . People in these parts say mining is in the blood. As far back as the 1870s, miners have worked deep down inside the shafts that burrow through southwestern Pennsylvania countryside, bringing up the coal that fueled the industrial revolution. . . . This community is no stranger to pain. On September 11th, Flight 93 went down just 10 miles from here in a field that used to be a coal mine. . . . A community built on a respected way of life, now pulling together.

—*NBC Nightly News* (July 27, 2002)

This language—full of truth and stereotypes, local news and national mythology—was typical of American news reporting in late July 2002, when an accident trapped nine workers in the Quecreek Mine in western Pennsylvania. A day after this report aired, the miners were rescued in an event that was hailed by the media, as well as the Pennsylvania governor and the U.S. president, as a miracle. Coal mine accidents have occurred with regularity for more than a century, and several explosions in this particular region of southwestern Pennsylvania have drawn national attention: 179 workers died in the Harwick Mine in 1904, 239 in the Darr Mine near Jacobs Creek in 1907, 195 in the Mather Mine in 1928, and as recently as 1962, 37 at the Robena Mine in Carmichaels. Yet nothing paralleled the international spotlight that shone on the rescue of the

Quecreek Nine, who were raised to safety on the Dormel Farms in Sipesville, a town not far from the field where United Flight 93 had crashed on September 11, 2001.

Journalists immediately made a narrative connection between the two events, focusing on characters whose symbolism was well understood by the summer of 2002. Among the locals interviewed by news media while the rescue was under way was Sipesville Fire Chief Mark Zambanini, whose company had responded to the Flight 93 crash less than a year earlier and who vowed, "We're going to succeed."[1] After meeting the miners, President George W. Bush declared, "It was their determination to stick together and to comfort each other that really defines kind of a new spirit that's prevalent in our country, that when one of us suffers, all of us suffer."[2] One reader letter appearing in USA Today claimed that "just as cops and firemen received our respect after Sept. 11, the miners who put their lives on the line every day deserve dutiful regard as well," while another reader wrote, "Ten months later, we now experience how this miracle of the miners turns the darkness into light."[3] The rescue was seen as a form of redemption not only for the losses of 9/11 but also for the declining economic climate in mid-2002, amid discoveries of widespread corporate fraud. CBS News reporter Jim Axelrod editorialized, "After a steady diet of Wall Street villains, it's kind of nice to feed on some lunch bucket heroes."[4]

Seven years later, as this chapter was being written, the "Wall Street villains" of 2002 were long forgotten, as the nation's top banks, insurers, and car companies filed for bankruptcy and federal bailouts while America descended into its worst financial crisis since the Great Depression. But busloads of tourists continue to pay tribute to the "lunch bucket heroes" at the rescue site, which is still a large, working farm. There, in a former auction-house building converted to a museum, they can see the yellow rescue capsule that brought each miner to the surface (the event's iconic artifact, whose ownership was unsuccessfully pursued by the Smithsonian) and hear an hour-long account of the three-day rescue delivered by Lori Arnold, the daughter-in-law of the farm's owners. Then Karen Popernack, stepmother of rescued miner Mark Popernack, takes visitors down to the rescue site itself, past a large statue of a miner and the state historical marker that was installed in 2006. They get international tour groups; they also get busloads of Amish people who want to see where a miracle happened, Lori Arnold explains. A group of Ohio Amish, she says, have volunteered to raise the building that will permanently house the visitors' center.[5]

The Arnolds' farm in Sipesville is one of two sites where the Quecreek rescue is memorialized. Twenty-eight miles away, Mark Zambanini's fire chief jacket hangs alongside clothing worn by the miners and their rescuers in the Windber Coal Heritage Center. During the four days in July 2002 when the miners were still trapped, the center's director, Christopher Barkley (who has "four generations of miners in the family") was a source for the national press. "We were able to educate the public that, yes, people are still mining . . . and that was a surprise to them," he says. He realized at the time that this was a special story because it occurred so near the site of the crash of Flight 93 and so soon afterward. "This was the good-news story. It brought us as U.S. citizens out of the doldrums . . . to be able to rescue nine blue-collar guys." The typical visitor to this museum—which occupies a former bank building and post office in this town named for the Berwind-White Coal Company—is in fact one who has just come from the Quecreek and Flight 93 sites, he notes.

Barkley led an interpretive team to create a "Working Underground Exhibit" that combines the Quecreek rescue story with the story of Flight 93. To him, the stories are united not only by place and time but also by theme: "Where a lot of lives are sacrificed, there's a lot of ties there, too. . . . A lot of miners lost their lives with black lung and silicosis" as well as in accidents.[6] Through interactive technology, this exhibit explains the process and dangers of coal mining while providing a detailed timeline of the Quecreek incident. The many rescuers as well as the miners are listed on a memorial wall, which also briefly explains the crash of Flight 93. Its written text declares, "The rescue underscores the resourceful, strong, resilient character of rural America, in that it was alive and well at a time when our country needed to rally around a success story, which shows we can overcome adversity as a people and a nation. . . . We are all capable of rising to the occasion in times of difficulty and danger, just like the passengers did on that fateful flight when they decided to challenge the terrorists."[7] Both those passengers and the rescuers, the exhibit text claims, represent "the best qualities of the American spirit," which "can be found in communities across this nation."[8]

Such interpretation draws and expands on mythic ideas about American exceptionalism, progress, and an innate "character" that makes heroism the inevitable response to crisis. Several scholars have examined the continuing strength of these themes in popular communication. In his study of journalistic narrative, Jack Lule defines myth as "a sacred, societal story that draws from archetypal figures and forms to offer exemplary models for human life."[9] In American mythology, notes Betty Houchin Winfield, that "exemplary model" is the ordinary man who does extraordinary deeds, "a publicly spirited, sacrificing citizen."[10] Janice Hume writes, "Heroes stand on a pedestal, true, but on our egalitarian society, that pedestal must be reachable for everyone; in America, a 'hero' is not royalty or deity, but an average person who, through adversity, strives to reach society's highest potential."[11] According to Susan J. Drucker and Robert S. Cathcart, the "hero myth" of any particular culture "is transformed in the telling and retelling," which must take place in a public forum.[12]

Like the heroic national narrative used by major news media to tell the Quecreek story, the Windber museum's exhibit tells a story that is as much about the "proud community" (a status "reachable for everyone") as it is about the miners and their rescuers. Yet within its claim of American exceptionalism also is a claim of regional exceptionalism, a strong statement about the character of "rural America," specifically Somerset County. It is not insignificant that this claim is made amid museum displays that chronicle the town's struggle through several strikes and that detail the dangers of work in the explosive, bituminous coal mines that remain in operation in western Pennsylvania, West Virginia, and Kentucky—conditions that, in truth, few Americans either experience or understand (let alone "respect," as the NBC reporter contended).

The story of the Quecreek rescue, as it is commemoratively retold today, illustrates John Bodnar's assertion that patriotic rhetoric "embodies both official and vernacular interests" in civic rituals that situate historically specific, local history within familiar national mythology.[13] Those interests are sometimes complementary and sometimes contradictory.

"We Owe Him Much": Memorials, Moral Imagination, and the Local Language of Loss

Several interpretive tensions—between pride of accomplishment and fear of danger, between company success and worker struggle, between loss and renewal—are evident elsewhere in Windber. Just outside the heritage center and across from the renovated 1919 Arcadia Theater sits a park containing a band shell and a coal miner memorial. At the center of the memorial is a statue of a miner, with a plaque in language typical of the year of its dedication: "This statue [is] presented to the citizens of this community by the district school-children and dedicated to the men of the mines who by their labor and loyalty have helped to make Windber one of the best towns in the nation . . . 1952."[14] In 2000, townspeople added a wall of bricks behind the statue, each containing a miner's name, personalizing the tribute.[15] Off to the side, however, is a clash of memory, a newer historic interpretation from 2003, the year when a state historical marker was placed here. It details the United Mine Workers' strike of 1922–1923 over "deplorable living and working conditions . . . families of strikers were evicted from company housing."[16]

The Windber statue is only one of many symbolic reminders of coal mining across Pennsylvania. While the industry has largely departed from the state's anthracite regions, and while it is significantly smaller even in the state's western bituminous regions, coal is still the central public identity of dozens of towns. It is the source of town names such as Minersville (the state contains two of these) and Coaldale (three). Miners are represented in public art, from the cast-iron doors of the State Capitol Building in Harrisburg to New Deal post office murals in dozens of cities and towns.[17]

Most public history tributes to coal mining emerged as responses to the large-scale collapse of this industry in the mid-twentieth century. "Deindustrialization set in hard on the anthracite region decades before the term was coined," writes Kenneth Wolensky. "By the 1960s Wilkes-Barre and Scranton were the only two urban areas in the country with double-digit unemployment rates."[18] Mining memorialization began in earnest during the 1970s, by which time nearly all of the major collieries of eastern Pennsylvania had closed. Bodnar notes that small-town observations of the nation's bicentennial were thematically patriotic but also quite specific: "Local activities revealed more of an attachment to vernacular and personal interests than to official expressions of patriotism."[19] Pennsylvania coal miner memorials dedicated in 1976 bear out his point. While their language and settings seem patriotic, the heroism they celebrate is distinctly local, and their dedication language emphasizes loss— loss of life and loss of the industry itself.

That year the citizens of Pittston unveiled a stone marker showing the full figure of a miner, in front of a large piece of coal, with this inscription: "This monument erected in commemoration of the American Bicentennial is dedicated to the coal miner of Greater Pittston in appreciation for his unselfish sacrifice of labor beneath the earth for the promise of a better future for generations to follow. We Owe Him Much."[20] Another bicentennial marker can be found in Lansford's John F. Kennedy Park, just opposite the road that leads down to the No. 9 Mine tour site. On both ends of a stone wall are etchings of working miners and chunks of coal, one of which sits atop a time capsule to be opened in 2076. The inscription on the front of the memorial is dedicated to all who died in area mines, both the deep mining "of bygone days" and more recent surface mining, and notes that the stone with which it was made was "salvaged" from the former coal company office.[21]

Local sacrifice remained a major theme of memorials dedicated during what Linda Shopes identifies as "the history-making impulse" of the deindustrializing 1990s.[22] One such site is broadly named the Pennsylvania Anthracite Miners Memorial, although its memory is specific to Shenandoah, where it occupies a prominent spot in the middle of town. Built in 1996, this tall, curving wall shows miners and their families in three scenes, surrounded by bricks containing miners' names and personalized dedications. A plaque on the monument contains this grim text: "Dedicated to the men who worked in endless night: Their coal oil lamps dimly lighted the dismal tunnels while silhouetting their blackened faces that portrayed their exhausting labors and dedication to their families. Through endless days they braved the cold, damp and dark—from sunrise to sunset—only God knew their fate."[23]

The Statue of Liberty is referenced on another marker, also called the Anthracite Miners Memorial, which invokes the verse of Emma Lazarus: "You gave us your tired, your poor, your huddled masses. . . . Many of them came to the Anthracite Regions." This one is in Forest City, which despite its name is a small town in the mountains north of Scranton. On the mountaintop are huge, white wind turbines, reminders of the industrial change that has come to the valley below. This memorial, too, was erected in the mid-1990s, "in memory of those who built our small towns and labored and died in the mining industry to provide for a better tomorrow."[24]

Similar language graces a stone some 350 miles away, near Fredericktown. On the grounds of Bethlehem-Center High School, it is a large and impressive memorial. (Still, I would not have found this without the help of a woman, who, answering my query in a local supermarket, drove ahead of me over several miles of winding roads to lead me there.) Four tall, black slabs list names and feature this inscription from its 2003 dedication: "To those men and women whose toil and determination have forged our future." In front of the walls of names sits a statue of a miner reading a book—the same design as the miner statue at the Quecreek rescue site—whose pose is explained in a poem at the base:

> They who work the mines and
> They who read great books are but one;
> Their name is *human*. By the labor
> Of their hands, through the exercise
> Of their minds, and in the strength
> Of their spirit, they will prevail.[25]

The verb tenses used here are unusual for a memorial. They are a reminder that coal mining is ongoing in this part of southwestern Pennsylvania, just twenty-five miles from the West Virginia border. In areas where the industry continues, the language of worker memorials is a blend of tribute to ideals and testimony to very real experiences.

Memorials in general are rhetorically ambiguous since they make note of death even as they celebrate progress. They can inspire what Dolores Hayden calls "moral imagination" at places "where memory has not resolved injustices" and where people publicly recall "isolation and exploitation, as well as connectedness." Such sites, she writes, yield "difficult memories."[26] Difficult memories are evident in regions where mining is a current or recently remembered activity; they also are expressed in towns where industry is gone but where there is still public memory of a mine accident or other violence.

One of several extremely deadly early twentieth-century accidents occurred at the Harwick Mine, where 179 workers were killed in 1904. Today, a small and simple marker pays tribute to "all Harwick coal miners." It stands next to a cart full of coal, outside the local firehouse in an otherwise residential neighborhood between Cheswick and Springdale, an area in which a modern mining operation is visible.[27] The language is somewhat grander on the marker that commemorates the victims of the 1940 Sonman Mine explosion in the town of Portage, also in western Pennsylvania. The gray stone memorial sits in a large municipal park, next to a public swimming pool. Its front side reads: "In loving memory of 63 brother workers who took the last trip on July 15, 1940 to work for the good of mankind"; the back side lists the men who were killed. This memorial is Stop 3 on the Portage "auto tour," a driving tour marked by road signs and explained in a printed brochure distributed at a local museum.[28] If you continue along the tour, you get to "Stop 5—Hughes Borehole," which has this explanatory text: "You will come to a large, red area with very few living things on it. In the middle of this area you will see water coming out of the ground. . . . This is the Hughes borehole. It was drilled to relieve pressure from an old mine. The red material you see is iron. . . . The water from the borehole enters the river and effectively kills most aquatic life for miles." And then there is "Stop 10—Acid Mine Drainage: Continue up Main Street until you come to the bridge. Safely park your vehicle and look at the stream under it. This is Trout Run. No trout live in it now. This stream has been polluted by acid mine drainage from the mines 'up the creek.'" Other stops include company-built miners' houses and Miner's Hall, the union meeting building for the United Mine Workers Local.[29]

This is a fascinating example of local heritage that celebrates the bravery and sacrifice of past workers while sharply criticizing the negative legacy of their industry. It further connects mine accidents with the need for unions. The same mix of messages can be found on an imposing monument located just inside the Pennsylvania border from West Virginia, on the northbound side of Interstate 79. Located at a state "Welcome Center" near the town of Kirby, the Greene County Coal Miners' Monument at first appears to be a tribute to former United Mine Workers (UMW) President John L. Lewis, whose figure is carved on the front side. But it really is a memorial to the thirty-seven miners who died in a 1962 explosion in the Robena Mine, owned by U.S. Steel as part of its coke-producing operation. The dead miners' names are listed on the front of this tall slab of granite, underneath a historical explanation of the explosion; on the back are the names of more than one thousand people who have worked in Greene County mines and donated money to build the monument. Here, the living and the dead are connected through memorial, and union organizing is understood as not merely historical. At the same time, this monument's main inscription is general and neutral, like that on the Harwick memorial: "Greene County, Pennsylvania proudly dedicates this monument to all coal miners."[30]

Memorialization has the potential to depoliticize labor history through its patriotic rhetoric and its tendency to mourn the industrial dead as a single group. The details of labor history, and especially labor unrest, tend to get smoothed out by the language of heritage culture, in which class struggle is understood as the inevitable sacrifice made by our immigrant ancestors who "pioneered" the country's growth. Yet the power of reminders of particular moments—of their horrible local impact despite "national progress"—is evident in the Sonman and Robena memorials. The names they list are testimony to workers' ethnicities, an acknowledgment of diversity that is specific and documentary rather than broadly celebratory.

Ethnicity and unionization also are interpretive themes at the site of the Lattimer Massacre. Located just outside Hazleton, in eastern Pennsylvania, this is the spot where fifty-seven immigrant men were shot and either wounded or killed by police as hundreds of striking miners marched from Harwood to Lattimer in 1897. It is a somber and moving monument, but because it sits at a three-way intersection in a suburban neighborhood, it looks as if it's in someone's front yard. Like several other miner memorials, it is very hard for an outsider to find; its location suggests that its purpose is local memory, not tourist information. The language on the stone monument, dedicated in 1972 by locals of the UMW and the American Federation of Labor and Congress of Industrial

Organizations (AFL-CIO), is strongly worded, noting that the unarmed miners "were simply shot down like so many worthless objects; each of the licensed life takers trying to outdo the others in the butchery." Above the names of the seventeen miners who died is a phrase—"Dedicated to these union brothers who made the supreme sacrifice"—that can be read as rhetorically linking their fate to the Civil War dead.[31]

At the Lattimer site, union activity, as part of local history, is interpreted as an act of national patriotism. In Scranton's Courthouse Square, UMW President John Mitchell, who brokered the settlement of the subsequent 1902 anthracite strike, stands in stone in an alcove under the words "Champion of Labor/Defender of Human Rights."[32] Mother Jones, too, is remembered for her involvement in the 1900 coal strike, explained on a state historical marker in Coaldale, located next to an unlikely kind of memorial—a bus shelter. On its three closed sides, the Coaldale No. 8 Miners Memorial bears these slogans: "A Car More a Day Means Extra Pay," "Did You Produce a Car More Today?" and "Everybody's Goal Is Mine More Coal." This structure functions both as folk art and as a reminder of what is now gone: coal mining and extra pay. Together with the marker honoring Mother Jones and a large chunk of coal on the ground, this park, which in 2008 was named Miners Memorial Park, is a labor history site. But the nonresident or non-coal-history expert would never see it unless they happened to drive by it, as I did, careening to the side of Route 209 to find out what on earth I had just passed.[33]

The Coaldale shelter is one example of a few memorials that seem haphazardly situated on the landscape and that certainly are not meant as tourism. In Minersville, a Rotary Club–sponsored statue of a coal miner stands atop a pile of coal, holding a lamp up and looking forward. Its somber dedication is meant "to commemorate in a very special way the many men and boys who lost their lives in the mines." Unfortunately, its impact is diminished by its backdrop, the large awning and bank of gas pumps of a Turkey Hill convenience store.[34] Even less gloriously located is the miner in the Frackville Mall food court. (On closer inspection, I realized that this statue, though listed under "monuments" in a guide to coal history sites, actually is a promotion for the Pioneer Tunnel and Coal Mine, a tourist mine nearby.[35])

More often, mining memorials are located near official buildings such as courthouses, banks, schools, and fire stations. They also appear near war memorials, as is the case in Summit Hill, Lansford, and Pittston. That connection is provocative, according dead miners the status of public servants and public heroes. Former mining engineer and Pottsville native Joseph W. Leonard III sees miners in these terms, reminding us that they not only "faced death each day" but also faced "years of gradual loss of quality of life and health resulting from workplace darkness, isolation, dust and smoke. . . . Perhaps the only difference between the well-known military hero and the unknown coal-mining hero is time."[36]

"Telling How Things Were": Logistics and Legacies in Mine Tours and Museums

Such reminders also are provided by the guides who lead Pennsylvania's five underground tours of former mines that have been "repurposed" for tourism. In the west, these include the Tour-Ed Mine in Tarentum, northeast of Pittsburgh, and the Seldom Seen Mine, northwest of Altoona. The Seldom Seen Mine is probably aptly named, given that it is located in a rural mountain area and open only four days a week during the summertime. As its own name suggests, many visitors to the Tour-Ed Mine in Tarentum are school groups from the local area (its website provides driving directions only from Pittsburgh), although I saw it on a summer day with a group primarily of adults.

These two mine tours in the state's bituminous coal region emphasize the *process* of mining—recent, rather than nineteenth-century industry—and the differences between shallow and deep mining. My guide at the Seldom Seen Mine focused his narration on the many ways miners could die or be injured on the job. The tour at the Tour-Ed mine is primarily a walk past a series of electrical machines, which are turned on to demonstrate their functions in extracting, culling, and moving coal. At both mines, you descend underground along a gradual slope in a "mantrip," a squat, yellow train of cars you can barely sit up straight inside, and in the mine itself, the ceiling is no more than six feet high. Both tours stress the dangers that can lead to explosions, and the guides, who themselves are former miners, explain the flooding that happened at Quecreek.

A woman in my group at the Tour-Ed mine said that her father had worked in this mine, and she had brought her children and grandchildren to see it. The guide replied that his relatives, too, had been miners, as he himself had been. He was laid off in the 1980s, when, as the source of coke, the bituminous mining industry suffered from its close relationship to the collapsing steel industry. He couldn't get rehired, he said, because younger miners were cheaper: "I just had to suffer it out until I could collect my miner's pension."[37] Here, the tour narration was about the recent working past, and even the present, as much as it was about distant labor history.

The dangers of mining and the hardship of mining community life are frankly discussed as well in the interpretation at the three anthracite mine tours in eastern Pennsylvania. When a newspaper travel writer took the Lackawanna Coal Mine Tour in Scranton, he noted that tourists "are meant to come back into the sunshine with a greater appreciation of a way of life that left deep veins of loss, misery and cultural trauma through successive generations of families in the anthracite fields of northeast Pennsylvania."[38] Yet these tours are historical since they document an industry—deep mining of "hard coal"—that has all but vanished.

In the Lackawanna Mine, guides tick off information in a matter-of-fact manner: what the purpose of the canary was, how blasting was done before electric power, how old you had to be to be a mule boy, what each type of worker was paid.[39] A similar presentation is made inside the Pioneer Tunnel and Coal Mine in Ashland, which has given tours since 1962 (this mine closed in the 1930s). There, in addition to their trip into the mine, visitors may take a short but bone-jarring ride in open-air cars down railroad tracks once used by the Philadelphia Reading Coal Iron Company. At the ride's turnaround spot, the guides point out, over the next mountain, the town of Centralia, where an underground coal fire has been burning for forty-eight years; nearly deserted, this town nevertheless draws a steady following of "disaster tourists," as Edward Slavishak has documented.[40] These two and a third anthracite tourism mine, the No. 9 Mine in Lansford, give visitors a sense of how deep anthracite mines were, how tiny the tunnels were that miners crawled through, and how much hard coal is still left under the mountains of northeast Pennsylvania.

As with the other anthracite tours, the narration in the No. 9 Mine is full of historical facts, yet on the tour I took, the guide also offered political and cultural context for miners' experiences in their own time (as opposed to our heroic notions of them now). In discussing the frequency of collapses and explosions, the guide explained that the miners were less valuable than the mules because there was a larger supply of immigrants than of mules. She (yes, a female guide in a mine) then stressed that, in the nineteenth century, ethnic diversity was not a rich and wonderful aspect of mining communities; it was a systematic hiring practice of mine owners who were intent on keeping their workers divided and distrustful. If workers could not speak English, let alone

one another's languages, and if they lived, by design of the mine company, in separate neighborhoods, they were less likely to identify the common concerns that would lead to unionization, she explained.[41]

While such negative specifics of labor history are often obscured by the public history celebrations of "cultural heritage" that are the subject of chapter 4, labor history survives in much coal-mining heritage. It is evident in memorials marking accidents and labor violence. The state's two main coal history sites, the Pennsylvania Anthracite Heritage Museum in Scranton and Eckley Miners Village near Hazleton, celebrate the "proud legacy" of ethnicity, yet they also are explicit about the financial hardship experienced by large families, the frequency of death in the mines, and the long struggle for unionization.[42]

Eckley, a Hazleton-area patch town where anthracite was mined from 1854 to 1963, was used as the set of the 1969 film *The Molly Maguires*—Paramount Pictures added a company store and a large, fake breaker, both of which remain—before it became a state "living history" museum. Although some people still actually live there, today this village is open to visitors who tour the preserved or restored houses, churches, and other buildings. In the "doctor's office," a house containing interpretation about how mine-accident victims were treated, a volunteer docent stressed to me that the village is "authentic": most of the buildings are original, and the stories the guides tell in each building are based on archival records. But mostly, she told me, she was glad that she could tell visitors "the truth" about life in a patch town because her grandfather had been a miner in this region and she remembered what it was like to be a child during the Depression.[43]

Her testimony is evidence that even at such official, state-funded history sites, the perceived authenticity of interpretation is influenced by volunteers. This is even truer of smaller museums, many of which are entirely dependent on volunteer staffers and therefore less likely to communicate with a broad public. Anyone seeking a comprehensive understanding of public history about Pennsylvania coal mining would find herself, as I did, driving from one small town to another in multiple trips planned around sites' limited hours.[44] Often I also was surprised by their locations. One "Anthracite Mining Museum" sits next to a water flume ride inside Knoebels Amusement Park near Elysburg, containing equipment donated by former miners in this area near the Poconos.[45] Other museums are tucked inside municipal buildings. The Coalport Area Coal Museum features mining equipment and memorabilia in displays lining the long hallway of a former school, built by the Civilian Conservation Corps in the 1930s, that now houses the town library and a day-care center.[46]

The Museum of Anthracite Mining in Ashland, while professionally curated and state funded, is located inside the Ashland Borough Hall, meaning that it is open only on weekdays and closed on the weekend—when the Pioneer Tunnel and Coal Mine across the street is most likely to have visitors.[47] The Coal and Coke Heritage Center, which documents the experiences of bituminous coal miners, is in the basement of the library at a branch campus of Penn State.[48]

Occupying the former Miners National Bank, the Williamstown Historical Society—like some memorials, a product of the town's 1976 bicentennial celebration—contains a second-floor exhibit that effectively uses photographs and artifacts to explain how work was done in the once-enormous colliery of the Susquehanna Coal Company where my grandfather worked. I was able to see it because my aunt and uncle knew of its existence and knew when it would be open (four hours every Monday in good-weather months). Its downstairs displays emphasize the local high school and the military service of young men from the area. Edith Umholtz, whose husband, Ward, had helped found the museum, was working there that day. When I explained who I was, within minutes another volunteer handed me photographs of the girls' basketball team and the Williamstown High School class of 1945, both including my mother. I encountered band uniforms, old dresses, pictures of churches, an antique sewing machine, a hand-wringer washing machine, and a horse-head costume from a local theatrical production as I headed upstairs to the coal mining exhibit.[49]

A similar array of small-town memory can be found inside the Broad Top Area Coal Miners Museum in the central Pennsylvania town of Robertsdale, once home to the Rockhill Iron and Coal Company and a constellation of mines, foundries, furnaces, and railroads. (The East Broad Top Railroad, now a tourist attraction, is nearby.) All of these industries are thoroughly explained, with maps, photographs, models, equipment, company records, and chunks of iron and coal. But the main floor of this museum, inside a former Methodist church closed due to dwindling population, is devoted to ordinary life. It displays furniture, clothing, census records, programs from town pageants, stereograph cards, sports uniforms and trophies, movie posters, school photographs and pennants, and military uniforms and medals. The latter items are featured in a section paying tribute to local soldiers of all wars, on the raised area that once was the church's altar.[50]

Indeed, every small-town "industrial" museum I visited in the course of researching this book had the same two features that are most striking in the coal mining museums in Williamstown and Robertsdale: they were as much about daily life as about industry, and they inevitably contained an exhibit about military service, usually emphasizing World War II. Like memorials, such gestures include the community in their conceptualization of heroism and invite visitors to compare the sacrifices of miners (or other kinds of workers) with the sacrifices of warriors.

"For Generations to Follow": The Persistence of Symbolic Heroism

In his study of mining landscapes, Richard Francaviglia writes, "Mining, like warfare, is the kind of activity that someone, preferably someone else, has to do. . . . Both . . . leave heroes and, significantly, are regarded with nostalgia only after they are finished, that is, become history."[51] Francaviglia's statement helps explain not only the more historical interpretation of anthracite (as opposed to bituminous) mining but also the ambiguity of the interpretive messages of coal heritage sites when they are considered collectively. On one hand, miners were (or are) heroes who have advanced the nation, supported by "close-knit" communities that have embodied "the best qualities of the American spirit." On the other hand, they were (or are) the "someone else" who have had to do a dirty and dangerous job and who often have died as a consequence.

In recent years the heroism of miners and soldiers has been further conflated by the factor of age: the last generation to work in a fully operating anthracite economy also was the generation that fought World War II and the Korean War. Many of those same men (and women, often widows) were involved during the closing decades of the twentieth century in the creation of the mine tours, memorials, and museums discussed in this chapter. Today many of them are the volunteers who promote and staff these sites, hoping to spur their towns' economic development as well as to preserve their own pasts.

Thomas Dublin and Walter Licht describe these people as "a largely elderly group . . . persisters who chose to stay and struggle rather than move to the more prosperous communities beyond the anthracite region."[52] The best the state tourism office can do in its advertising promotion of this area is to refer to "the tough beauty of these hardscrabble towns," quoting one local man as saying, "Been here all my life and I'll die here, too. My plot's already bought and paid for."[53] One wonders what will happen to these historical sites when this generation is gone, or perhaps later when their children or grandchildren no longer visit to remember. Many of the baby boomer offspring of the "persisters" are already gone, scattered to other towns and cities where newer industries offer employment.[54]

The resulting demography of the anthracite region was symbolically captured in a front-page photograph appearing in the *New York Times* in 2008
showing an elderly woman walking with a cane in front of two coal-themed
outdoor murals in Pottsville. The occasion for national attention to this small
Schuylkill County town was the possibility that the county courthouse and
prison—where in 1877 six of the Molly Maguires were tried and hanged—was
considering switching from coal to less-expensive natural gas heating. "You
can't pay millions of dollars for nostalgia," the chairwoman of the county com-
missioners was quoted as saying in the *Times* story, which ran with the headline "King Coal County Debates a Sacrilege."[55] A Pottsville man who had spent
thirty years working in the mines told the Harrisburg *Patriot-News,* "Coal miners kept this county going. . . . What do they do? Turn their backs on them."[56]

In western Pennsylvania today there is a different debate, focused less on
the departure of industry than on the growing criticism of coal mining's environmental impact and on recent claims that coal-burning power plants now
can be made "clean," producing less pollution. Proponents of the survival and
growth of the bituminous coal industry continue the elision of coal mining and
military service. In an effort to recruit more miners, in 2007 one Pittsburgh-
area coal company began running ads with the slogans "We mine the coal that
powers the nation" and "We're working down here to keep America running
up there" (a *New York Times* business article about this campaign was titled
"They're Looking for a Few Good Coal Miners").[57] The industry also commu-
nicates its message on billboards that line the Pennsylvania Turnpike. "Electricity," reads one, with the letters spelling "city" in black: "Without Coal, Most
Cities Would Be Dark." "Welcome to Coal Country," reads another, which continues, "Coal. Pennsylvania's #1 Fuel for Electricity. Now Clean and Green with
New Technologies." These are sponsored by a lobbying group called F.O.R.C.E.,
which stands for Families Organized to Represent the Coal Economy and has
the website www.families4pacoal.org.

Although at first it may seem specific to current events, this group's name
is squarely within the rhetoric of news media and local history accounts of the
Quecreek rescue, and these messages along the state's main highway are reminders of the continuing symbolic power of the small town, the "proud community that supports its own when trouble strikes."[58] That symbol is based not
just on material realities of the present but also on public memory of the past.

Current debates about and understandings of coal mining are indeed
threaded with the past, with memory stories that simultaneously, if contradic-
torily, invoke ghosts of warrior heroes and sacrificial victims, opposing forces

of coal companies and unions, and feelings of national pride and local outrage. Much public history about coal mining conveys loss, nostalgia, and tribute to the "old soldiers" of a passing generation. Yet the heritage narrative is also, to use the language of the Pittston memorial's inscription, "for generations to follow."

Memorials are most abundant in areas where mining is largely gone. They and the few surviving breakers are reminders that "work was and is central to life here," writes Ken Wolensky. "In anthracite country the air may now be cleaner, the water less polluted, and the landscape less scarred where reclamation has taken hold. Yet industrialization and its human and environmental costs cannot be easily exiled from historical memory."[59] In the state's western, bituminous coal fields, mining heritage is something more than memory; it is social and political rhetoric. Understood in that sense—as a set of ideals emphasizing sacrifice and community that are actively recalled today—coal mining's past is very much present.

"FROM OUR FAMILY TO YOURS"
Personal Meanings of Work in Factory Tourism

Americans grow up with Pennsylvania in their closets, in their toy boxes, in their kitchens. They know crayons, Slinkies, Zippo lighters. They know the Jeep without knowing it was invented in Butler. We're branded as authentic. As much as they know Gettysburg and the Liberty Bell and Valley Forge, they also know ketchup and crayons.

—Lenwood Sloan, Director of Cultural and Heritage Tourism, Pennsylvania Tourism Office

Even as factories themselves have been disappearing from the landscape, in recent years tourism literature has increasingly promoted the state's many "factory tours." The curious can visit the Utz Potato Chip factory in Hanover, the Martin Guitar Company in Nazareth, and the Yuengling Brewery in Pottsville, as well as museums that celebrate Crayola Crayons and Zippo lighters. York, home to the Harley-Davidson motorcycle plant tour, calls itself "The Factory Tour Capitol of the World."

The familiarity and nostalgic appeal of such products have made them effective subjects of public history as well. In 2008, the State Museum of Pennsylvania mounted an exhibit called "Made in PA." While it included interpretation and artwork about the coal, iron, and steel industries, this display was dominated by brand-name products, including Mack Trucks, Quaker State Motor Oil, Yuengling, Rolling Rock and Iron City beers, and Slinky, whose repeating musical advertising jingle wafted out of the exhibit.[1] Quaker State Motor Oil and Rolling Rock Beer are no longer made in Pennsylvania, but other well-known names remain, and several invite the public to watch their products being made.

Factory tours have been given in Pennsylvania for more than a century, since the H. J. Heinz Company opened its doors to the public beginning in the 1890s. "Some 20,000 visitors were trooping through the Allegheny factory annually at the turn of the century" to watch workers in the Pickle Works, the Baked Bean Building, and the Bottling Department, Robert C. Alberts writes in his history of the company.[2] The Heinz tour emphasized the care and cleanliness with which its condiments were made and packaged, as well as the founder's success story, featuring, by 1905, "The House Where We Began." According to Roland Marchand, "The plain two-story house in Sharpsburg, Pennsylvania, where Henry Heinz had first prepared horseradish sauce in 1860, had arduously been lifted from its foundations and floated down the Allegheny River to nestle in the courtyard of the huge Heinz plant in Pittsburgh. It served to narrate, architecturally, an edifying story of success through diligence and morality."[3]

In the opening decades of the twentieth century, amid concern and legislation about food safety, tours were meant to reassure the public that such products, even if mass-manufactured, were made by wholesome, careful individuals who took pride in the details of their work. At Heinz, visitors watched hundreds of "spotlessly clean girls" as they "packed, inspected, corked, capped, and labeled" pickles, notes Alberts.[4] During the Depression, tours also were part of an effort to improve corporate image in order to counter distrust of big business. Appeals were made to the public in friendly, conversational language.[5] In 1938, Hershey Chocolate promoted its factory tours with an advertisement in the format of a letter printed on company letterhead:

> To People Everywhere and Especially Children:
>
> The people of the United States are the largest consumers of chocolate and cocoa products in the world.
>
> Children and grown-ups like to eat chocolate because it is so delightful.
>
> Wouldn't you like to see how it is made? Then come to Hershey, Pennsylvania some day and our guides will take you through the factory and explain it. Sixty to seventy thousand people go through our plant each year.
>
> Why not you? We will welcome you.[6]

Food manufacturers led the factory-tour trend, and they dominate factory tourism now. In the middle decades of the twentieth century, the offerings were thematically much broader, thanks to thriving industrial production and the growth of family automobile travel in the postwar era. By the 1950s, Pennsylvania state tourism literature declared, "No other state offers the wide variety of different family tours to interest children. From steel mills and aluminum plants to hat factories and paper mills along with an exciting visit to the Hershey Chocolate Co."[7] Among the thirty-three businesses listed in 1950s and 1960s editions of a "Pennsylvania Plant Tours" brochure were the U.S. Steel Homestead Works, the Patterson Lumber Company in Galeton, the Berkshire Knitting Mills in Reading, and the Scranton Lace Company.[8]

Today there are about two dozen plant tours operating in Pennsylvania, but they aren't of steel mills or textile mills, and some of them aren't even of factories. The current incarnation of this phenomenon confirms Stephen V. Ward's observation that today "tourism promotion [is] linked to wider themes," such as hospitality, food and beverage, entertainment, and retail.[9] Blending these themes especially well are companies that manufacture three products of which Pennsylvania leads the nation in production: potato chips, pretzels, and chocolate.

Lancaster County's tourism office (officially, the Pennsylvania Dutch Convention and Visitors Bureau) promotes a "Sweet 'n Salty Trail," with local snack food and candy companies mapped along a driving route. A travel writer for the *Washington Post* enthused, "A trip here is a yummy exercise in between-meal noshing: warm, soft, salted pretzels straight from a brick oven; chocolate Wilbur Buds (a squatter version of the Hershey's Kiss); penuche fudge; chocolate toffee crunch; peanut-butter cups nestled in a rich cookie coating. . . . Pretzels are a mainstay. This twisted treat is to Pennsylvania what pizza is to New York or coffee to Seattle."[10]

Most of the large chip and pretzel companies are in adjacent York County, which also uses the phrase "Sweet and Salty" to group them together as a themed day trip. Drawing on a former state slogan, their marketing material promises, "You've got a friend in Pretzelvania."[11] For more than a decade, York County has held an annual event when area businesses open their doors to tours or expand their tour hours and offer free admission. First called "York Manufacturers Days," this event now is billed as the "Made in America Tours." Its promotional language promises "an exclusive, behind-the-scenes look at the making of some of America's favorite products. Step onto manufacturing floors for a first-hand look at American craftsmanship."[12] This event's tours, especially the one of the Harley-Davidson motorcycle plant in York, have received national and international press coverage.[13]

Of all of the sites discussed in this chapter, the one most visited (by far) is Hershey's Chocolate World. Some five million people come here every year, even though it's no longer possible to tour the actual chocolate factory, as it was when I was a child. Instead, Hershey gives "The Great American Chocolate Tour," a ride through explanatory displays within a retail and entertainment center whose entryway is flanked by smaller replicas of the real factory's smokestacks (which visibly rise over Hershey less than a mile away). Chocolate World sits just outside the entrance to the real draw: Hersheypark, a major amusement complex that has grown over the past century from the "picnic and pleasure ground" Milton S. Hershey built for his workers in 1907.[14] Only the smell of chocolate coming from the plant reminds visitors that factory work continues adjacent to this massive playland.

While Hershey is an exceptionally successful tourist attraction, it is promoted in combination with many of the other destinations discussed in this chapter, and its tourism narrative is consistent with the stories told at the other factory tours. Its product also is typical of what tourists are most likely to see being manufactured across the state today—either food or leisure/lifestyle products. Understood as American brands, these companies' products blend together thematically. At the Pennsylvania companies that invite tourists, the meaning of American industry, past and present, is explained in remarkably similar ways.

"Hands-on Discovery": Work as Play

Did you know that 75 percent of all of the country's pretzels are made within 100 miles of Lancaster County?[15] In Hanover, Snyder's produces 40 pretzels a second. And in Hershey, they make 33 million Kisses a day!

The narration of factory tours is filled with facts, especially numbers—measuring quantity, size, weight, speed, cost—to convey the superlative dimensions of manufacturing, even if the products themselves are quite small. Walking visitors through windowed hallways on the level above the factory floor, the Snyder's tour guide spews out figures. The company manufactures several kinds of snack foods in its 300,000-square-foot facility that operates 7 days a week, 24 hours a day, shipping to 43 countries on 5 continents. There are 400 workers here and 1,000 total at all of their plants. It takes 10 minutes to get from a potato to a bag of potato chips. They go through 450,000 pounds of potatoes every week and 28 tons of pretzel salt every month. Using "the largest pretzel ovens in the world, made only for Snyder's" ("you won't see them anywhere else"), they produce 10 million airplane-sized bags of pretzels per month—240 of them per minute. When all the pretzel ovens are running at the same time, they produce 40 pretzels every second, which over a 2-hour period would amount to 14 tons of pretzels, the weight of a school bus![16]

This narrative style is used at other companies as well. At Harley-Davidson in York, visitors learn that a single bike has 1,300 parts, that their giant metal-shaping machines stamp out 700 fenders per shift, and that just two machines have forged a total of 303,479 kickstands over the years.[17] The Mack Truck assembly plant in Macungie (near Allentown) rolls out 36 trucks, or one every 13 minutes, during a typical workday, and Mack makes 75 percent of all the garbage trucks in America.[18] In just 13 years, production at Tröegs Brewery in Harrisburg has risen from 1,500 to 30,000 barrels a year; each batch they brew fills 25 barrels, or 300 cases, of beer.[19] The Wilbur Chocolate Factory in Lititz makes 240 million pounds of chocolate a year, while the Hershey factory needs "approximately 50,000 cows to provide the 700,000 quarts of milk for *one day's* production."[20]

Described as an accumulation of astonishing numbers, manufacturing seems wondrous. (At Snyder's, the pretzels do make a remarkable sight, as hundreds of thousands of tiny snacks dance down conveyer belts through the large factory.) This barrage of data implies that what we're seeing is a scientific process, measured, regulated, accurate, predictable, and reliable in its result. At the same time, these many facts and figures are delivered in a way that blends information and entertainment and that has the gee-whiz quality of a trivia game.

The statistics-filled introductory film at the Herr's potato chip factory tour is narrated in part by "Chipper," a talking chipmunk. A stuffed version of Chipper is available in the Herr's large gift shop, along with "Tate Herr," a furry potato with happy human features and little arms and legs. As these examples and the school bus analogy suggest, many of the factory tours are geared toward children. This has been the case for more than half a century, as Hershey's 1938 invitation makes clear, and factory tours long have been popular with school groups and families. In 2007, the Children's Museum of Pittsburgh mounted an exhibit, called "How People Make Things," inspired by the factory tours given on the popular public television show Mister Rogers' Neighborhood, filmed in Pittsburgh beginning in 1968.[21]

A thematic focus on play is unsurprising at sites that interpret the manufacture of products for play, such as the Crayola Factory in Easton. The actual factory manufacturing crayons is indeed in Easton, but this site is, like Chocolate World, a tourism venue in another part of town, advertised as "A Hands-on Discovery Center." Inside, the manufacturing process is reenacted on a small scale—a couple of men operate a wax melter, a crayon mold, and a label machine, and then children are given the freshly made crayons. There is a large area with a variety of surfaces on which children can draw with crayons, chalk, and markers. After they're finished drawing, children wash their hands and are funneled into the other tourism site that shares the building, the National Canal Museum.[22] Because of its incongruous combination with crayons, this museum explains canal boat transportation (which ended more than 150 years ago) in a child-sized display of canals and locks through which children push toy boats.[23]

Outside Hershey's Chocolate World, employees costumed as the Hershey-owned candies—a Hershey Bar, a Kiss, a Reese's Peanut Butter Cup, and a Kit-Kat Bar—mingle with tourists coming in from the vast parking lot. Inside this complex are three attractions that represent factory work. "The Great American Chocolate Tour" simulates the chocolate-making process, complete with a heated tunnel; audio narration explains the stages of production over the Hershey's Chocolate theme song, apparently coming from the singing, animatronic cows positioned at the start and end of the ride. In an area called the "Factory Works," already-wrapped Kisses come down a chute, children put them into a round bowl shaped like a gear wheel, a hard-hatted adult worker puts this onto a conveyor belt to go "through the factory," and at the other end of the area, the gear-shaped bowl comes out and is placed into the children's hands. (Then their parents have the option of buying it.) The most recent attraction is a chocolate-bar assembly line on which children can "wear authentic factory aprons and hair coverings" and choose the type of chocolate and the fillings that go into their own candy bar.[24]

Children also can be "workers" at two pretzel companies. Although its production is now in the city of Reading, the Sturgis Pretzel House remains in charming small-town Lititz, on a street full of eighteenth-century Moravian stone houses. Billed as "America's Oldest Pretzel Bakery," it contains five original kilns in which pretzels were baked when the company began in 1861. In this preindustrial building, each visitor hand-shapes a pretzel from a lump of dough while the guide talks about the origins of pretzels: the word came from "pretziola" (which means "little treat" for children); the shape was meant to look like the shape of children's arms when they prayed (crossed over their chest); the knot signified the marriage of the children's parents.[25] With less historical flourish, children who take the "Intercourse Pretzel Factory Tour"—actually a 15-minute demonstration in a room off the gift shop—line up along a low counter and are shown how to roll out and then twist the pretzel dough.[26]

"You Know It's Quality": Work as Craftsmanship

I suspected that the children on my tour of the Revonah Pretzel Factory in Hanover had already been to Lititz and Intercourse because they were surprised and disappointed not to be allowed to play with the pretzel dough at this small York County company business. Located in the same town as the giant Snyder's and Utz companies, Revonah (the name is Hanover spelled backward) combines a close-up view of the processes of hand-rolling and twisting pretzels with a sense of production in significant quantities, up to 15,000 handmade pretzels per day. Every step of the process—making and shaping the dough, soaking for color, spicing, salting, and baking—is visible in this 80-year-old building. The company is as old as the building, although it has changed hands several times, including brief ownership by Snyder's. Along with their pretzels, the shop sells T-shirts that say on the front, "Revonah" and "Hand Made," and on the back, "The Best Pretzel in the World."[27]

The best potato chip in the world—I have concluded after much research—is Martin's Potato Chips, whose small factory in Thomasville distributes to only five counties in Pennsylvania and part of Maryland. Explanations are provided by employees stationed beside each part of the chip-making process (peeling, slicing, cooking, drying, salting, and packaging), and visitors actually walk through the plant, passing within a foot or two of the chips swirling in boiling oil and bouncing along conveyor belts. This site, too, has a hands-on feeling, even though its processes are automated, because visitors watch the transformation from potato to chip and are handed fresh chips just out of the salting machine.[28]

Martin's Potato Chips and Revonah Pretzels are both part of the York area "Made in America Tours" and are both good examples of what people experience when they "step onto manufacturing floors for a first-hand look at American craftsmanship."[29] Paradoxically, most sites that bill themselves as "factory tours" stress work that is done by hand, by individuals rather than machines (even if the individuals are operating machines). This modern-day "craftsmanship" is explained as fidelity to historical manufacturing techniques, as a resistance to commercial pressures, and as the personal touch of individual workers.

Stories of the Land, the visitor-orientation film for the Susquehanna Gateway Heritage Area, takes up this theme, noting, "At one time, almost anything you can think of was made right here in this area. That's because a strong work ethic and pride in craftsmanship have been passed down through generations. . . . Machines have always driven industrial innovation, but it takes the human mind to foster the idea and the human hand to run them."[30]

Visitors to Tröegs Brewery in Harrisburg are allowed to handle and taste the barley and hops that go into the beer made in this "independent craft brewery."[31] Like Tröegs, Straub's Brewery in the town of St. Mary's brews in one small plant and sells its product regionally. Their guides explain that their beer is considered "hand-brewed" because certain functions, such as pouring in the grains, are done by hand, even though the brewing, bottling, capping, and boxing processes are automated. This point is underscored by the highlight of the tour, when, at one station on the assembly line, the guide reaches in and pulls out, for each visitor, a bottle of beer, freshly filled, still labelless and capless. Adding to this feeling of personal informality and welcome is the "endless tap," where visitors may take a glass and pour themselves a beer (or several) before and after the tours.[32]

The actual handling of the product is a subtheme in several of the tour narrations. The recorded tour narration on Utz's self-guided factory tour (dubbed the "Chip Trip") concludes by telling visitors, "No matter where you find Utz products, you can be assured that they were handled by Utz people from beginning to end."[33] In both the Lititz Chocolate Factory and the Wolfgang Candy Company in York, tourists see women hand-dipping candy in a kitchen behind glass, even while automated production goes on elsewhere in the plant.[34] At the Susquehanna Glass Factory in Columbia, visitors watch women etch designs onto glass products, and the tour guide emphasizes "how many hands these glasses pass through"; the company's brochure celebrates "100 Years of Quality" and promises, "We make it Personal."[35]

Certain businesses advertised as part of "factory" tourism are in fact workshops where a few skilled craftsmen hand-make products. In 2010, the "Made in America" weekend included a new site, Bluett Bros. Violins, where those instruments are handcarved by a master luthier and his three apprentices in a four-room shop.[36] This setting epitomizes state Cultural and Heritage Tourism Director Lenwood Sloan's definition of the local "ambassadors" who reenact "craft traditions" in cultural tourism programs. Visitors, says Sloan, want to see "the master, the journeyman, the apprentice, the intern, the whole process of passing down traditions, laying on of hands . . . the passing from maestro to apprentice. That's part of our heritage."[37] At George's Woodcrafts, near Marietta, every furniture item, whether a dining room table or a bed or a rocking chair, is made entirely by one man who then signs his work. The tour brochure makes this point clearly: "Each piece is made by a skilled craftsman who takes pride in his work." My guide there said to me, "When you see it made by hand, that's how you know it's quality. Not some mass-manufactured stuff from Ohio."[38]

A few company tours are able to effectively blend the seemingly contradictory narrative themes of craftsmanship and mass-production because they use historic machinery. Visitors to York Wallcoverings watch wallpaper being freshly inked on paper threaded through an enormous printing press that dates to 1898; a video shown in the adjacent showroom explains that "historic presses create a painterly effect that cannot be duplicated by modern presses." It also notes the company's "humble beginnings with just a handful of workers and a few presses," and uses the words "pride," "craftsmanship," and "artistry" to describe its workers and its products.[39] At the Family Heirloom Weavers Mill Tour in Adamsville, owner David Kline personally gives tours, but the machines communicate the message. Here, nineteenth- and early twentieth-century looms clatter and clack, making the extraordinary sound of automated *wooden* parts, as they create coverlets, drapes, and pillowcases in eighteenth- and early nineteenth-century patterns. This company, which also has a more modern plant in Red Lion, has supplied the period rugs for nine presidential houses and Colonial Williamsburg and made the costumes for the Civil War film *Cold Mountain*. While other sites claim to be historically authentic because their work is done by hand rather than by machine, these sites' authenticity lies in the industrial machinery itself.

More often, company tours stress the historic techniques used within what is otherwise largely a modern, automated production process. In Mount Joy, near Lancaster, Wilton Armetale, a company that makes metal alloy "serveware" (bowls, platters, pitchers, and mugs), dates only to the 1960s, and most of its production involves electric machinery. Yet its tour guides and brochure emphasize that one part of its metal-making process, in which the product is shaped by washtubs full of gyrating rocks, is a "technique . . . perfected long before the American Revolution."[40] Seltzer's Lebanon Bologna once gave tours of its Palmyra plant, but now only a "video tour" is shown in an old school-house building that houses a little Seltzer's shop and a charity clothing shop. Its narration emphasizes the importance of the smokehouses "built entirely out of wood," where the meats are "slowly cured over hand-tended hardwood fires," just as the process was done in 1902, the year the company was founded. The video goes on to note that while newer manufacturing processes "may be faster and less expensive, only this centuries-old process" results in such a fine product.[41] The tour brochure given to visitors at the Yuengling Brewery highlights the company's antebellum beginnings and construction: "David G. Yuengling, a German immigrant who settled in Pottsville, founded the brewery in 1829, when Americans were just getting used to their newly elected president, Andrew Jackson. The original name was the Eagle Brewery to identify with the qualities of strength and pride, symbolic of the American eagle. Like many old breweries, this one was built on a mountain so that tunnels dug through rock could take advantage of the natural cold temperatures necessary for aging and fermenting."[42]

The Yuengling tour takes visitors through cool, underground chambers where this process continues today, even as bottles fly through capping and labeling machines aboveground. Similarly, the tour and museum at the Martin Guitar factory in Nazareth stress the importance of handcraftsmanship and attention to the sanding and shaping of the wood, within a building that is clearly a very large factory. "When you buy a Martin," reads a worker's testimony inside the museum, "you're buying a person's hard work and skill. It's not like going out and buying something that's just stamped out."[43]

"Some People's Priorities Don't Change": Work as Family

The founders of Martin Guitar, Yuengling, and Straub's all are identified, in interpretive materials, as German immigrants who settled in small towns during the nineteenth century and built successful businesses that are still in the family; Yuengling and Straub's are run by the fifth generation, and Martin Guitar by the sixth.[44] "Continuous operation under family management is a feat bordering on the remarkable," says the historical profile on Martin's website. "In or out of the music industry, C. F. Martin has few rivals for sheer staying power."[45] Yuengling claims to have "the longest uninterrupted history of management by a single family" in the brewing industry and attributes the company's longevity to its retention of "family values."[46]

Company promotional language often invokes the general concept of family to suggest connections among the workers and between workers and visitors. "From Our Family to Yours" is the tagline in the logo for the Wolfgang Candy Company, which specializes in samplers sold as fundraisers by school and church groups.[47] Asher's Chocolates, in the Philadelphia suburb of Souderton, "remains the oldest continuously family owned and operated candy manu-facturer in the United States," and it invites visitors on its self-guided tour to "watch your favorites being made right before your eyes from timeless recipes handed down through four generations."[48] At Wilbur Chocolate, video nar-ration emphasizes that the best chocolate comes from cocoa beans grown on "small, family farms" and hand-harvested by "experienced farmers" who have done this work "for generations" (albeit in South America).[49] In a regional mag-azine article about tours at Wilton Armetale, co-owner John Wilton "credits his father with a sound piece of advice: 'treat everyone who works with us like family and it will in turn come back to you.'"[50] In York, tour guides refer to the "the Harley-Davidson family of dealers, riders, and workers."[51]

Several tours feature the founder's own life story, and inevitably it is one of ingenuity, hard work, and unwavering values. Utz Potato Chips has remained in the hands of the same family for three generations since 1921, when it was founded by Bill and Salie Utz, whose large portraits hang above the entry stair-way to the company's self-guided tour. In an introductory video and from visi-tor center displays, we learn that Bill (referred to as "Grandpa Utz") saved the money he made working in a local shoe factory, while Salie ("Grandma Utz") "used her knowledge of good Pennsylvania Dutch cooking" to make the first chips in their summerhouse, and over time their small venture grew into a great company that nevertheless is still a local company. The video closes by pay-ing tribute to the "hundreds of Utz people, many of whom have been with the company for decades . . . local employees" who are featured in old photographs that line the walls.[52] During one of my tours of Martin's Potato Chip Factory in Thomasville, a guide told this charming origins tale: One day little Harry Mar-tin stopped on his way home from school and bought a bag of Utz potato chips (boo!). When he got home with them, his mother, who ran a greengrocery, said, "Oh, Harry, if you want potato chips, I'll make them for you!" And so she did. And she kept making them. . . . Harry grew up and married a woman named Fairy (yes, Fairy), and they established the company in 1941. Although in the 1970s the company changed hands, members of the Martin family, including Fairy, continued to work there until recently.[53]

At the Herr's Potato Chip Factory Tour in Nottingham, visitors learn that the Herr family are Mennonites who founded the company in 1946 "in a shed on the family farm" in Lancaster County; because of their religious beliefs, there is no production on Sunday. A company history booklet sold in the tour site store explains that, when twenty-one-year-old Jim Herr was searching for a career, "he expressed his desire to do something that would help people." He took out a loan to buy an existing, small potato chip company, and, although he struggled at first, "because he had an obligation to meet, he pressed on." He and his wife Miriam ("Jim and Mim") built a successful business only to see their plant burn to the ground in 1951. They started anew in Nottingham (close to Philadelphia and the Delaware border), where the company is in its second generation of family ownership, run by their son Ed Herr.[54]

The ultimate founder's story, however, is that of Milton S. Hershey, a parable told inside a new museum called "The Hershey Story" and on the two trolley (bus) tours that depart frequently from Chocolate World. In these and many other accounts, Milton Hershey's life is described as a tale of overcoming obstacles, living cleanly, and being loyal to local people. Impatient to make a name for himself, he quit school at age fourteen and failed at early business ventures in Philadelphia, Denver, Chicago, New Orleans, and New York City. He did not succeed until he came home to central Pennsylvania, where his Lancaster Caramel Company flourished; he sold it in 1900 for $1 million and founded the Hershey Chocolate Company. "He had his share of hardships," the trolley tour guide says, but "he never gave up," following the admonition of "Mama Hershey": "Milton, a Hershey never quits." The trolley goes past both Highpoint, Milton Hershey's mansion, and "the Homestead," where he was born in 1857 to Mennonite parents whose "ancestors immigrated here from Switzerland in order to escape religious persecution," the guide explains.

Hershey's mass production of chocolate made the treat so inexpensive that "a child could afford it." As time went on, this democratic vision extended to labor as well. During the Great Depression, the narrator explains, Hershey not only built much of the town but also kept his workers employed: "not one person lost his job." The tour bus passes the double-gabled "worker houses" of a "model town," and the guide says, "Mr. Hershey toured other factory towns and didn't like what he saw. You'll note that those other factory towns, they're not here anymore. Hershey is." Hershey extended his paternalism to orphaned boys, for whom he built a school at the request of his wife, Kitty, when they couldn't have children. Yet no amount of riches mattered when she became ill with an incurable neurological disease and died at age forty-two; the broken-hearted "Mr. Hershey always carried a photo of Kitty in his wallet." Despite his many accomplishments and great wealth, the guide explains, "Mr. Hershey always said that the best thing he did with his life was to marry Kitty," adding, "It's incredible how some people's priorities don't change. Mr. Hershey stood for basic values. . . . Mr. Hershey always put other people's needs before his own. . . . Mr. Hershey is one of those great American heroes that we don't hear enough about today."[55]

"An American Icon": Work as Legacy

With its founder's narrative and its "Great American Chocolate Tour," Hershey is one of several companies that describe their own values as American values and tell their own history as emblematic of American history. In such an account, the company's values and history combine to create a product that stands for the nation. Celebrating the 2007 centennial of its most famous sweet, the Hershey Museum mounted an exhibit called "Kisstory" that promised to tell "The Story of an American Icon."[56]

Tour guides at the Yuengling Brewery talk of the crisis of Prohibition in the 1930s and then the challenges of modernization and expansion in more recent decades (challenges some other breweries such as Rolling Rock did not weather without being bought by big companies and moved out of state). The company's loyalty to and success in Pottsville are also understood as a kind of redemption for the collapse of the anthracite coal industry in the mid-twentieth century. Yuengling "is a survivor," an authentic product from small-town America whose integrity is intact despite a changing global business climate. Its tour brochure boasts that the company's survival is "a testament to American entrepreneurship. Its legacy is one of a successful business against all odds, and a . . . channel into our own past."[57]

Because Harley-Davidson is based in Milwaukee, Wisconsin, the tour of its York, Pennsylvania, assembly plant tells an American story rather than a local one. An introductory film explains that the company began in 1903 in "a small shed" with just four workers and since has survived hardships including the Great Depression, a hostile-takeover bid in 1969, increasing global competition after it became the only remaining American motorcycle company, inept ownership in the 1970s (the company was saved when it was bought by a group of Harley-Davidson managers, including a grandson of one of the co-founders), and near-bankruptcy in 1985. The film's historic portion ends with the statement that "in many ways, the history of Harley-Davidson mirrors the history of the nation" because it "absorbed the blows" of the twentieth century and survived.[58]

Harley-Davidson also credits its customers for the iconic status its products have achieved, and factory tour visitors are addressed as part of the "legacy." At the start of the tour, they are asked, "Do you ride?" and then, "Do you ride a Harley?" (and, if so, what model?). Martin Guitar pays the same respect to people who come to its factory in the town of Nazareth. The staffer at the front desk asks, "Do you play the guitar?" and if the answer is yes, they're invited to go back to an area where several models hang on the wall, waiting to be lifted down and played. The tour guide begins by asking the same set of questions: Who plays? Who owns a Martin? What model? For people who own these products, their visits are understood to be something more than tourism; they are referred to as "members" at Martin and as "owners" at Harley-Davidson.[59]

Both plants have large visitor centers to accommodate the many people who come—according to their tour guides, fifty thousand a year at Martin and eight thousand a year at Harley-Davidson—and both have been the subject of travel journalism.[60] One article in the *Cleveland Plain Dealer* called the York motorcycle company a "shrine."[61] Another, in the *New York Times,* called Martin Guitar visitors "pilgrims" and told the story of Beverly Goskowski, "whose horn-rims showed a studious side, but whose leather jacket whispered, 'rebel.' . . . 'I came here seven years ago with my granddad,' she said. 'He passed over the summer, and I guess I'm trying to recapture the fun we had when we first came. Or to say goodbye to him.'"[62]

Martin anticipates its visitors' desire to connect with the past, as well as the guitar-making process, by housing a museum that tells the story of the company and contains dozens of special guitar models made for certain events or performers (among them Johnny Cash, Dolly Parton, Paul McCartney, Eric Clapton, and others). At the museum's entrance is this text: "Martin Guitars have bridged generations, helped define American musical culture and yet stayed close to their 1830s roots. Their simplicity, craftsmanship and superb tone are timeless. They are truly America's Guitar."[63]

This sort of rhetoric is taken to an extreme in another site that attracts "pilgrims," the Zippo/Case Museum in Bradford, a remote town in north-central Pennsylvania. The company claims to have had "thousands of visitors from over 120 countries around the world," who are referred to as "collectors" in promotional materials.[64] Zippo began during the Great Depression amid the collapse of the oil industry in this part of the state. Its founder, George Blaisdell, had failed at school and at investing but went forward with his new idea even though "nobody had any faith in it. It seemed like a foolish, harebrained idea. . . . Imagine: manufacturing and marketing a lighter for $1.95 when that amount of money fed a family."[65] Today, Bradford's tourism icon is a cigarette lighter, which, like the Kiss in Hershey, adorns street lamps. The Zippo factory is still in operation in Bradford but is not open for tours; instead, the company's story is told in a large, retail-oriented visitors' center. Primarily, this is the story of Zippo lighters, although it also historicizes Case Knives, a company

Zippo purchased in 1993. A museum is devoted to "the rich history of these two American icons."

Like other company founders with humble beginnings, J. Russell Case "rode a horse and buggy selling knives made by his father," the tour brochure informs visitors. A film inside the museum starts and ends with black-and-white footage of little boys playing baseball, as the narrator intones, "a small town, a summer's day"; at the end, a father hands a Case pocketknife to his son. One section of the museum focuses on the Zippo lighter in wartime, especially World War II, and much is made of Ernie Pyle, who wrote about the lighter in one of his syndicated newspaper columns from the front; there also is a sculpture of two soldiers huddled together in a bunker, lighting cigarettes. Other parts of the museum feature Zippo advertisements and clips from famous films in which the product was used, confirming its status as "an American Icon." An enormous gift shop features clothing and keepsakes marked with the company logos, as well as the products themselves in many designs and colors. The day I was there, these knives and lighter display were surrounded by teenage boys, and the company's website encourages visits from Boy Scout troops.[66]

Boys appear frequently in the factory tour narrations that emphasize iconic products; so do references to sports or war (surviving "blows") and to popular-culture masculine ideals ("Walk the Line," Harley-Davidson invites factory tourists in its advertising).[67] Behind the great product is, or was, a great man who once was a regular boy. This prototypical boy faces setbacks, but—thanks to his religion, his mother's unshakeable faith in him, and his wife's love and help—he survives and then thrives. He passes the business down to his sons (or in Hershey's case, the orphaned boys who became his surrogate sons) while building a community of workers who are also "family." These employees take pride in the aspects of their work that are hand-done and in their obligation to carefully handle the product from start to finish. That product is not just a commodity—a pretzel, a bottle of beer, a chocolate bar, a cigarette lighter, a motorcycle, a guitar—but a legacy preserved for you, the visitor, and for your children and grandchildren.

"What Would Milton Do?" Fissures in the Factory Tour Narrative

Factory tours are among the activities featured on *Explore PA*, a public television series documenting travelers' themed weekend trips across the state. On one episode, two young women friends from Harrisburg attend the York

Fair ("America's first fair"), go kayaking and horse-riding, and take tours of the Harley-Davidson and Martin's Potato Chip factories. The show also mentions Wolfgang Candy and Family Heirloom Weavers. Astride a Harley, the show's hostess says, "Who knew watching people work could be so much fun?"[68]

At most of the sites discussed in this chapter, the visitor experience is designed to be interactive and entertaining, and work is described as creative fun or skilled craftsmanship. On some tours, visitors meet workers who explain what they are doing, and several of the tours are given by employees who normally work on the factory floor. Mostly, though, visitors are kept away from the workers, or their attention is diverted by the barrage of amazing numbers. In a few places, including Hershey, Crayola, Wilbur, and Zippo, visitors never see factory workers at all; instead, they watch multimedia presentations or simulations of the work. At these and other tour sites, the star of the show is the product itself—the costumed characters and toys, the beers visitors are handed, the specially designed lighters they can buy, the motorcycles they can mount at the end of the tour. That disconnect obscures the truth that most factory labor is neither creative fun nor skilled craftsmanship but just work, and work that is decreasingly unionized or stable.

Occasionally economic realities intrude (and even less occasionally they are intentionally introduced) into the tour narratives, as when my group's "Mack ambassador" assembly plant tour guide revealed that the only part of their trucks customers can be sure was made in America is the little bulldog hood ornament.[69] While the assembly operation remains in Pennsylvania, Mack headquarters is moving from Allentown to Greensboro, North Carolina, a significant economic loss that has attracted local press coverage. The string-making operation of Martin Guitar in nearby Nazareth has been moved to Mexico, our tour guide said, though she assured us that no one was laid off; they were just reassigned.[70] I heard exactly the same phrase on tours at Herr's Potato Chips and Harley-Davidson, during discussions of the effects of newly automated processes.

In fact, Harley-Davidson cut several hundred jobs at the York plant in 2008, and in May 2009, the company announced that it was considering shutting this plant down entirely. Both developments made front-page news.[71] For local tour-takers like me, that knowledge gave new meaning to the proud statement, on one wall of the visitor center, that "many of the employees here have tenure spanning decades."[72] When local Harley owners held a weekend festival benefiting the Muscular Dystrophy Association in June 2009, a newspaper reporter interviewed one man who explained what the riders and the event stood for:

Paul Melachrinos, a member of the Cumberland Valley Hog Chapter, said he wishes there were more folks . . . willing to support American-made brands and "take pride in what this country has to offer."

"They're supporting the people in Springettsbury Twp. [home to the York plant]—that's thousands of jobs," the Mechanicsburg resident said. "You're buying a piece of America when you buy a Harley-Davidson."[73]

Even more headlines were devoted to the labor situation at the Hershey Chocolate Company that emerged amid massive tourism promotion of the one-hundredth anniversaries of both Hersheypark and the Hershey Kiss in 2007. During a summer-long celebration, schoolchildren sang "Happy Birthday" to a fifteen-ton chocolate Kiss in Chocolate World and students at the Milton Hershey School "aimed flashlights toward the sky to spell out the words 'thank you'" on the anniversary of Milton Hershey's birthday.[74] *USA Today* published an article titled "Hershey Honors Its Past, Looks to the Future," which reported, "The model factory town built a century ago by chocolate magnate Milton Hershey (and still the hub of the Hershey chocolate empire) offers everything from thrill rides to a history lesson in American ingenuity, all in a bucolic setting that seems to draw more vacationers every year."[75] No mention was made of the news the company had announced that spring: the likelihood of worker layoffs, outsourcing of production to Mexico, and the possible sale of all or parts of the company.

In the Harrisburg newspaper, headlines were very different: "A Lot of Fear," "Kiss Jobs Goodbye," and "What Would Milton Do?"[76] The *Patriot-News* interviewed the granddaughter of H. B. Reese, founder of Reese's Peanut Butter Cups, now owned by Hershey, who said of the possibility of a sale, "It saddens me terribly."[77] One Hershey resident wrote to the paper that the layoff plan "is not in the spirit of Milton S. Hershey, who never laid off a person during the Depression, and it will break the spirit of our town and the towns around us that need their jobs to keep everything going. . . . Think of Milton S. Hershey, his success and what he would do."[78] An eighty-three-year-old alumnus of and former houseparent for the Milton Hershey school told a reporter for the local CBS News affiliate, "Mr. Hershey never, never, never—he wouldn't have done that to his people. He was a family person."[79]

As this book was being finished in 2010, Hershey was still Hershey, having decided against a merger with British competitor Cadbury, and the York Harley-Davidson plant was still operating, after its greatly reduced workforce accepted a new contract including wage cuts and additional job eliminations.

These two situations make visible the tensions between corporate public relations efforts and current economic realities. More tellingly, they are fascinating
examples of how the common themes of factory tourism—the product-as-
American-icon and the heroic founder who treats his workers and his town like
family—can be turned on their heads and used as forms of criticism. Precisely
because the mainstream tourism narrative stresses the survival of American
business and casts workers as family members, it is publicly jarring when that
story goes wrong and when economic losses are interpreted as moral betrayal.
For now, though, tourists flock to Hersheypark every summer, bikers arrive
daily at Harley-Davidson, and children munch on pretzels and chips in Hanover. In a state full of empty factory buildings, famous brands live on, trans-
forming work into tourism—an industry of its own.

"STEEL MADE THIS TOWN"

An Unfinished Story in Uncertain Times

We should build a museum that does for Pittsburgh what the Rock 'n' Roll Hall of Fame did for Cleveland: make it a tourist destination. . . . Instead of spending more time searching for the perfect marketing slogan, isn't it time to focus our collective efforts on showcasing the one thing that already defines our city to the rest of the world? Let's use our steely resolve to send a message loud and clear, "Yes, we're the Steel City—and darn proud of it."

—Letter to the editor, *Pittsburgh Post-Gazette*, November 19, 2002

When the American steel industry collapsed in the closing decades of the twentieth century, the blow was felt perhaps most painfully in Pennsylvania, home to the largest plants of U.S. Steel and Bethlehem Steel. Together, these two companies had forged the ingredients of the nation's greatest bridges and skyscrapers, as well as huge battleships engaged in both World Wars. The wave of abrupt plant closures across the state in the 1980s had social as well as economic consequences, bringing to an end not only jobs but also a way of life that had defined entire towns and cities.

Since then, a range of public debates have taken place regarding how steelmaking and its losses should be publicly remembered. In some cases, the dispute is over who should get to tell this story; in other cases, it is over the question of whether or not the story should be told at all. Especially in the face of real need for economic development—new high-tech businesses, new tourism and hospitality venues—why insist on reminding everyone that a town or city was once, perhaps too recently, full of smoky industry? "The steel heritage people—that's their mission, but they're the only people who talk about that," one museum director told me.

In recent years they have been talking a lot, and the desire of former steel-workers and steel communities to be culturally compensated for their economic losses has attracted federal and state monies as well as press coverage. Due largely to the efforts of the late U.S. Representative John Murtha, who represented an area including Johnstown, federal funding created the Southwestern Pennsylvania Heritage Preservation Commission in 1988 "to develop and enhance old industrial sites to promote tourism."[1] In the same year, a Steel Valley Heritage Task Force was created in the Pittsburgh area, funded in part by the National Park Service, and other redevelopment programs were funded in that region by the Heinz Endowment.[2] Over the past two decades, these efforts have resulted in a series of worthy if largely unconnected heritage projects, many of which are still just beginning to address the subject of steel. In Bethlehem, where steelmaking's departure is most recent, it is still unclear whose vision will prevail among several proposals for commercial and cultural projects drawing on the city's industrial past.

"A City Recast?" The Transformation of an Industrial Symbol

Of Pennsylvania's steelmaking sites, Pittsburgh is the most visible symbol of the industry and its loss. Writing in 1992, the year of the one-hundredth anniversary of the labor battle that made Homestead famous, William Serrin described the public response to these initiatives, which was, in short, unhappy. The citizens of Homestead didn't want parks and museums; they wanted their jobs back. They resented the hypocrisy of sudden public interest in the area, writes Serrin, whose account summarizes a common criticism of industrial heritage in general:

> In its tragedy, Homestead became fashionable, as what might be called "working-class chic" or "working-class voyeurism" arose. For this to happen, it was necessary that the mill be closed and the workers disappear. When the Homestead Works was operating and Homestead was a dirty steel town, people from outside paid no attention to it. They had no desire to go to a dirty steel town or to hang around with steelworkers. But once Homestead was a relic, Homestead was the rage. There were study groups and committees, historical exhibits, film proposals, lectures, brown-bag lunches, dinners, economic analyses, historical surveys, oral histories, a

case study of disinvestment and redevelopment plans in the Monongahela Valley done by the Harvard Business School.[3]

Despite the initial interest of outsiders, the region's tourism promoters have
been skittish about fully embracing a heritage story about steelmaking. Instead,
the gist of their tourism message since 1990 has been that the worst is over
and that visitors now will be delighted to discover a clean and modern city.
One state tourism guide tells readers, "Contrary to popular belief, Pittsburgh is
no longer the smoky, blue-collar steel town of years past. Today it is a vibrant
cultural center offering world-class events, attractions, shopping, sporting activities and exceptional accommodations, all in a historical yet progressive setting."[4] Another calls the area "A City Recast," explaining, "There's a fire burning
in Pittsburgh, but it's not the white-hot heat of a blast furnace. . . . Like SoHo in
the sixties, something is rising from the ashes of old industry in Pittsburgh. Its
name is Art."[5]

Travel journalism has taken this view as well. In 1998, the *Toronto Globe and
Mail* called Pittsburgh "The Comeback Kid," noting, "Less than a century ago,
Pittsburgh was the Gotham of Grime . . . a city of smog so dark and unrelenting
that streetlights blazed at noon. . . . Today, Pittsburgh is well worth exploring,
for its art, its incredible array of architecture, and its omnipresent sense of history. Even if that history is only partially visible today."[6] This theme was well
established by the time of the city's 250th anniversary in 2008. "Pittsburgh has
undergone a striking renaissance from a down-and-out smokestack to a gleam-
ing cultural oasis," declared the *New York Times,* while the Associated Press
advised tourists to "take what you think you know about the Steel City, wad it
up into a little black-and-gold ball and throw it away. . . . Tourists who visit the
city realize it's no longer a smoky steel town but a city with a thriving cultural
district, world-class universities and an impressive vista."[7] A writer for *USA
Today* suggested that the city take up a new slogan: "Pittsburgh: Who Knew?"[8]

The resonance of all of these comments depends on fairly fresh public memory of what is "no longer." One travel article published during the anniversary
year noted that the city's residents "still give directions based on where things
used to be" and referred to "the 'Pittsburgh diaspora,' created by the exodus that
drained the city of its population when steel collapsed."[9] In its coverage of the
international G20 economic summit held there in 2009, the *New York Times*
reported, "Even though Pittsburgh has remade itself by attracting young professionals with university hospital jobs, the city, for many, remains a symbol of

the collapse of the nation's industrial base and the loss of manufacturing jobs."[10] Another newspaper covering the summit explained steelmaking as "inheritance" passed from father to son over time. "Pittsburgh used to be a 'like father, like son' city. The steel mills forged together generations like so many links in a chain," read the article's deck, over a photograph of a former steelworker and his young-adult son (who, hardly unfortunately, went on to become a medical doctor, but "remains a steelworker's son at heart").[11]

In public communication and popular culture, steelmaking long has been described through masculine metaphors. One is sports, notably the athletic "grit" (and recent winning dominance) of the city's professional football team, the Steelers. This spirit was described as "tough, working-class, blood and guts" by a former Steeler interviewed for the documentary Gridiron and Steel, aired in 2002 on Pittsburgh's public television station; the DVD version of this program features the silhouette of a football player walking through flames and the tagline "the mills are gone but the fire burns on."[12]

Another metaphor is war. Writing about public art and other tributes to steelmaking proposed so far in Pittsburgh, Kirk Savage compares these tributes to military monuments: "While the battlefield and the steel mill both brought fire and smoke and waste, they also produced masculinity and power. War built 'men' and nations; steel mills built 'men' and the infrastructure of the modern world. The mythic qualities of the men who made steel—toughness, bravery, endurance—are the very qualities that define a warrior."[13] For more than a century, in storytelling and artwork, the Pittsburgh steelworker was symbolized by the folkloric character of Joe Magarac, "the steelworkers' equivalent to the lumberjacks' Paul Bunyan," writes Janet Marstine. This seven-foot-tall Slavic character, himself made of steel, "turned out 2,000 tons of steel a day" and "could form molten steel with his bare hands, cut sheets of metal with his teeth, and a stop a train with one arm."[14]

Conversely gendered is commentary on the area's modern landscape, so greatly changed in just two decades. A large portion of the site of the now-demolished Homestead plant, which once stretched for miles on the banks of the Monongahela River, is now "The Waterfront," an entertainment and shopping complex including a hotel, chain restaurants, a movie theater complex, and a landscaped, outdoor shopping mall. When this primarily feminine world of leisure and retail first opened, it attracted much academic derision. Up from this site soar the only physical remnants of the mill, a dozen tall, brick venting stacks whose insufficient presence concerns critics. Calling the complex a "strip mall," Jefferson Cowie and Joseph Heathcott refer to the "twelve ghostly smokestacks disembodied from any other reference to the old steel mill—like sentries guarding access to an already forgotten past. . . . They stand merely as commodified quotations from a distant modern epoch, which do little more than offer a bit of nostalgia and character to an otherwise nondescript, post-modern retail landscape."[15]

This level of condemnation is a bit unfair, as I discovered when I went there. There are plenty of references to the old steel mill. Waysides provide histori-cal information, many of them lining a walking path along the river. Pieces of industrial equipment, including a Bessemer converter and a train engine once used on a narrow-gauge track inside the vast mill, are displayed on the grounds in between the restaurants. I stood for a while beneath the twelve tall stacks, near a large wayside display that attracted the attention of a group waiting, on a summer evening, to get into the Longhorn Steakhouse. One of them, a middle-aged woman, started talking about her father's work inside the plant. Smiling, she remembered how, as a child, she had looked at the buildings, stretching along the river as far as she could see, and wondered where they ended. Such a comment might be an example of what Cowie and Heathcott call "smokestack nostalgia,"[16] and yet it is a local, not tourist, account, distinct to an individual with a particular past, and it is her story to tell. Her wistful memory also had a surprising conclusion: she then mentioned that her father's friend, another steelworker, had committed suicide.[17]

Thematically, there are several ways to tell Homestead's story: as the site of a violent labor strike that was unsuccessful but ultimately led to unionization of the industry; as the single plant that, once, produced one-third of the nation's steel; or as the setting for one of the most symbolic episodes of unexpected job loss in American history. The last possibility, like local memory of coal-mining disasters, invites "moral imagination," a reaction in which "difficult memo-ries, and the anger they generate" undercut narratives of American industrial might.[18] In 2006, twenty years after the Homestead plant shut down, a reporter for the *Pittsburgh Post-Gazette* interviewed former steelworkers and described their feelings as "a mixture of pride, resignation and bitterness at the way the company treated the mill workers" at the end.[19] In her ethnographic study of laid-off autoworkers in Kenosha, Wisconsin, after the closing of a Chrysler plant there in 1988, Kathryn Marie Dudley writes, "Plant closings . . . provide the occasion for an important kind of ritual communication in American so-ciety. Every participant and bystander in a local plant-closing drama is drawn into a national 'conversation' about cultural values. How should labor be val-ued? How do people demonstrate their moral worth? Who has the right to make decisions that will affect the whole community? What kind of country was America in the past, and where are we going in the future?"[20]

Who Are "the Lords of the Mon"? Elevating and Eulogizing the Worker

The same questions have been asked within the public dialogue that has ensued since the collapse of the steel industry in Pennsylvania, and an interesting blend of heritage narratives has emerged in attempts to answer them. A leader in that effort is a group called Rivers of Steel, based in Homestead and funded by the Steel Industry Heritage Corporation, a coalition of government and private interests. Over the past decade, Rivers of Steel has developed curriculum plans and programs for school groups, mounted museum exhibits, organized oral histories that have led to radio shows and an online database, and offered public tours of the city, the river, and the Homestead site. Central to all of their interpretation is their mission to convey the worker experience.

When Rivers of Steel began giving public tours of the Carrie Furnaces, an enormous, intact relic that sits on the north bank of the Monongahela, it solicited input from former steelworkers, who were invited to "make appointments to give a short oral history of their working experiences to a Rivers of Steel staff member," explained a notice in the *Pittsburgh Post-Gazette*. The article went on to say, "Those stories will be woven into guides' narration during the tour. Steelworkers who feel comfortable standing in front of people and sharing their tales will be asked to do so before tour groups."[21] I encountered two such men when I took the tour in 2007.[22] One, who handed us samples of the three ingredients of steel (iron ore, coke, and limestone) as he explained the steelmaking process, was eighty-three years old. The other was much younger, having begun there at age eighteen in the 1970s. He described working there as a rite of male passage and as a matter of pride that came from doing your job well and working together with your buddies. Both men confirmed that it was a hard job, hot in the summer and cold in the winter and always dangerous, but that on the whole it was a good job they regret losing.

Narrated by them and by Rivers of Steel Communications Director Jan Dofner (who began by introducing herself as the daughter of a steelworker), the tour was full of details about process and equipment, nearly all of which went over my head. But it seemed to be well understood by the other twenty people in my tour group. Most of them, it turned out, were former steelworkers and their families, and some jumped into the conversation with references to other plants and memories of their closings. They could envision what I—probably the only real tourist in the group—could only imagine, the sight and sound and feel of a live plant.

Unlike the interpretation of iron furnaces, oil drilling, and lumbering, this tour narration did not include a reminder that this placid present site was once filled with flames and noise. Yet, like the woman waiting for dinner at The Waterfront, Dofner did share her childhood memory of the river valleys, filled with one plant after another, all emitting fire and smoke . . . a picture she remembers as a beautiful sight. The Carrie Furnaces complex—which was saved and given national historic landmark status because, until its end, all of its functions were hand-controlled—is now beautiful in a different way, a rusted colossus whose massiveness is stunning. Steven High and David W. Lewis use the phrase "the deindustrial sublime" to describe this aesthetic of abandoned plants and factory buildings that cultural geographers call "industrial ruins."[23] They write, "Industrial ruins are memory places, for they make us pause, reflect, and remember. But remember what, and to what end? To answer this question we must go beyond a vague, melancholy regret."[24]

One reminder—one check on the temptation to wax nostalgic over a "landscape of lost industry"—sits right next to Carrie Furnace: the Edgar Thomson Works, a huge, operating mill with flames flying out its top, a plant that, according to our guide, produces 20 percent of all U.S. steel today. This is the "new" steel industry, however, highly mechanized with fewer workers; the town around it is Braddock, the *New York Times*' chosen symbol for the current recession.

Rivers of Steel, which hopes eventually to build an interpretive center on the Carrie Furnaces site, currently tells several kinds of stories about the area's steelmaking past in a variety of venues and formats.[25] Dofner also gives a "Lords of the Mon" tour aboard a riverboat on the Monongahela, explaining the industry that used to line its banks, and a bus tour called "Babushkas and Hard Hats," which provides a mix of cultural and industrial history (when I took the bus tour in 2009, once again the other members of my group interrupted her talk with memories of their own; they, too, were locals in search of personal memories).[26] Visitors on foot may stop in at the Bost Building, which was used as a headquarters for the steelworkers' union and the press during the 1892 Battle of Homestead and now houses the Rivers of Steel offices. Here the organization holds screenings of old films and newsreels about steelmaking and has changing exhibits (I saw one about worker safety and another about the lesser-known companies referred to as "Little Steel").[27] In conjunction with the Westmoreland Museum of Art, it also produced a multimedia project titled *Born of Fire,* including a book of steel-themed artwork, a DVD featuring historians and former steelworkers, and a CD of labor folk songs.[28]

The latter is an example of the relatively rare inclusion of labor activism in industrial heritage culture. In the Pittsburgh suburb of Aliquippa, once home to steel-industry giant Jones and Laughlin, there is a blue state marker and a stone-and-metal plaque listing the names of the workers whose firings resulted in the passage of the 1935 National Labor Relations (Wagner) Act, which for the first time formally legalized labor unions. These tributes, along with a vernacular shrine with a wooden cross, sit just outside a tunnel in which workers once staged a protest; over that tunnel now is a sign reading "industrial park." Located at the bottom of a highway exit in another depressed town, this is public history that a visitor would see only if she were looking for it, as I was, or if she took a wrong turn off the main road.

Labor history is told more effectively the Pump House, another structure on the Homestead site that survives due to its historic value—it was the building from which steelworkers staged their 1892 confrontation with Pinkerton guards—and due to a mid-1990s preservation campaign by a group called the Battle of Homestead Foundation.[29] Now maintained by the Steel Industry Heritage Corporation, it is the departure point for Rivers of Steel tours, it houses a small exhibit about the strike, and it hosts lectures, photography and art exhibits, storytelling, and musical performances about industry.

From the ceilings of this building hang banners depicting individual steelworkers for each decade of labor at Homestead. Especially because of their folk art style, these figures appear as symbols of labor history. Yet they also have the odd effect of depoliticizing the exhibit about the strike by reindividualizing workers. A brochure available inside the Pump House describes the banners as "A Memorial for America's workers" but contains this predictable heritage explanation: "The idea is that any visitor who ever had a relative or neighbor who worked the mills might be able to find some portrait here that resembles 'GranPap Joe' or 'Uncle Stush.'"[30]

Indeed, the main social group in industrial heritage narratives is not the union but the family: long-ago workers matter because they were our grandparents or great-grandparents, and because (therefore) they were just like us and our own children. The Pennsylvania public television travel series *Explore PA* explains many aspects of the state's history through the lens of family. In one episode, the producers send a family from the Lehigh Valley (home to the shuttered Bethlehem Steel, although this ironic connection is not mentioned) to visit the Pittsburgh area. The narration makes several references to the steel industry, but always as a comparison—for example, "While Pittsburgh is best known for its steel industry, Pittsburgh was also a major glassmaking center." We see the family create glass paperweights at an artist's studio; we watch them learn rope making at Old Economy Village in nearby Ambridge. At the Heinz History Center, the family inspects steelmakers' protective gear but is more delighted by the "giant pickle" in the Heinz exhibit. Then they visit a modern art museum called The Mattress Factory and go shopping at Station Square, with no mention of what that complex used to be (the grandest station of the Pittsburgh and Lake Erie Railroad Company).[31]

The steelmaking outfit that this family saw at the Heinz History Center is gone now. Previously the museum's permanent exhibit was a chronological account of the city's role in American westward expansion and industrial growth. In 2008, the year of the city's 250th anniversary, the museum unveiled a new exhibit meant to provide "inspiration as well as information," according to CEO Andy Masich, by recounting the past as a series of "innovations" in all categories of life.[32] This theme enables a blending of otherwise very different topics: the launch of the Lewis and Clark Expedition (1803) with the birth of commercial radio (KDKA in 1920) and the debut of *Mr. Rogers' Neighborhood* (1968); the development of the polio vaccine (1952, when Jonas Salk was working at the University of Pittsburgh) with the building of the Brooklyn Bridge (1870–1883) and the Ferris Wheel (1893) (engineers John Roebling and George Ferris were Pittsburghers); and the inventions of the Jeep (1940, in nearby Butler) and the Big Mac (1967, by a Pittsburgh McDonald's franchisee).

Heavy industry is in this mix, though largely in its middle. Exhibits calling the city "A Crucible for Industry" and "The Birmingham of America" describe the rise of the steel industry in the nineteenth century. In a geographical stretch, the exhibit also takes credit for Edwin Drake's 1859 oil strike in Titusville, described as "north of Pittsburgh" (it is one hundred miles away). Another section recounts "The Darkest Month," December 1907, when more than seven hundred coal miners were killed in four accidents in western Pennsylvania. Steel comes back into the story near the exhibit's end, in the second-to-last room.

I had seen the previous version of this exhibit and been struck by the emotional rawness of its display of U.S. Steelworkers' lockers left hanging open, as though the men had walked out yesterday. The new exhibit explains the collapse of steel as just "a chapter in this region's history," an episode in an evolving story that is, on the whole, a story of progress. Moreover, the fate of this industry is the narrative device through which Pittsburgh's story is conclusively connected to the story of "the nation." Wall text offers steelmaking's eulogy. It begins, "When former steelworker Blaine Popp entered the Homestead mill on its final day of operation, a century of noise had been silenced, the molten metal now cold." Here is the usual nod to the representative common worker as the main character of industrial public history. But quickly the language changes and the worker disappears from this story, lost amid vague phrasing:

> The economic and personal hardship, the uprooting of families, the questioning by individuals and communities posed a great challenge. But the city responded and remade itself as it had done so many times before. New industries, centered on medicine, technology, the environment, and education, took root. . . . This region faces the same challenges as the nation—preserving the environment; developing new, clean sources of energy; providing safe, efficient, affordable healthcare; developing and applying new technologies; and staying safe in uncertain times. These challenges present opportunities for creative thinkers and for Pittsburgh to build on its tradition of innovation. [33]

While optimistic, this presentation of the city's recent past suggests that its outcome was inevitable. "Treated like an advancing weather front, the 'gales of creative destruction' have taken on a natural quality," write Steven High and David Lewis about such explanations. "It just happened."[34] Because this story's closing "chapter" features medical technology and the environment (the themes of the exhibit's final room), the city's trajectory seems to have been almost scientifically determined—a conclusion quite similar to those of oil and lumber heritage narratives, as discussed in chapter 3. The exhibit's overall theme of "innovation" cushions the blow to the steelmaking industry by recasting it as just another good idea whose time has come and gone. A Pittsburgh public television documentary that was done in conjunction with the anniversary exhibit sounds this note clearly at its end, as its narrator moralizes, "We have to remember that Pittsburgh has profited from new ideas and new ways of doing things. . . . We have to remain curious and smart and clever. . . . Whether it's robots or vaccines or videogames, or something we haven't thought of yet, we need to be ready to be ingenious. . . . We need to remember the spirit that figures out how to make things."[35]

In understanding the end of an industry as just another change in a longer story of progress and "spirit," we learn little about the political and economic circumstances that hastened its demise. "The resulting story of 'community lost' presents residents as innocent and passive victims in the face of dislocation," people who unfortunately must accept their fate, write High and Lewis.[36] There is no room in such a eulogy for public anger, although it is still palpable in many cities and towns across the state.

"Never in My Wildest Dreams": The Stalled Story in Bethlehem

That anger has been one of several factors in more than a decade of debates over how steel history should be told on the former site of Bethlehem Steel, once the nation's second-largest steel producer, which in 1995 ceased production after 122 years, subsequently declaring bankruptcy. In 1989, a reporter for the *Christian Science Monitor,* assessing redevelopment plans proposed there at the time, predicted that Bethlehem would become "a model for old industrial sites." Written while steel was still being made in Bethlehem, albeit on a greatly reduced scale, the article noted:

> This city on Pennsylvania's Lehigh River has already begun to write the next chapter for the historic site. Rising out of the soot, say company officials, will be a National Museum of Industrial History—a Smithsonian Institution affiliate—hotels, stores selling blue jeans, new restaurants, an IMAX theater, and even a pair of ice-skating rinks. The 160-acre rehab will be called "Bethlehem Works," as in "the steel works." The $400 million effort is an attempt by the city to rebuild its future from its past. . . . The rapid pace of this city's transition from rust bucket to showroom model has already garnered attention.[37]

More than twenty years later, one project has been completed amid the huge blast furnaces and giant sheds still standing on the former plant site: the Sands Casino Resort Bethlehem. It is in a new building, not a reclaimed one, with lights resembling rods of hot steel dangling from the ceiling and bars named Molten and Coil positioned among more than three thousand slot machines on its main floor. When it opened in May 2009, this casino, Pennsylvania's largest, was expected to draw as many as sixteen thousand visitors per day.[38] Because a new entrance ramp allows the busloads of gamblers to enter the casino directly from the highway, though, it is unlikely that many of them see the rest of Bethlehem. Other promised attractions—a hotel, shopping centers, an arts complex, condominiums, a public broadcasting facility, and a museum about industry—remain in the planning stages, repeatedly delayed by a poor economy. The casino's gift shop promotes the Sands brand, not local history, although it does sell a coffee table book of photographs of the plant in its heyday, as well as paperweight-sized (2" x 3" x 3") steel beams engraved for the occasion of the casino's opening—for $50 each.[39] The only other attraction on the land surrounding the plant is the Steel Ice Center, an ice-skating rink that opened in 2003.

In their study of the departure of steelmaking from Youngstown, Ohio, Sherry Lee Linkon and John Russo, co-directors of the Center for Working-Class Studies at Youngstown State University, identify the issues that arose among those who wanted to tell its story. Among them were the difficulty of raising money to preserve and maintain huge buildings; the challenge of re-creating the intensity and enormity of the steelmaking process; the question of whether public memory should be in the hands of officials (a museum or government-run site) or grassroots, neighborhood groups; and the psychological and political tensions between the obligation to preserve the past and admonitions (and need) to "get over" it. They write that "finding a way to remember the past that neither idealizes nor dismisses the events and experiences that shaped a place is not simple, especially in a community that has seen so much conflict and so much loss."[40] The same concerns have arisen in Bethlehem.

The planned project that has received the most attention over the years—indeed, for a decade it has maintained a website that suggests that it actually exists in bricks and mortar—is the National Museum of Industrial History, which will have Smithsonian affiliate status.[41] "This was the headquarters of the largest shipbuilder in the world from World War I to World War II, so the impact of Bethlehem Steel not only on the community but also on the nation is a significant story," says Steve Donches, a former Bethlehem Steel vice president and the planned museum's executive director. But the museum's interpretive premise is even broader, aiming to survey "the achievement of American industry in helping to build our country. As far as we know, there isn't any other place in the U.S. that has attempted to address industry in its broadest sense."

Using machinery from the 1876 Centennial Exhibition in Philadelphia, previously on display at the Smithsonian, this museum will explain major nineteenth-century industries, including textile production and railroading. And, using what remains of its own equipment and buildings plus multimedia technology, it will attempt to relay to visitors the experience of steelmaking. "We can create heat and smoke and the image of flowing hot metal . . . and the sound," says Donches, whose vision is to "put people in the face of fire and make them feel like they were actually on a casthouse floor watching hot metal come out of the furnace. The technology is out there to do almost anything." Comparing this experience to the appeal of railroad steam engines, "that big power machine that lights people up," Donches describes the imaginative experience for tourists: "There's a romanticism about steelmaking, about the heat and the hot metal and the size of things."

The planned museum is meant to serve local people as well as tourists. In one building, says Donches, there will be a large map of the former plant "so parents and grandparents can point to it and say, 'There's where I worked.' People worked for the company for forty or fifty years. It was a way of life. There was a pride that just became a part of you. You were helping to build America. You know that what you were producing was going into building and ships and bridges and skyscrapers all over the country."[42]

Some area residents want to tell another story, a smaller but, in their view, more important one, about local more than national pride and about the town's lingering feelings of loss and betrayal. The difference between these two possible narratives was subtly suggested by the phrasing of former steelworker Peter de Pietro, who told the *Allentown Morning Call* in August 2006, "Steel made this town and it is important to preserve history like that."[43] In this memory formulation, the town did not merely, or even mainly, make steel for America; instead, steel made the town, and it is the town's past and present that are most important to publicly interpret. Allen Sachse, executive director of the Delaware and Lehigh Valley National Heritage Corridor, agrees. "We've got to make sure that the people story stays in the process and not just the industrial story. That's the challenge. It's easy to look at what the company did nationwide, but to keep the interest long term you need the people story."[44]

The "people story" was told in an award-winning documentary produced by the Lehigh Valley PBS affiliate, WLVT, that first aired in 2003. Its overarching narrative was grand, a tragedy that felled "the plant that helped build America, bridge America, and defend America," but its stars were local residents. Several of them, near tears, expressed their continuing disbelief at the company's fate, with phrases such as, "Never in my wildest dreams." Of the still-standing plant site, one elderly worker commented, "My friends, many of my men . . . are just brokenhearted when they look at it." His comment was followed by a woman's voice saying, "It's just really hard to imagine that a company like Bethlehem Steel that I read about in my history book is just gone, like it never happened."[45]

To prevent that eclipse and to preserve their own place in history, former steelworkers have created the Steelworkers Archives to collect oral histories and artifacts from Bethlehem workers.[46] This group is one of the many members of the Lehigh Valley Industrial Heritage Coalition, along with local arts organizations, tourism promoters, and the National Museum of Industrial History (whose industrial artifacts from the 1876 Centennial Exhibition have sat for nearly a decade inside a warehouse near the Lehigh Valley airport). Another voice in this debate has come from the Mid-Atlantic Regional Center for the Humanities, an academic coalition that secured federal funding to hold public meetings and that in 2007 offered an alternative plan for site interpretation, which would "highlight the human scale, the lives lived around and because of the Steel."[47]

Honoring those lives is the aim of the Steelworkers' Memorial Park, which features a statue of a man holding up a steel beam and is paved with bricks engraved with the names of former steelworkers. A small sign explains this, and contains this text: "Let this hallowed ground last forever as tribute to the thousands of men and women who worked in our city's steel industry," a quote from the park's 2001 dedication by Donald T. Cunningham Jr., then mayor of Bethlehem (identified on the sign as "the son and grandson of steelworkers").[48] When the project was announced in 1998, Cunningham told the local newspaper, "In this city, we haven't spoken about recognizing all the workers for the past 100 years or more who made the Steel plant move. . . . People worked 12 hours a day for pennies, and it was a tremendous sacrifice."[49]

This small plaza is hard to find, tucked under the Fahy Bridge between an exit ramp and a waterfront complex including a gym called Steel Fitness. It is the only official labor memorial on Bethlehem's landscape. That said, it is nearly impossible for any visitor not to notice the huge blast furnaces that, even silent and smokeless, continue to dramatically dominate the city's skyline. Their fate still unknown, they are, for now, the steelworkers' memorial of this city, as well as the proverbial elephant in the room. They are striking reminders of assumptions about economic development and the postindustrial future that have not come to pass, here and elsewhere across the state.

Unraveling "the Mystery of Steel": Steelton, Coatesville, and Johnstown

The plant in Bethlehem is only one of several sites in Pennsylvania once owned by Bethlehem Steel. Two others continue to make steel under the new ownership of the world's leading steelmaker today, ArcelorMittal, which resulted from the 2006 merger of European and Indian companies and has purchased failing mills across the world, downsizing and specializing the work they do. One is in the aptly named town of Steelton, near Harrisburg, where seemingly empty mill sheds stretch for miles along the Susquehanna River. The fact that industry continues there is visually apparent only from the back side of the plant, where nighttime travelers passing on Amtrak trains between Harrisburg and Philadelphia may be surprised to see flames shooting out of the mill. Founded in 1865 as the Pennsylvania Steel Company to make rails for the Pennsylvania Railroad with iron ore from the nearby Cornwall Iron Furnace, this plant helped to pioneer Bessemer steelmaking and once employed more than nine thousand workers.[50] Today its workforce stands at seven hundred.

The company has promised to hire more workers if its property is reclassified as a "Keystone Opportunity Zone," which would erase much of the firm's tax obligations.[51] The borough itself has announced a redevelopment project called "The New Steelton," a plan "to renovate the blue-collar town with new offices, storefronts, gaslight-style streetlights and a grand plaza across from Borough Hall within a decade," explained a local newspaper in 2006.[52] In early 2010, the plan was still in place, and the borough's website bore the slogan "The New Steelton: Our Renaissance Continues."[53] But no construction had begun, due in part to the poor economy and in part to the refusal of some local businesses to make way for it, prompting the borough to begin eminent domain seizure proceedings. The redevelopment plans include cosmetic references but no historic interpretation, and none is evident in the town's landscape today. Of the 131 state historical markers mentioning steel, not one is in Steelton.[54]

The second still-operating plant is in Coatesville, a town that was described as "a weary, two-mile stretch of mostly departed commerce" in a Philadelphia newspaper report on a series of arsons that took place there in 2008 and 2009.[55] What this article referred to as "the old Lukens Steel plant" continues to turn out its specialty product, boilerplate steel, with a small workforce. The original company began in the late eighteenth century as an iron furnace and for much of the nineteenth century was run by a woman, Rebecca Lukens. Today a local historical organization called the Graystone Society is planning to tell its story in a National Iron and Steel Heritage Museum. The nineteenth-century homes of Rebecca Lukens and her daughter and the former company headquarters, now home to the society, are already open to visitors. The first two sites conjure a distant past, but the latter contains a startling reminder of very recent history, an exhibit noting that Lukens made the steel "trees" at the base of the World Trade Center buildings—the ground-floor, arched exterior walls that looked like tuning forks and were left standing as mangled monuments after the 2001 attack. Several were recently returned to Coatesville, and the plan is to display them on the museum grounds.

Eugene DiOrio, the society's vice president and a former Lukens executive, believes that this site is well suited for heritage tourism because its past is thematically connected to the history of the early republic (and thus dovetails with the colonial story told in nearby Philadelphia) and yet industry continues here. That advantage "makes us a more vibrant place," says President Scott Huston, a direct descendant of Rebecca Lukens. Somewhat ironically, part of their interpretive challenge will be to convey that steel is, in fact, still being made here. Today, says Huston, "The process is more hidden from the general eye . . . the public perception of a busy mill is smokestacks, and lots of smoke." Another plus is the site's compactness; compared to the sprawling land of Homestead and Bethlehem, "the buildings are big enough to convey the bigness of steel-making, but small enough to be understandable and affordable to maintain."

Their museum would be in a historic brick building that would include a theater and equipment exhibits and—pending the cooperation of Arcelor-Mittal—would allow visitors to tour the nearby operating plant as well. Huston says that they are using the word *national* "because the story here is so big . . . it covers a lot of time" and because their geographic setting is foundational in industrial history, extending back to a time when iron-making was not just an industry but, says Huston, "It was a science. It was a true American craft. It was an art."

Such language aligns their vision more with public history about the iron industry—which tends to be remembered as part of a preindustrial era of rural craftsmanship—than with urban public memory of the steel industry. Yet Huston also refers to Lukens workers as "the people who fought the Industrial Revolution," a phrase that blends colonial imagery with that of a more recent past. In this sense, their vision coincides with the interpretive premise of planned projects in Homestead and Bethlehem. DiOrio, too, uses the word "romance" to describe steelmaking: "Watching a furnace being tapped—it's a glory." Huston expands on this theme, adding the kind of military metaphor common to civic presentations of steelmaking history: "Working in a steel plant is like hell on earth. But there's nothing like the experience. It's awesome. It's dirty. It's hot. Who were these people who fought in the trenches for forty, fifty years? It's about the technology, the process, but mainly it's about the guys in the plant. The story is about the people who made it happen."[56]

While they await the building of the museum, the Coatesville organization makes much the same point in its website description of the return of the World

Trade Center trees, which in April 2010 were draped with American flags and transported from a New York storage facility on flatbed trailers. As they traveled through New Jersey and into Pennsylvania, they were "greeted with great fanfare all along the route, with fire companies draping flags from their ladder trucks along the way," the account explains, adding, "It is appropriate that these artifacts should come home to Coatesville as they were made here. Here they will be displayed in a large area as a reminder of the events of 9/11. The trees will be freely accessible to the public, so all can see them and pay tribute to the victims, survivors and the First Responders who were there in New York on that September day in 2001, and also to the steelworkers from Lukens Steel who made them in the first place."[57]

This is a dramatic, symbolic gesture that transforms the Coatesville story from local history to national memory. Another site that tells a national story in a local venue is Johnstown, the third area where industrial heritage projects have emerged after the closing of a major Bethlehem steel plant. There, mills once stretched for twelve miles along the Conemaugh River. As in Bethlehem itself, steel was still being made at the plant (formerly the Cambria Steel Company) when the first funding was secured for a heritage plan.

"Back in the early 1990s, there was a federal heritage commission working in this area," says Richard Burkert, executive director of the Johnstown Area Heritage Association. "There was a group of folklorists and they were training former steelworkers in didactic methodology, to tell this story from the perspective of the worker. They took a group of industrial workers and were training them to be tour guides. But there was no place for them to actually work." There were plans for a national historic site, but then Bethlehem Steel shut the plant, "and suddenly ten thousand men were thrown out of work here. The idea of going forward with a national park that was a steel mill didn't seem expedient; the political moment was lost." The Johnstown Redevelopment Authority acquired four of the buildings, one of which, an 1862 octagonal blacksmith shop, was preserved with all of its forging equipment. The eventual plan for this building is to have blacksmiths interacting with visitors while forging iron.

In the meantime, the Johnstown Heritage Discovery Center does offer the kind of multimedia presentation envisioned by planners at the other sites. "In 1992, two weeks before Bethlehem Steel closed, we sent a film crew into the plant," says Burkert. "When we were done I had two and a half hours of the best footage of a steel mill that anyone certainly has anywhere in the United States. . . . What we're trying to do here is not just tell the history of the steel industry but . . . to give people a sense of being there, in front of a rolling mill."

He also wanted to tell a story of technology—"in the 1850s, this was the Silicon Valley of industrial America"—and "a story of achievement, what a group of mill men and engineers and capitalists were able to do."[58]

The resulting twenty-five-minute film, called *The Mystery of Steel*, debuted in 2009. Shown across three screens, it tells the history of steelmaking, and not just locally—making Johnstown the first public history site to tell a national steel story. Its footage from inside the plant is indeed dramatically glorious. Its narrative also is telling in an era of continuing debates about how steel history should be interpreted. There is a nod to people rather than things ("But it was not the bricks, mortar, and machines that would set Cambria apart. It was the workers of the valley and their leaders."), but it is a particular kind of person-alization. This is a story of long-dead great men, described as technological "pioneers," and of a town that was, by the 1860s, "the liveliest iron and steel center in the country, with the most inventive minds gathered there. Men came to Johnstown to be part of the future." We learn that, by the early twentieth century, the Cambria plant produced two million tons of steel per year, and we hear that steel was "a new material that made it possible to build bigger, higher, and stronger" as we see pictures of skyscrapers, bridges, trains, and ships. The narration attributes the "steep decline" of the U.S. steel industry in the 1980s to "foreign competition and overcapacity." Then we see scenes of production from 1992, as heat lamps go on and off to create the feeling of heat inside the plant.

Despite the way this industrial story actually ended, the film's main narrative is an extremely positive one, almost in the language of mid-twentieth-century celebrations of the steel industry. This tone and plot are possible because of its narrative focus on the distant past, an era when "pioneer" detective-entrepreneurs solved "the mystery of steel." More recent history—workers' loss of jobs and lifestyle—is hinted at in the images we see in its conclusion. But these workers also are conduits to our own experience of that "mystery," as the warmth of the heat lamps and the film's triumphant music redirect our atten-tion to the exploding molten liquid.[59]

What makes this kind of traditional heritage narrative work in the Johns-town museum is its broader institutional setting. Its message is contextualized by the strongly pro-worker (or at any rate, pro-immigrant) story in the Discov-ery Center's main exhibit, as well as in the Wagner-Ritter house, a nearby build-ing interpreting the domestic daily life of townspeople. When I saw the film, it was surrounded by a traveling photography exhibit titled "Steel: Made in Penn-sylvania," which previously had been on display at the State Museum in Harris-burg and at sites in Bethlehem and Homestead. This small but powerful set of haunting images by photographer Don Giles captured both the postindustrial interior of the deserted buildings of Bethlehem and the work that continues in Steelton and other plants. Collectively they conveyed a feeling of survival as well as a kind of loss that transcends locality.[60]

Finally, the story of steel is told here against the backdrop of the town's real tourism draw: the story of the Johnstown Flood, one of the greatest industrial moral tales of American history and popular culture. Its Flood Museum, also run by the heritage association, recounts the 1889 disaster in which more than twenty-two hundred people, mainly working class, were killed when, due to soil erosion caused by industrialization, a dam north of the city broke and the town was inundated during several days of heavy rain. "The Johnstown Flood is an absolutely amazing episode in American history that really gets at the short-sightedness and the heedlessness of consequences of rapid development and unwitting exploitation of the natural environment," says Burkert. "You have everything there—the industrial financiers from Pittsburgh, the workers; when people were killed, the media interpreted this as the robber barons get away with murder. It peels back the layers of industrial America and exposes its true form in an appalling way."[61]

This may be true—and the Johnstown Flood surely is a sober footnote to the celebratory story of American industrial progress—but its appeal lies in its tragedy and melodrama. Those narrative qualities explain why, in its own time, the flood spawned popular songs, silent films, and a Coney Island attraction dramatizing the disaster. Even today, the Johnstown Flood National Memorial, run by the National Park Service at the site of the burst dam, shows a film that tells a gothic horror story of "the wave of death," featuring eerie images, including the floating body of a woman in a gauzy white dress. We learn about the tragedy through a fictional survivor who walks through the town's Grandview Cemetery in the rain and speaks for the dead:

> I have heard the echoes through the grass, their lost voices still muffled by the veil of death. . . . They are all here, the rich and poor, the strong and the weak, the very young and the very old. They all died equally in the eyes of the Lord. . . . I hear them weeping. . . . I sense a reunion of souls, remembering the fateful storm that bound them together. . . . Each lost voice screams back in pain. . . . Each stone tells of a different path to eternity.[62]

How can industrial history compete with that?

"Staying Alive": Steelmaking's Special Memory Challenges

The drama of steel industry history seems to lie in simulations of steelmaking's flames, noise, and heat and in reconstructions of the lives of typical immigrant workers, whose very ordinariness seems, in retrospect, heroic to their descendants and inheritors (us). As is the case with oil and coal heritage, the political, economic, and environmental histories of steelmaking are less tellable, at least not with the level of consensus that the flames and the immigrants tend to secure. Consensus is important for commerce as well as for closure.

The heritage organizations in Johnstown and Homestead have so far done an impressive job of balancing those needs and of representing a range of narrative perspectives—worker as well as corporate, scholarly as well as genealogical, local as well as national. "No one likes the story when you tell the other side of it; if both sides are mad at me, I know I've told a good story," says Rivers of Steel Executive Director August Carlino. Steelmaking history, he says, is "too big of a story not to tell. And if we don't tell it, somebody else will tell it. And we—we being the community—might not like it."[63]

The downside of attempting to represent a range of points of view (and political interests) is the possible interpretive paralysis in which, presumably, everybody's story should be told and every building should be saved. In an article about the heritage plans in Johnstown and Homestead that in the 1980s and 1990s attracted considerable federal government interest, Thomas E. Leary and Elizabeth C. Sholes explain:

> In both projects . . . the original goal became lost in a mélange of unrealistic and unrelated plans. As the number of preservation targets multiplied and became geographically more widespread, costs for site acquisition and development skyrocketed. The focus on steel became subordinated to other more easily obtained, though less original, preservation objectives such as railroad museums and community folklore studies. Multijurisdictional heritage partnerships, created to assuage government cost-cutters, were unable to mobilize sufficient resources to carry out any of the original large-scale plans. The National Park Service looked at steel sites and flinched.[64]

Their description of these two sites' situation two decades ago could describe the apparent situation in Bethlehem today. Steel's place in current tourism promotion of that city remains oddly elliptical. In one *Explore PA* episode on Bethlehem, steelmaking is mentioned as only one of several industries that made the city prosperous, and when the visiting family goes to the Steel Ice Center to learn how to skate, no mention is made of where it is or why it's there.[65] But the ice rink's name is one of a number of rhetorical references to steelmaking, and the youth hockey team that plays there is called the Bethlehem Blast. A ten-year-old restaurant called the Bethlehem Brew Works serves entrees including Bessemer's Bratwurst, Slag Pot Meatloaf, Rigger's Ribs, and a Pig Iron Pulled Pork Sandwich.[66] In nearby Allentown, a new professional baseball team, a triple-A affiliate of the Philadelphia Phillies, is called the Lehigh Valley IronPigs. The team's gray swine mascot is named "Ferrous, derived from the chemical name for iron," reported the *Philadelphia Daily News* when the IronPigs debuted in 2008.[67] Steel is increasingly visible in popular culture—the commercial uses of its legacy—even as debates continue about its cultural meaning and as public historians seek a lasting narrative that does justice to this industry's rise and fall.

That challenge is daunting, as I realized during the three summertime visits I made to Pittsburgh in search of that story. Most public interpretation of steelmaking history is done on the city's South Side, the base for Rivers of Steel activities. Once home to the workers as well as the steel mills, this area is now filled with microbreweries, coffeehouses, and trendily dressed young people zooming by on bicycles. I was nearly run down by one of them as I wandered around trying to find the Steelworkers Memorial, whose design was described by Kirk Savage as a "ghost mill . . . a sequence of simple structures—shed, rail tracks, ladle for molten steel—hovering in midair above a curving 'wall of memories' intended to make the steelworkers' past come alive."[68] Fortunately I had written this down, because I would not have been able to guess what it was meant to depict or convey. I also couldn't find a "wall of memories," just this raised, modern, metal sculpture, standing in a little park below the bridge leading to Hot Metal Street. Had I not been actively looking for it, I would have mistaken it for the usual kind of river park artwork, an artifact of the upscale present rather than a reference to the industrial past.[69]

Later that same day I took my second of the three tours given by Rivers of Steel. I previously had taken its tour of the Carrie Furnaces, where the sheer size of the surviving structure and the presence of former steelworkers inspire the visitor's close imaginative engagement with what once occurred there. The organization's other two tours are packed with historical and industrial information, but their interpretive goals are undermined by their settings.

On the "Lords of the Mon" riverboat tour, two live narrators (amplified to be audible to passengers sitting on the outdoor decks) described the area's many industries and their interdependence, noting how the river and the railroads enabled the mills to get a steady supply of the steelmaking ingredient of coke from surrounding towns. Pieces of coke were passed around, and passengers on the inside areas of the boat could try on steelmakers' protective gear and see photographs of what the riverside used to look like, lined with mills and filled with flames and smoke. As we approached the Edgar Thomson Works, the narrators reminded us that the old industries were still, to an extent, going on along the river, adding that coke was still being made in Clairton and river barges were still being made in Brownsville.

And yet—as at former iron furnaces and oil-drilling sites—the realities of industrial history were very hard to imagine as the boat glided down this now-clean river, lined with pleasant foliage, on a warm, sunny day. Even as twelve connected barges full of coal passed beneath the railings of our boat, so did a swarm of jet skiers. Even as a freight train with more than one hundred cars, some reading "CSX Coke Express," clicked along tracks on the other side of the river, it seemed small compared to the complexes just behind it, which include The Waterfront in Homestead, a water amusement park, and Station Square. Once the site of the Clinton Iron Works as well as the great terminal of the Pittsburgh and Lake Erie Railroad, Station Square is now a riverside attraction whose high water fountains and spotlights draw boaters' attention to the branded façades of its chain restaurants and stores. And we were, of course, on a riverboat. When the historical narrative ended, the speakers emitted ragtime and Dixieland jazz, neither within the actual memory of even the elderly passengers, a musical gesture toward a distant time, not a recent past.[70]

I had a closer view of Pittsburgh's renovated waterfront the following summer when I took Rivers of Steel's "Babushkas and Hard Hats" tour in 2009. Chapter 4 describes the "Babushkas" part of this tour, its thematic emphasis on ethnic traditions and food. The tour also provides much explanation of steelmaking (the "Hard Hats" part). Inside the Pump House, we were invited to don a steelmaker's protective suit and helmet and to participate in a demonstration of how three ingredients interact to create steel. The morning tour had begun with a detailed discussion of industry, as Jan Dofner gathered the fourteen of us in the outdoor plaza of Station Square.

Surrounding us were a Hard Rock Café, a Lone Star Tavern, and a Joe's Crab Shack; front and center in the plaza were water fountains and an impressively large Bessemer converter with a state historical marker next to it. Our guide took us to stand near the converter while she explained what different workers did and how dangerous their work was. She offered some industrial history of the city and repeated a nineteenth-century reporter's famous comment that Pittsburgh once "looked like 'hell with the lid off.'" She noted that Mount Washington, the cliff behind us that now is a sightseeing spot, was once called Coal Hill. She said, "This was an industrial complex like the world had never seen before."

Then, suddenly, we could hardly hear her. Promptly at 9:00 A.M., even though there was almost nobody on the plaza except for our group, water began gushing from fountains behind the industrial relic of the Bessemer converter, and music blared across the plaza from several large speakers. Jan Dofner shouted out the ingredients of steel—iron ore, coke, limestone—but whatever else she was trying to tell us was drowned out by the Bee Gees. The day's pop music soundtrack for this retail complex had begun with "Staying Alive."[71]

MADONNA OF THE TRAIL

N·S·D·A·R· MEMORIAL
TO THE
PIONEER MOTHERS
OF THE
COVERED WAGON DAYS

"WHAT'S THE USE OF WOND'RIN'?"
The Questions of Industrial Heritage

Lycoming County has provided stable jobs for many and fortunes for a few. Settlers transformed its pioneer villages into thriving communities where generations of immigrants found opportunity and made homes. However, Lycoming County's century of great prosperity and productivity ended in the 1960s. . . . Companies began exporting jobs, leaving those that did not undercut and out of business. This book is a nostalgic tribute to the hardworking people who built Lycoming County and, in doing so, built America. It is a message of loss and, sometimes, a message of corporate abandonment.

—Robin Van Auken and Louis E. Hunsinger Jr., *Images of America* (2005)

This passage, from the introduction to one title in a local history picture-book series, begins with typical heritage language—full of settlers, pioneers, immigrants, and thriving communities—but then takes a less pleasant turn. Occasionally, through mixed messages like this one, the unhappy feelings of local people caught in economic change make their way into industrial heritage interpretation. "Just beneath the surface of much heritage discourse seethes social rage, for the relative quietude of heritage communication joins dialectically with the anger of the outraged," James F. Abrams writes about Pennsylvania's former coal-mining towns. "Heritage discourse and social rage are but two sides of the same coin."[1]

Such tensions certainly are part of the current development of steel-industry heritage, which celebrates workers of a century ago rather than the more recent days of the industry, a more demoralizing era. Stories of sacrifice, even crisis, in industry are included in industrial heritage, but they tend to tell of long-ago losses, such as the early twentieth-century coal-mining accidents somberly marked on memorials across the state. Heritage tributes are less comfortably paid to those with fresher wounds. The less glorious circumstances of recent and even continuing industry are among the themes that rarely make their way into heritage narratives. This chapter considers a set of questions about what is missing from the stories told in the preceding chapters.

What Industry Does Not Qualify as Heritage?

Cultural narratives are by definition, as Raymond Williams once wrote, "a continual selection and re-selection of ancestors."[2] In order to remember, we must also forget; we must make tacit choices about what people, events, and stories are less important to preserve and "pass on" as heritage. Pennsylvania has, in the past, been home to industries that are less well remembered at museums and heritage sites, some on a relatively small scale, such as auto manufacturing in York, and some on quite a large scale, such as glassmaking in Pittsburgh. They are left out of the story either because their particulars are less dramatic than those of other industries in their areas or because—like locomotive manufacturing in Erie or silk mills in Allentown—they were in cities where industrial heritage culture has not yet taken hold (as discussed in the next chapter).

Other industries are not (yet) well recalled because they do not yield strong narratives of lessons learned and they have uncertain legacies. One especially compelling example is the nuclear power industry. Pennsylvania has the distinction of being home to the nation's first commercial nuclear reactor (in 1958 in the Pittsburgh suburb of Shippingport) and its worst commercial nuclear power accident, in Unit 2 of the Three Mile Island plant near Harrisburg in 1979. Lonna Malmsheimer did oral history interviews with local residents during the year after the accident. Writing in 1986, the same year Unit 1 restarted, she declared, "Few Americans . . . have any difficulty calling up an image of Three Mile Island's cooling towers in the bucolic middle landscape of central Pennsylvania, now the icons of a dramatic encounter with the machine in the garden."[3] More than thirty years later, that dramatic encounter is largely (even locally) forgotten. The state museum's industrial section includes a kiosk-style display playing corporate videos, made by the power company during the 1980s, next to a model of a "Rover," the machine built to go inside the radioactive reactor during the cleanup.[4] A state historical marker stands along the road leading to the island, but the on-site visitor center is closed now, and Unit 1 continues to operate. Despite avowals to the contrary just after the accident, the industry itself not only has survived but seems poised to come back into fashion as a "green" technology. In 2010, Exelon, Three Mile Island's current owner, donated a quarter of a million dollars to fund watershed-improvement projects of the Schuylkill River Heritage Area.[5]

Industrial heritage culture also distracts our attention from the fact that Pennsylvania's most celebrated "former" industries—coal mining, oil drilling, lumbering, steelmaking, and railroading—are in fact still going on, somewhere in the state, albeit on a smaller scale and with a shrinking workforce. Driving away from the reconstruction of nineteenth-century Drake Well, one rounds a bend on the state highway and sees rows of circular oil tanks in the valley's surviving refineries. Passengers on the tour bus that goes to the ruin of the Carrie Furnaces can't help but notice the flames shooting out of the Edgar Thomson Works across the road. At Steamtown, on a pedestrian bridge that enables visitors to walk over railroad tracks to a shopping mall, I watched as a little boy pulled his father along, shouting, "Train! Train!" His father knelt down, looked, and said, "Oh, it's just a real train." It was not the "Big Boy" steam engine that makes hourly short runs carrying little boys and their fathers; it was merely an ordinary freight train carrying . . . *coal.* I remember my own reaction to the ride around Horseshoe Curve during Altoona's summer "Railfest": when the train pulled up, the lovely, early twentieth-century Pennsylvania Railroad cars in front were followed by—ugh—*real* Amtrak cars, complete with filthy windows.

The current vestiges of Pennsylvania's famous industries are not as charming as their re-creations. Robert Thayer uses the term "technological landscape guilt" to describe Americans' uncomfortable psychological relationship with modern technology even while we express nostalgia for lost industries (after cleaning them up). He writes, "Nostalgic technologies have acquired considerable visual status and are now often proudly displayed on the landscape. This technology lies in the realm of the ideal image, providing assurance of a continuum of culture anchoring us to our heritage, harkening back to the good old days, when things were supposedly better."[6] But we do not have the same fondness for, or even awareness of, current industry that is visible on the landscape.

One reason may be that heritage culture does not create a narrative bridge between departed industries and continuing ones. Consistently it devotes less attention to causality and context than it does to community and cultural traditions. As Mike Wallace notes, heritage sites tend to re-create "lost" industries without offering political and economic explanations for their loss. "Tour guides at industrial museums tell me people repeatedly ask them: 'Why did the factories leave?' and 'Where did they go?'" he writes.[7] Lizabeth Cohen has argued that the interpretive preference for culture over politics—"this nostalgia for a self-contained cultural community of family members, neighbors and ethnic groups that permeates our presentations of industrial history in the era of deindustrialization"—ultimately "represents a reluctance to look critically at capitalism, both for the life it has offered its workers and the responsibility it may bear for the present industrial crisis."[8] The current recession and the weak state of unions today remain unacknowledged in industrial heritage narratives. Instead we learn about folk dancing and wheat threshing, pierogies and halupkies, and the "social goulash" of symbolic ethnicity.

Who Is "Ethnic"?

Heritage narratives (in general, not just industrial) describe America as a country of immigrants who came here in search of a better life, and immigration is central to the notion of an American national character and "destiny." There are at least two problems with this definition: there were some native occupants of the country prior to European immigration; and not all "immigrants" came willingly for a better life. Industrial heritage interpretation struggles with representations of Native Americans and African Americans. Both groups do tend to be included among the "diversity" themes of interpretation. For instance, mixed in among the testimonies about Polish foods, Italian lacemaking, and Croatian band music on Rivers of Steel's "Tradition Bearers" website are segments called "Native Traditions" (a powwow and a medicine woman) and "A Charge to Keep" (African American church music and a hairdressing shop). But these groups' nonimmigrant status makes it necessary to interpret their experiences through a different thematic lens.

What's most surprising about the appearance of Native Americans in industrial heritage is that they're in the story at all. But they are. Like the other kinds of "ancestors" who are celebrated, Native Americans are recalled through the lenses of culture, mechanical ingenuity, and pioneer mythology. Native American musicians or dancers are now commonly featured in many "ethnic" festivals with industrial themes. "Made in PA," the state museum's 2008 exhibit touting products manufactured in Pennsylvania, began its chronology with Native American arrowheads.[9] When the former Lancaster-York Heritage Region changed its name to the Susquehanna Gateway Heritage Area, its thematic focus shifted from the agricultural heritage of the Amish to the "special landscape" that was home to the Susquehannock Indians hundreds of years ago.

Recently this heritage organization has mapped a "Native Lands Heritage Trail" marked by waysides that situate those Indians chronologically before a more familiar story of German immigration; in this story, the region is a place "where many stories come together—a place that many peoples have called their Native Land."[10]

Other museum exhibits and heritage media also salute these earlier residents for "teaching us" about environmentalism, a gesture that seems antithetical to the memory of industry and that catapults these "ancestors" into the present. In a public television documentary made for the 2009 oil sesquicentennial and now shown at Drake Well, a modern-day member of the Seneca Indian tribe, wearing a Native-patterned, woven vest, explains to a museum staffer how his ancestors used oil as paint and medicine, and says, "This is a gift from the Mother, a gift coming from the Earth."[11] Because they are understood as uniquely connected to the Earth, Native Americans tend to appear in heritage interpretation of oil, lumber, and agriculture, all industries interpreted as forms of nature and elements of the environment. A film shown at visitor centers in Lancaster and York begins by remembering "these native people," whose "footsteps mapped this land long before the Europeans settlers came. . . . They were the first farmers, and the first caretakers of this land."[12] Like the western European "settlers" who followed in their footsteps, Native Americans ultimately are remembered as pioneers in the wilderness.

So are African Americans, who tend to be recalled in industrial heritage interpretation in terms of two kinds of "journeys"—geographic mobility toward freedom in the industrial north, and then economic mobility through their inclusion in certain industries. Slave escape routes were significantly connected with Pennsylvania industries, including iron furnaces near the Mason–Dixon Line, farms all across the state, and the various industries of the northern tier. At the ruins of Caledonia Furnace, now in a state park about fifteen miles from the Maryland border, a wayside explains that the furnace foreman was a conductor on the Underground Railroad, that some free blacks worked at the furnace, and that, because it was owned by abolitionist Thaddeus Stevens, the Confederates destroyed the furnace and town on their way to Gettysburg.[13] In Lancaster, "Amish Experience" tours include one in which an actor plays an escaping slave and tourists visit Quaker cemeteries where two conductors are buried.[14] Along the state's eastern border, the narrator on the New Hope and Ivyland Railroad tourist train points out a large stone farmhouse that once was a safe house.[15] The Williamsport Trolley Tour travels across Freedom Road, where free blacks lived in the nineteenth century; its narration explains that a local lumberman,

Daniel Hughes, helped more than three thousand slaves escape by taking logs down the Susquehanna River to Maryland and then guiding slaves along its canal path on the northward journey.[16]

Industrial museums are paired with Underground Railroad history sites in two *Explore PA* public television shows, which are also good examples of the unlikely combinations of activities promoted in "cultural tourism." In one episode, two "gospel-singing" sisters from Harrisburg go to northwestern Pennsylvania for a weekend that incongruously mixes a lesson on oil history at Drake Well, snowmobiling, and clay pigeon shooting with a stop at abolitionist John Brown's farm outside Meadville (through which, we learn, twenty-five hundred escaping slaves passed).[17] In another episode, three African American friends (also women) from Philadelphia go ice fishing, get manicures, stay overnight in a Scranton hotel that once was the great Lackawanna Railroad Station, and visit the Anthracite Heritage Museum, where they admire the coal sculptures done by African American artist C. Edgar Patience. A trolley bus takes these women to Underground Railroad sites including a church and a cemetery, where they meet the family of an escaped slave who is buried there. They also learn quilting techniques during a visit to the Center for Anti-Slavery Studies in Montrose. At the latter, Cindy Wooden, a local historian who also runs a bakery, explains how the patterns of quilts hung outdoors identified escape routes and safe houses; she told me the same story when I attended the Pennsylvania Heritage Festival held each fall at the Bradford County Farm Museum in Troy.[18]

It is interesting that in both of these television episodes, music is involved. The women admire a church organ in one episode and a piano in an antique store in another; the visiting African American women's own musical talent is acknowledged; the young descendants of the escaped slave, standing in the graveyard where he is buried, sing "Amazing Grace" to the Philadelphia friends. Here, it is music rather than food that—reenacted and experienced by women—transforms politics into culture, much as food is used in Pittsburgh-area heritage culture. There also is a segment on black church music in Rivers of Steel's "Tradition Bearers" online oral history videos.

The *Explore PA* shows note that many escaped slaves remained in northern Pennsylvania and became 'Pennsylvanians who changed our nation.' How they did so remains vague, however. At least so far, in industrial heritage presentations African Americans are remembered more often as former slaves freed through the help of white industrialists than as workers themselves. The one exception is the railroad industry, in interpretation that focuses chiefly on the distinctly racialized job of Pullman porters. It is hard to miss the talking replica of a porter who enthusiastically greets visitors at the entry of the Railroaders Memorial Museum in Altoona.[19] The Railroad Museum of Pennsylvania has held an exhibit about this profession, and on its website goes "beyond the stereotype of porters" to address the use of slave labor in building railroads and passenger segregation during the Jim Crow era.[20] *Rising from the Rails,* a film about these workers based on a book of the same title, was screened in 2007 at Steamtown, whose permanent exhibit includes a porter among the figures representing the many types of people who rode and worked on the railroads. Explanatory wall text contains this quote from a real porter in 1931: "I am one of the six thousand colored men who will be at the doors of your Pullman cars tonight, waiting to greet you and watch over you as a mother hen watches over her chicks."[21]

Where Are the Women in Industrial Heritage?

The railroad museum's online history also features a photograph of two Pullman porters solicitously helping a white woman, dressed all in white, down from a train car: "Miss Phoebe Snow." This is actually a publicity photograph of Marion Murray, an actress who "played" this early twentieth-century advertising character who took "the Road of Anthracite" and is discussed in chapter 2. Phoebe's appearance and testimony promised not only the cleanliness of travel on the Lackawanna Railroad but also the security and purity of female passengers at a time when a growing number of real women were traveling on the railroads.[22] Ads pictured Phoebe interacting with, in addition to African American porters, assorted working-class men of the railway, including the conductor, brakeman, oil man, fireman, signal man, and ticket clerk.[23]

Phoebe was one of the first female figures employed to promote industry, adding freshness and glamour to products that were dirty or nondescript, such as coal and oil, or standing for the purity of manufactured food. Among Phoebe's contemporaries were the potato-chip-snacking "Utz Girl," another illustrated character who has morphed from a flapper in the 1920s to a child today, and real workers also serving corporate public relations purposes, such as the "spotlessly clean girls" visitors to the H. J. Heinz Company saw filling jars with pickles and ketchup.[24] In the early 1960s, the Pennzoil motor oil company held a contest in which young women vied for the title of Penny Pennzoil, a model who would travel the world making promotional appearances with the product. The winner, Nancy De Celle, returned to the oil region for the 2009 Drake

Well sesquicentennial, posing for visitors' pictures, holding up an oil can next to old advertisements featuring her twenty-four-year-old self.[25]

Female characters appear not only as symbols but also as predictable characters in heritage stories about the great men of industry. As discussed in chapter 6, company history is often told in heritage tourism as a tale of a young man who overcame obstacles in order to make his vision a reality, usually in part because of the encouragement and often the help of a mother or wife. Like the Madonna of the Trail, these women stood solidly by, steadfastly certain of a better future. An account sold in the gift shop of the Herr's Potato Chip Visitor Center describes Mim (Miriam) Herr, the founder's wife, as "Jim's loyal partner" who "worked diligently in the plant alongside her husband. . . . For Jim, Mim was indispensable."[26] Milton Hershey's life story is bookended by inspirational women: on one end, his fiercely determined Mennonite mother Fannie ("Milton, a Hershey never quits!"), and on the other his beloved wife, Kitty, whose death at an early age inspired him to establish a home for orphaned boys.[27] Among the "legendary ladies" profiled in guides distributed at state welcome centers are the mother of Andrew Carnegie, the daughter of Henry Clay Frick, and both the wife and mother of H. J. Heinz. The latter's biographical sketch explains, "In his will, Heinz described his mother as 'a woman of strong faith, and to it I attribute any success I may have attained during my life.'"[28]

"Women of strong faith" appear among the ordinary characters of industrial history as well. Near the end of the main exhibit in Pittsburgh's Heinz History Center is a kitchen tableau representing a typical, postwar-era steelworker's home. From speakers above the exhibit comes a wistful song that plays over and over, and is still quite audible in the adjacent exhibit on the collapse of the steel industry. The song is "What's the Use of Wond'rin'?" from the Broadway musical Carousel, the stand-by-your-man declaration of a battered wife in a nineteenth-century New England mill town.[29] I didn't know what to think. Was this an unfortunate choice or a bold statement? What are we meant to imagine about the steelworker's wife? This was a rare moment when the predictable portrayal of women as the "home life" of industrial communities contained a jarring reminder that their lives often were unhappy and their alternatives few.

Women's day-to-day hardships are recognized and interpreted at most of the museums, as well as a few of the coal-mining memorials, I visited across the state. An exhibit at the Coal and Coke Heritage Center, near Fayette, is based on an oral history project that became a book, Common Lives of Uncommon Strength: The Women of the Coal and Coke Area of Southwestern Pennsylvania, 1880–1970.[30] As the book's title suggests, it contains relatively recent women's history. In most public interpretations of women's role in the industrial house-hold, the common wife of the common worker is recalled through a longer historical lens. Hard as her experience was, she is saluted as a pioneer, and her challenges are reenacted cheerfully. At harvest days and festivals held at farming museums and iron furnace sites, female reenactors bake bread and pies, spin wool, sew quilts, make soap and candles, weave hay into wreaths, and churn apple butter.[31] Visitors to Eckley Miners Village see a costumed woman energetically putting clothes through a wringer on the back porch of the "1880s house."[32]

Such domesticity frequently is conflated with ethnicity. In Eckley's gift shop, I bought the *Coal Miners' Gourmet Cookbook,* subtitled *Fine Old European Recipes.* This is one of several sites that sell recipe books in which local women recall how to make Polish, Welsh, German, Irish, or other foods. The home is commonly interpreted as the place where "tradition"—immigrant identity—was kept, a place of ritual resistance to the modern, industrial world urging workers to assimilate. A house exhibit titled, merely, "At Home," sits among the displays about Altoona's various ethnic groups in the Railroaders Memorial Museum.[33]

The Altoona museum also remembers women as workers, and it is one of several sites that document American women's industrial work during the Second World War. Here, there is a model of a woman in railroad gear holding a lantern and throwing a track switch, labeled "Molly Pitcher, 1942," as well as a floor-to-ceiling reproduction of a 1940s Pennsylvania Railroad advertisement saluting the women who worked for the railroad.[34] Among the reenactors on the Bellefonte Historical Railroad is woman dressed in a WWII-era cap and skirted uniform and identified as "Cora the Conductor."[35] The famous "We Can Do It!" poster of an arm-flexing Rosie the Riveter hangs in the Heinz History Center.[36] A section of the Piper Aviation Museum in Lock Haven, which once manufactured small ("Cub") airplanes in the former factory buildings of the Susquehanna Silk Mill, is devoted to women who served as WASPs, Women's Airforce Service Pilots, ferrying planes around the various theaters of war. This exhibit has many photographs of the women and a copy of their mascot, a Disney character named Fifinella, "a female gremlin," which during the war Disney allowed them to paint on their planes and wear on their uniforms.[37]

As such names suggest, these wartime workers are remembered as spunky helpmeets, patriots who were willing to temporarily pitch in during a crisis and were surprisingly successful. Similar explanations usher a handful of "great women" into the mainstream industrial heritage narrative of innovation, vision, perseverance, and courage. Chief among them is Rebecca Lukens, who owned and personally supervised the Brandywine Iron Works (later Lukens Steel) in Coatesville. Her significance in American industrial history is acknowledged in a number of books as well as Philadelphia's science museum, the Franklin Institute.[38] Yet, like other accomplished women of the nineteenth century, she is largely remembered as a widow whose success was an unexpected outcome of necessity. She herself advanced this impression in her memoir, which is quoted in a booklet published by the local historical society and available to those who visit her house on the grounds of the future National Iron and Steel Heritage Museum: "This was his dying request—he wished me to continue and I promised to comply. Indeed I knew well I must do something for the children around me. . . . Necessity is a stern task mistress; and my every want gave me courage; besides . . . where else could I go and live? . . . The workmen were tried and faithful, and so with some fear but more courage, I began to struggle for a livelihood. . . . Now I look back and wonder at my daring."[39]

Presented as protectors—as women who "dared" because they felt a need to take care of others—even women who *opposed* industrialization are now remembered as being among its heroines. The author of investigative journalism that exposed the business trust built by John D. Rockefeller and other oil and railroad barons more than a century ago, Ida Tarbell is now claimed as part of oil country heritage. It is an uneasy pride. The historical marker outside her childhood home identifies her as a "noted oil historian." Drake Well Director Barbara Zolli, who sometimes dresses and speaks as Tarbell for special events, notes that the museum has plans for a new exhibit on Rockefeller and Tarbell, to be called the "Big Business of Oil."[40] Due to state budget cuts, its development has been postponed; in the meantime, a larger-than-life-sized cutout of Tarbell's head and shoulders, labelless, is propped inside the entryway.[41] She is better explained in the Venango Museum of Arts and Science in nearby Oil City, where a life-sized wax figure of her sits at a desk beneath reprints of her articles for *McClure's* magazine. On one wall of this exhibit are photographs of Ralph Nader and of Woodward and Bernstein of Watergate fame, with the explanation: "Ida Tarbell's groundbreaking reports about Standard Oil paved the way for today's consumer activists." Through this interpretation Tarbell becomes an inspirational crusader standing up for ordinary people, a prescient caretaker of "our" modern rights. Thus she makes narrative sense here even though she once posed a threat to the industry whose heritage is celebrated all around her.[42]

Another western Pennsylvania crusader remembered in similar terms is Fannie Sellins, an organizer for the United Mine Workers who was shot and killed in western Pennsylvania in 1919. Tucked inside a hillside war memorial the town of Natrona, where she died, a wayside labels her "An American Heroine."[43] A local historical society pamphlet contains this curious blend of protest and pride: "What Sellins and countless others worked for was nothing less than the dignity of workers whose sweat and blood helped make the nation a world power."[44] Noting that "an estimated 10,000 mourners attended her funeral," exhibit text in the Heinz History Center explains, "In death, as in life, she served as a key symbolic figure in the ongoing labor movement."[45]

Whether they are Fannie Sellins or Phoebe Snow, female characters do tend to appear in industrial heritage more often as symbols of labor than as laborers themselves. In public memory as well as academic scholarship, "industrial history" is defined as the story of the heavy industries populated by men, notes Maurine Greenwald. Acknowledging women's presence in the textile industries, domestic service, and clerical work, she writes, would "broaden the diversity of occupations and avenues from which the working class was made in the nineteenth century and remade in the twentieth century."[46] Instead, heritage interpretation casts women as relational rather than central to the operation of industries, even in the face of evidence to the contrary. I was struck by the irony of this quotation, taken from a set of oral histories done by the Railroaders Memorial Museum and used on a wall plaque (the italics are mine): "'Railroad women are proud. They're hard-working. They're mothers, they have children, they are wives.'—Theresa Wilt, Conrail *secretary.*"[47]

The garment industry in particular was populated by hundreds of thousands of Pennsylvania women. It initially was a "companion industry" to coal mining, employing the daughters and wives of miners, but it became economically central in many towns when the anthracite industry began its decline in the 1930s. A state historical marker in Wilkes-Barre notes the size and force of this female workforce, which, under the mid-twentieth-century leadership of Min Matheson, organized more than 160 chapters of the International Ladies Garment Workers Union totaling eleven thousand members.[48]

The textile industries are documented in several museums in eastern Pennsylvania, including the National Canal Museum in Easton, the Independence Seaport Museum in Philadelphia, the Schuylkill River Heritage Center in Phoenixville, and the Lehigh Valley Heritage Center in Allentown. Photographs in the latter museum show women—not one, not a few, but vast numbers of them—who once worked at the Allentown Silk Ribbon Company, the Adelaide Silk Mill, the Keystone Silk Mill in Emmaus, and the Pabsit Mill in Slatington.[49] Also impressive are the huge spinning machines in the back room of the Pennsylvania Anthracite Heritage Museum in Scranton. This museum's orientation film notes that "by 1910, nearly 20,000 women and 5,000 children were employed by the silk companies," and a masterpiece created by them is on display—the area's contribution to the 1893 Chicago World's Fair, a large bedspread bearing the name of its maker, the Wilkes-Barre Lace Manufacturing Company.[50]

Yet all of these exhibits are in museums primarily devoted to, and named for, other industries; they are adjuncts. There is no museum in Pennsylvania about the textile industries. There are plans in Scranton to create a lace museum that tells the story of the Scranton Lace Curtain Manufacturing Company, a progressive firm that in the early twentieth century initiated profit-sharing and health benefits for its hundreds of female employees.[51] For now, passengers on the caboose ride out of Steamtown might notice the fading words "United Silk Mills" on the back side of the building that houses the Electric City Trolley Museum.[52]

Where Are the Workers in Industrial Heritage?

Thus the working women of one of Pennsylvania's largest industries remain largely unremembered. Or, like Mim Herr and Rebecca Lukens, like Pullman porters, like the wartime "Rosies" and even Ida Tarbell, they are understood to have pitched in and done their parts in a bigger story of American progress. In this industrial pageant, many actors, even though they may have had their differences in the past, together produced a great future. This is, writes Diane Barthel, a "social progressivist narrative that has an inevitability about it, and the tourist leaves the exhibit with a Panglossian sense of living in the best of all possible worlds."[53]

In his study of Welsh industrial heritage presentations, J. Geraint Jenkins similarly found that the country's industries are looked back on as bucolic and harmonious enterprises in which even industrial disasters and labor activism were proof of worker nobility. As he and other scholars have noted, this vision diminishes understanding of how truly awful industrial work once was, how poor the quality of life was in industrial towns, how little harmony prevailed between owners and workers, and how little harmony often prevailed among

workers themselves. Part of the problem is the presentism of heritage interpretation, especially the trend toward encouraging visitor identification with
historical characters whose values are presented as being just like ours today.
While such techniques may help make people of the past more interesting,
"we must also acknowledge how their worlds differed from ours," notes David
Thelen, and we should understand that those differences were starkly economic
and political as well as social.[54]

Writing in 1990, Kenneth Foote called for public commemoration of industrial labor, arguing, "In retrospect the success of the American labor movement
is remarkable given the forces arrayed against it from the mid-nineteenth century onward. Rights that modern workers take for granted were won at a high
price in struggles as heroic as any in American history. The movement is replete
with martyrs and heroes, myths and legends, but nowhere in the United States
are these marked by anything more than modest local memorials." Among such
sites he listed were the Lattimer Massacre Memorial outside Hazleton and the
state historical marker that was erected outside the Pump House on the centennial of the Homestead Strike. More than two decades later, his observation that
worker memorials are local phenomena, "tucked away in odd corners" of the
landscape, remains largely true.[55]

The prototypical worker may be the star of industrial heritage exhibits
today, but he is an individual. Labor organizations tend to appear in heritage
interpretation only when they are part of historical dramas, such as the 1892
Homestead Strike in the steel industry or the resistance and execution of the
Molly Maguires in the anthracite region during the 1870s. Almost always these
are lesson-filled anecdotes, seen as episodes of valorous sacrifice for the future,
so that—like the Johnstown Flood—labor activism is remembered as a matter
of deviation from industrial progress. Philip Jenkins calls the current heritage
story of the Molly Maguires a set of "romanticized tales of apolitical victims
slaughtered by evil capitalists," a narrative formulation in which neither "evil"
capitalism nor labor violence is the norm.[56] In being rhetorically set aside in
this manner, labor activism is depoliticized. It also is historically entombed in
the long-ago past, understood as something that is over and gone.

Just as current industry is overlooked by heritage presentations, so are current industrial workers. There are hundreds of thousands of Pennsylvanians
still doing industrial jobs, even in what is called a postindustrial world. They
are not accorded the reverence of workers from bygone days; they are usually
not noticed much at all, unless something goes wrong. One consistent theme
in news coverage of coal-mine accidents is reporters' surprise that men are still

going underground to mine coal. As discussed in the introduction to this book, working-class people are a useful, and predictable, symbol in journalism during a political election or an economic recession, but general lack of interest in the actualities of current industry leads to little public understanding of labor today.

Worker hardship makes sense only as a struggle of the past, not the present, within industrial heritage narratives whose plotline is one of inevitable progress. Writing about the automotive industry, Kathryn Marie Dudley notes the problem with public notions that "the decline of manufacturing is a kind of linear evolution from an industrial past to a postindustrial future." In fact, she argues, "Dislocated industrial workers, their families, and their communities are struggling to preserve a way of life against the threat of social disorder. What we see is not a value-neutral evolution in technology, but a battle for culturally contested terrain. . . . To understand the meaning of industrial change in the United States, we need to focus on how people make sense of their lives in the face of ambiguous or shifting cultural values."[57]

In several small museums, amid the usual displays of local pride and national patriotism, it was evident to me that residents also felt betrayed by history. I was especially struck by this sense in the "oil heritage region." Although most tourism literature in this area focuses on the oil boom of the 1870s, two major motor oil companies, Pennzoil and Quaker State, operated here until around 1990. They did not go out of business; they were sold to big oil companies in California and Texas, and their departure put entire towns out of work. A volunteer staffer explained this to me in Emlenton's Pumping Jack Museum, which occupies that town's now-closed high school. Her tone of astonishment made it clear how shocking this loss was and still is for area residents. This museum is, like many other local historical societies, a celebration of the town's past and its place in an economically and politically strong America. But this celebration is a kind of objection as well, an insistent statement of what once was there, what remains in living memory even if it has been taken from the landscape.[58]

The same point is made in nearby Oil City. Its Venango Museum of Art and Science is full of historical and scientific displays about the glory of oil. But the first and last thing I saw was the organ. A 1928 Wurlitzer sits beneath two golden eagle ornaments that also were rescued from the town's long-shuttered movie palace, the Latonia Theater; its carousel-style percussion instruments are perched overhead. As she closed the museum, the lone staffer asked me if I'd like to hear this instrument play. The snare drum trilled and the doors swung open in front of the ceiling-high pipes, and I heard the opening notes of "When You Wish Upon a Star." As I watched the organ's computer-programmed keys press out the song, I looked up at a sign hanging on the wall above. It reads, "The past stays with us."[59] Most of the oil industry did not, but the Wurlitzer survives to remind us: *This is what we once were.*

EPILOGUE

The Future of Pennsylvania's Past

On this site in 1997 the citizens of Bristol and the surrounding community witnessed one of the most dramatic examples of volunteerism in modern Pennsylvania history. . . . With the goal of restoring the historic and environmental treasure known as the Bristol Borough Delaware Canal Lagoon . . . corporations provided services and equipment valued in the hundreds of thousands of dollars, and union members donated thousands of hours of skilled labor. They sought no other compensation than the satisfaction of a job well done . . . for generations to come. This beautiful site is their legacy.

—Bristol Borough Delaware Canal Lagoon Restoration Project

This explanation, on a sign at the entrance to a public park in the eastern Pennsylvania town of Bristol, describes the ideal situation for heritage projects, in which all kinds of local people come together with no interest other than to create a lasting legacy. At the same time, it pays special tribute to organized labor, and on its backside are almost memorial-style lists of the names of the men who did the work, under their respective union chapters names and numbers.

A mosaic inlaid in the ground below the sign tells visitors that Bristol was "Settled by the World's People" in 1681. Its industrial history is especially rich, due to its location on the Delaware River. In addition to the river, an important canal and several railroads have passed through it, and, over three centuries, the town has been home to sawmills, textile mills, and shipbuilding. The "lagoon" marked the end of the Delaware Canal that had "moved the coal that fueled the Industrial Revolution," the *Philadelphia Inquirer* explained in an article about historic preservation plans there in the early 1990s. "Once a classic case study of a dying Rust Belt town, Bristol Borough is emerging as a success story," this newspaper predicted at the time.[1] The Pennsylvania Department of Conservation and Natural Resources erected historical waysides with titles such as "Life Along the Canal," "Canal Boats," and "Mules and Men."

But neither these signs nor the restored lagoon is what a visitor to Bristol first notices. Still standing is the massive former Grundy Woolen Mill, with a clock tower and a tall smokestack that reads, in vertical lettering, "Grundy." (The town's library, museum, and recreation center also are named for the Grundy family, who founded the mill here in the 1870s and ran it for nearly a century.[2]) I used to wonder about this every time I traveled by train between Philadelphia and New York and noticed the large sign on one side of the mill building advertising condominiums in "The Powerhouse at Grundy Mill." I went to the web address given on the sign, where I found an artist's renderings of the spacious interiors of "Loft Condominiums" and a beautifully remodeled, lagoon-side complex that promised to be "Bucks County's Most Unique Transit Oriented Development."[3] The website invited prospective buyers to get on a mailing list. I put in my information. I never heard a thing.

In the summer of 2008, I finally visited Bristol. On the town's eastern side, a leafy and lovely area, restored colonial and Victorian homes line the Delaware River. On its western side, nearer the strip-mall-lined Bristol Pike and the train tracks, is the mill building. Its size—its sheer survival—is impressive. But in 2008 it was still unoccupied, its restoration only half finished. In the adjacent lagoon park, the DCNR signs explaining canal life were covered with graffiti. The following year, its developers gave up, selling the property to Habitat for Humanity, an outcome that left townspeople feeling "cheated, lied to and taken advantage of," a local newspaper reported.[4] Ironically, because this project has failed, this former mill building is now set to house not upscale commuters who would "revitalize" the town but working-class people.

Still "Shaking off the Ashes of Industry": Cities in Transition

Bristol's heritage plans and redevelopment hopes, born during the optimistic 1990s, ground to a halt during the terrible economy of the following decade. In this, it is typical of many industrial heritage initiatives, which are realities in theory more than in practice. Like the Grundy Mills condominium complex, the National Museum of Industrial History in Bethlehem has existed online, fully formed, for a decade, but it is nowhere to be found in Bethlehem. The Adelaide Silk Mill in Allentown and the Grimshaw Silk Mill in Reading are now apartment buildings, but the cities around them have not yet embraced their considerable industrial history as a way of reviving their economies.

Neither has Erie, another city in transition. In 2002, the local newspaper published an article titled "Erie Shakes off Ashes of Industry, Attempts to Dress for Company." "Tucked into the heart of the Rust Belt, Erie still is perceived by some as nothing more than a dying industrial town," it reported, while noting new efforts to draw tourists to the city.[5] Even in 2007, the *Erie Area Visitor Guide* began bluntly, "Fifteen years ago, travel and fun along Erie's bayfront were unimaginable."[6] Today its chief tourist attraction is Presque Isle, a state park in a much cleaner Lake Erie, where waysides detail the area's past. Long a great fishing and shipping port, one panel explains, Erie became a metalworks manufacturing center in the early twentieth century: "Immigrants flocked to Erie for jobs in iron, brass, and steelworks."[7] Industrial history is halfheartedly embraced in the Erie Maritime Museum, a state-run site located in a former electric company generating station. A small exhibit inside its entryway notes this fact and goes on to claim that Erie "was once known as the 'Boiler and Engine Capital of the World.'" But this is a maritime museum, and its main attraction sits outside on the water, a replica of the brig *Niagara,* the victorious vessel in the Battle of Lake Erie during the War of 1812.[8] The visitor leaves knowing how sails are raised and knots are tied and cannons are fired but not knowing much about Erie's industrial history.

It also is in a maritime museum, at completely the other end of the state, that industrial history is halfheartedly embraced in the city that is shockingly missing from the Pennsylvania industrial heritage story: Philadelphia, once called the "Workshop of the World." Inside the Independence Seaport Museum is a display about that city's industrial past, including an old advertisement bearing its former industrial moniker. The city's science museum, the Franklin Institute, devotes one large room to railroading, with an enormous Baldwin Locomotive as the focal point.[9] But neither of these museums is primarily about industry. Philadelphia lies within one of the state's heritage areas, the Schuylkill River Heritage Area, and the city is featured in a 2010 documentary about this region—but again the focus is water. Past industry is mentioned in this film only as the source of terrible pollution that has since been cleaned up.[10]

The region's waterways were reclaimed in the closing decades of the twentieth century, following a mid-century cleanup of Philadelphia's public face—the restoration of an identity to what it now seems always to have been. In fact, as Charlene Mires notes, the 1876 Centennial Exhibition had virtually ignored the city's colonial history in favor of its mechanical might; that event was not an ode to political revolution but rather a tribute to industrial revolution, "a celebration of the progress of the United States in the century since" the founding fathers had met in Independence Hall.[11] For more than half a century, the city promoted its industry as a tourism draw. When it was published in 1937, the Federal Writers' Project book about Philadelphia noted that it was "the country's leading district for textiles and the home of the largest saw-making plant in existence. Other famous Philadelphia-made products are radio reception units, hats, streetcars, automobile bodies, cigars, and carpets." The guide concluded by suggesting city tours, one titled "Through Industrial Philadelphia, City Tour 9," which not only described many of the city's major businesses—the Stetson Hat Company Plant, a textile mill, two hosiery plants, the Philco Radio and Television Corporation Plant, a printing company, a saw maker, and a sugar refinery—but also gave instructions on how people could visit them.[12]

The idea did not take hold. Instead, these industries gradually left Philadelphia while the process of "obscuring the nineteenth century" began downtown, and Independence Hall reclaimed the core of the city's public identity.[13] Much of the city's landscape nevertheless bears the marks of industry, including many factory and warehouse buildings. Some, especially those lining the Delaware and Schuylkill Rivers, have been converted to upscale condominiums or trendy business complexes. In the city's Manayunk area, once home to textile and paper mills and called "the Manchester of the United States," a nineteenth-century textile mill building is now a local brewery whose customers "can still find the scale, now an antique, that was once used to weigh the wool brought into the factory."[14] But other hulking industrial structures stand empty, with broken windows and vandalized brick walls. Perhaps because so much of the unattractive landscape of Philadelphia's "smoky" past is still visible, there is not yet much nostalgia for its lost industry, and the city's tourism continues to feature the Liberty Bell and Independence Hall.

Eighteenth-century history also dominates tourism in Bethlehem, where visitors can take in Moravian heritage year-round in "The Christmas City." The city's steel heritage remains mired in funding problems and interpretive disagreement, a contest between what Kenneth Warren calls "rather uneasy alternatives."[15] As he suggests, the most criticized outcome of that site's decades of development planning, the large slots casino that opened in 2009, is likely to be a main sponsor of whatever industrial heritage story does eventually get told in this city. "If Bethlehem Steel had closed in 1949 instead of 1999, it's conceivable that the state would have been involved in that development," says Robert

Weible, the state's former director of public history. "But now the emphasis is not on public education; it's on economic development."[16]

Questions of Funding, "Friends," and Focus for the New Industrial Story

It seems inevitable that Bethlehem's heritage will represent a mix of commercial and cultural interests, and that it may indeed end up being "a model for old industrial sites . . . rising out of the soot"—if in a way somewhat different than the *Christian Science Monitor* predicted more than twenty years ago.[17] Not far from Bethlehem is the intended site of a new agricultural museum that will showcase an 1872 structure well-known in central Pennsylvania as "The Star Barn." Its new owner, a company called Agrarian Country, is moving the barn from its longtime location in Dauphin County, where its proximity to Interstate 283 has hastened its decay, to a site in Lebanon County "near the Hollywood Casino at Penn National Race Course." There, a local newspaper reported, the barn will become "an educational center devoted to agriculture . . . a $10 million hands-on exhibit and education complex that would showcase 30 or more working agricultural enterprises. . . . The barn raising will be accompanied by a music festival, an agricultural foods festival and Civil War reenactors."[18]

The future of industrial heritage—and of public history in general—is increasingly up to private funders, whether they are casino companies or development corporations with euphemistic names or small-town historical societies. In 2009, the Pennsylvania Historical and Museum Commission, one of the oldest and most active state historical agencies in the country, cut opening times for many of its sites and announced plans to lay off a third of its employees. Major renovations have been repeatedly postponed for the permanent exhibits of two of the oldest commission sites, the state museum in Harrisburg, where a Conestoga wagon and a Tin Lizzie still greet visitors to the exhibit "Man and Machine," and Drake Well, where the top of Ida Tarbell still sits without explanation, propped inside the front doors.[19] Today the state budget has little room for history, despite the commission's 1945 charter vowing a lasting commitment to the preservation of historical records and properties. The 2010 federal budget also cut funding for heritage area programs. To survive, government-run historical sites must raise their own money, through active "friends" groups and community outreach, an outcome favoring sites with the most friends or wealthiest communities.

This economic situation has several implications. One is that, more and more, history will need to be entertaining. An example from the private sector, the transformation of the nature of factory tours from the middle of the twentieth century to its end, is revealing. Current factory tours explain not how clothing is made or ships are built but how potato chips, pretzels, beer, and motorcycles come to be. Interactivity is a growing emphasis of all kinds of historical sites, whether it takes the form of a caboose ride, the chance to make your own pretzel, a race to get your toy canal boat through the locks, or a 3-D or IMAX movie. Scranton tourism materials jointly promote the Lackawanna Coal Mine Tour and the Electric City Trolley Museum with the phrase "Rock and Roll"; visitors here also get free Yuengling beer when they take "*The Office* Tour," a four-hour bus ride whose narration explains the city's industrial past while noting locations mentioned on the television show.[20] Media fantasy blends with transportation history in special events held at the Railroad Museum of Pennsylvania, including a program of "Trains in Motion Pictures," "Hogwarts Express Parties," and "Polar Express Parties."[21] The only permanent change to the state museum in recent decades has been the addition of the "Curiosity Connection," a child's play area, dominated by a giant yellow chick, just off the lobby.

As several of these examples suggest, museums increasingly cater to families with young children and to school groups, including a growing population of homeschoolers and their parents. The importance of school groups may partly explain the growing tendency to interpret the industrial past in terms of technology, science, and nature or environmentalism. In its advertisements, the Pennsylvania Tourism Office packages seventeen of the twenty-four state-run historic sites as the "Energy Trail of History." These include some obvious choices such as Drake Well and the Anthracite Heritage Museum, some conceptually creative choices such as the Erie Maritime Museum ("the power of the wind") and the Landis Valley Museum ("horse power"), and some real stretches such as William Penn's summer home ("Pennsbury's gardens are excellent examples of period recycling and energy efficient horticulture") and the Pennsylvania Military Museum ("Manpower supplied the energy").[22] Through this prism, past industry is retrospectively understood as responsible for the beautiful nature all around us today, a very strange lesson indeed. Presentations of industry as science—a matter of minerals chemically interacting and steam-powered pistons moving and water flowing over wheels—further flatten the political, economic, and social history of labor, rendering the industrialist as merely the man with a great idea and the worker as merely the transformer of nature's bounty. Understanding industry as the scientific process that produces our modern conveniences today further diminishes the truly vast scale on which manufacturing once operated.

The difficulty of conveying that sense of scale, of depicting what industry once really looked like, is among the most pressing economic challenges of industrial heritage. In the face of often great unhappiness from former workers and local residents—for whom empty mills and factory buildings are the last evidence of a lost way of life—historic preservationists and heritage organizations must make choices. "You can't save every building," says August Carlino, executive director of the Rivers of Steel Heritage Area. "It's impossible. You have to choose what you save and what you leave behind."[23] Ken Wolensky of the state's Bureau for Historic Preservation agrees: "Only a piece can be preserved, something representative, to survive and be interpreted."[24] Moreover, as Bella Dicks notes, "Heritage production involves both salvaging the past and staging it as a visitable experience."[25]

Indeed, I learned that if I was to observe any appreciable number of visitors at industrial history sites, I needed to go not merely to destinations but to "experiences," themed events such as harvest festivals, fall-foliage train rides, battle reenactments, or Memorial Day homecoming weekends. Because they have the qualities of ruins, former (or reconstructed) industrial sites lend themselves especially well to Halloween themes. In October, the Tour-Ed mine near Pittsburgh is transformed into a "haunted mine" filled with zombies; outside Philadelphia, the West Chester Railroad becomes "The Great Pumpkin Express."[26] At Eckley Miners Village, a tourism publication promises that "visitors may creep through the village either on foot or in a wagon to encounter a frightening array of characters. 'The Count' and his servant ghouls lead the walking tours. . . . Visitors . . . may watch classic horror movies in an auditorium while awaiting their turn to enter the dark streets of the village."[27] In nearby Jim Thorpe, ghost tours are given at the Old Jail, where seven of the Molly Maguires were hanged.[28] Year-round this site is promoted more for its supernatural qualities— much is made of the "handprint on the wall" that supposedly confirms the innocence of one of the condemned men—than for its labor history. In this sense it joins Centralia and Johnstown as an example of "dark tourism," a growing phenomenon in which visitors seek out sites of disaster and death.[29]

The public face of the industrial heritage landscape also depends increasingly on regional coalitions and cooperative fundraising and marketing. Such logistics determine the survival of some industrial history sites and the creation of others. Three of the public history professionals I interviewed while researching this book noted the odd disconnect between the most popular and profitable state-run historic site, the Railroad Museum of Pennsylvania, and its location in the middle of Amish farmlands in Strasburg (as well as the irony that one cannot get there by train). One said, frankly, "The railroad museum should be in Altoona, not in Lancaster. But it's in Lancaster because that's where the tourists are. The question isn't how to educate the public about history; it's 'where do you get the audience?'"

From Culture to Commerce: "Timeless Authenticity" in the Heritage Marketplace

The question of where, and how, you get the audience has produced shifts in how regions are identified and how historical subjects and eras are connected in public storytelling. Cross-promotion is the goal of the *Explore PA* television shows and "Shunpiker" advertisements, and it is a requirement for designation as a state or federal heritage area. These trends, plus the growing popularity of costumed reenactment, dovetail with the emergence of "cultural tourism" and the blending of history and retail. The state tourism office promotes a twelve-county region of forestland as a way to connect with the land through selective shopping, assuring visitors, "In the Pennsylvania Wilds, we value authenticity—the company of unpretentious people, the enduring quality of nature, and the timeless appeal of handmade goods. Our towns and villages attract artists and artisans who appreciate our values and contribute to our regional identity by creating beautiful and functional items you won't find anywhere else."[30]

This marketing rhetoric is typical of the growing commodification of memory-fueled concepts such as authenticity and nature, woven into nation-building stories. One such retail heritage fantasy can be found (in fact, it is impossible not to notice) beside Interstate 78, midway between the two casinos that are the intended partners of the planned National Museum of Industrial Heritage and the planned agricultural heritage complex. At the junction where the interstate crosses State Highway 61, which winds northward toward Minersville and the anthracite region, stands Cabela's, a megastore devoted to hunting and fishing. I stopped there to find a kiosk that shows the Schuylkill River Heritage Area's short video about the "three revolutions," located in the store's vestibule.[31] What is all around it says far more about heritage culture. This outdoorsman's palace, which opened here in 2003, recalls the preindustrial nostalgia of much heritage tourism. Folklore scholar Simon Bronner describes the sculpture at its entryway, "paying tribute to America's pioneer heritage. A

Native American sits in the rear of a canoe while a buckskin-clad white adventurer stands at the front, taking aim with a cocked musket." The store's interior, which features a shooting gallery, floor-to-ceiling aquariums full of freshwater fish, a "mountain" dotted with animal mannequins, and a waterfall descending into a trout pond, "enacts a rags-to-riches mythology for self and nation and ensures that gold and manifest destiny can be achieved for folksy types panning for the American dream."[32]

Heritage-themed products and experiences are abundant across Pennsylvania—tradition and authenticity are for sale, it turns out, nearly everywhere—though not all are quite this commercial, and some do serve history as well as heritage. As I was finishing this manuscript, I received an email from the Rivers of Steel heritage organization inviting me to visit a "Holiday Heritage Market" at the Pump House in Homestead. Its text provided a good historical explanation of the labor conflict that took place there in 1892, in addition to a good explanation of what I could buy on this site 2010: "Authentic, ethnic heritage art such as Bulgarian-Macedonian pottery, Hungarian wood carvings, Native American beadwork and pre-colonial maps. . . . Swiss chocolate and Scottish shortbread can be sampled and purchased, along with Greek and Hungarian entrees. Planned art demonstrations include Slovenian Polka music."[33]

Such "cultural tourism" offers so many points for entry into the past, enticing appeals through which we may feel a sense of connection to those who came before us. Yet it constructs a notion of identity, and of the past itself, that is thematically and temporally jumbled: chronology disappears, causality is vague, and contexts are fluid. Against such a blurry backdrop (somewhat paradoxically) certain ideas have come to stand out, often through sheer repetition. The presumably universal nostalgia for "authentic ethnicity" is one of them; the memorialization of labor history as patriotic sacrifice is another; the understanding of environmentalism as the outcome of industry is a third. Certain events also emerge as dominant in heritage memory, not only occupying their own times but oozing into other eras as well.

A "Tragic Struggle of Brothers" in a Simpler Time: The Story After Living Memory Is Gone

During the three years I spent traveling the state looking for industrial history, I was struck by how often I found, instead, the Civil War. Skirmishes take place along the routes of tourist trains across the state. At Eckley Miners Village, a woman costumed in Victorian black told me about wartime mourning rituals in a coal town while reenactors marched in formation and fired cannons in a field behind the breaker; the glory days of the oil boom were recalled by members of the Bucktail Regiment in Titusville.[34] At the Landis Valley Museum, Lancaster's agricultural heritage site, I walked through a field of pitched tents where Union soldiers whittled sticks and polished their guns, and listened as one explained his rations to spectators.[35]

In recent Civil War interpretation, not military strategies but "the small towns and families who endured our most personal war are the heroes." This language is from a state tourism office campaign called "Civil War Trails," which declares in its promotional materials, "Diaries Speak Louder Than History Books."[36] Its more than forty "Story Stops" (interpretive waysides) recount Civil War history in the towns that circle Gettysburg. Some of them explain the role of industries in the war and the reasons central Pennsylvania was such a coveted prize for the Confederacy: its railroads, its iron furnaces, its textile mills, and its agricultural production.[37] More of these signs, though, offer anecdotes about local residents whose individual deeds contributed in some way to the buildup to and aftermath of the Battle of Gettysburg. These are not generals; they are "heroes less known."[38] This vernacular focus allows for a rather hazy notion of the war itself, a conflict now understood as a collection of "stories of those who fought for their beliefs during this dark time in our nation's history."[39]

Recent trends in public memory of the Civil War may foretell the future of other kinds of heritage storytelling as well. In 2001, when I first visited the newly opened National Civil War Museum in Harrisburg, I was stunned by its perfectly even-handed interpretation. In each of its themed rooms (weapons, flags, uniforms, music, "the home front," various battles), Confederate artifacts are on one side and Union artifacts are on the other side. The museum was created to offer, according to its mission statement, "a balanced presentation of the American peoples [sic] struggle for survival and healing."[40] A decade later, this kind of presentation is common in Civil War interpretation, including that of the new National Park Service Museum and Visitor Center that opened in Gettysburg in 2008. Its theme is "A New Birth of Freedom," and it is everyone's rebirth, a shared, patriotic redemption. Increasingly understood as "a tragic struggle of brother against brother" fought by "soldiers and citizens who forged a stronger nation," the Civil War offers a model for public understanding of the Industrial Revolution, as it, too, recedes into the distant past—a story that could not have unfolded otherwise, a tale with only heroes, courageous citizens who "took care of their own" and ultimately strengthened the nation.[41]

Public memory of the Civil War began as a local (and distinctly *not* nar-ratively even-handed) phenomenon in the late nineteenth century, when me-morials and museums were founded by people who could remember the war or who wanted to pay tribute to their fathers and other townspeople who had fought in it. To an extent, this is the phase industrial heritage is in at the mo-ment. Very many of the sites I visited while researching this book are small-town venues run by volunteers motivated by their own work experience or by their desire to pay tribute to their parents. The stories they tell are particular and proud, even defensive, a tribute to departed heroes who once stood for the greatness of their towns and their ethnic identities. But who will run these museums in another generation, and what story will they tell? Already the in-dustrial heritage story is becoming much more general, a broad celebration of working-class identity (at least for those of us who no longer have it), an af-firmative social identity in which ethnicity is a badge of honor worn by nearly everyone. In that view, the Industrial Revolution was a difficult but inevitable episode of heroic sacrifice that ultimately gave us our modern world of lifestyle conveniences and beautiful landscape.

Like public memory of the Civil War, the industrial heritage narrative al-ready has begun to change, and it will continue to do so in order to meet the changing memory needs of future Americans. As Robert Archibald notes, "His-tory provides the context from which every generation extracts new meanings germane to their concerns."[42] Yet certainly some aspects of the broad heritage story discussed in this book will have continuing public resonance.

If the history of heritage has taught us anything, it is that the imaginative appeal of a simpler but nobler past—a time when our ancestors sought a better life, knew who they were, and worked hard—is not diminishing. In the 1930s, Civilian Conservation Corps workers re-created the Hopewell Iron Furnace as a tribute to a lost agrarian life, "a twentieth-century idea about the nineteenth century, the Norman Rockwell view of American history," notes the site's su-pervisor, Edie Shean-Hammond.[43] Today's heritage projects pay tribute to a lost industrial life, a twenty-first-century idea about the twentieth century. A cen-tury from now, it's likely that, somehow, our own lives too will be interpreted as a "simpler time" to which people will, for varying reasons, want to feel a connection.

That desire has considerable staying power indeed. Heritage culture matters because it is a public expression of our wishes of the present and because those wishes have implications for the future. What story we continue to tell will de-termine, in part, whose ancestors we become.

Notes

INTRODUCTION

The epigraph to this chapter is drawn from David Streitfeld, "Rock Bottom for Decades, but Showing Signs of Life," *New York Times*, February 1, 2009, p. A16.

1. John Luciew, "Welcome to Steelers Country," *Harrisburg Patriot-News*, February 1, 2009, pp. C1, C3.

2. Writing about this series, a columnist for the *Columbia Journalism Review* commented, "So it sounds like the newness of the recession that we get from the national narrative isn't so new in Pennsylvania." (Katia Bachko, "Talking Shop: Dennis Roddy: *Pittsburgh Post-Gazette* Reporter Talks About the Recession's Effects in Western Pennsylvania," *Columbia Journalism Review*, May 28, 2009, accessed May 30, 2009, http://www.cjr.org/campaign_desk/talking_shop_dennis_roddy_1.php).

3. Michael Powell, "Democrats in Steel Country See Skin Color, and Beyond It," *New York Times*, October 27, 2008, p. A1.

4. One example is Scott Horsley, reporter, and Steve Inskeep, host, "GOP Ticket in Hershey, Pennsylvania," *Morning Edition*, National Public Radio, October 29, 2008, accessed via Lexis-Nexis academic database.

5. John Marchese, "Scranton Embraces the 'Office' Infamy," *New York Times*, October 21, 2007, "Television" sec., p. 1.

6. "VP Debate," *Saturday Night Live*, first aired on October 4, 2008, on the National Broadcasting Corporation (NBC) and reshown in several broadcasts of the *Saturday Night Live Presidential Bash*, including January 18, 2008; accessed January 19, 2008, http://www.nbc.com/Saturday_Night_Live/video/clips/vp-debate-open-palin-biden/727421/.

7. ABC News and *USA Today*, "50 States in 50 Days," special edition DVD included in *America Speaks: The Historic 2008 Election* (Chicago: Triumph Books, 2008); Don Frederick, "Hillary Clinton Returns to Her Roots in Scranton," *Los Angeles Times*, March 10, 2008, accessed February 16, 2010, http://latimesblogs.latimes.com/washington/2008/03/clinton-in-scra.html; and Katherine Seelye, "One Clinton Hometown Sees Her in Images Befitting a '50s Movie," *New York Times*, March 10, 2008, p. A13.

8. Robin Roberts, "Whistle-Stop America: Voices from the Train," in *America Speaks: The Historic 2008 Election* (Chicago: Triumph Books, 2008), 11.

9. Author's attendance, in the spirit of thorough research, at Springsteen's concerts in Hershey, Pennsylvania, on August 19, 2008, and May 15, 2009, with Denise Graveline; Bruce Springsteen, "American Land," on *We Shall Overcome: The Seeger Sessions—American Land Edition*, Columbia Records, released August 25, 2006, accessed February 16, 2010, http://www.brucespringsteen.net/songs/AmericanLand.html.

10. Herbert J. Gans, *Deciding What's News: A Study of CBS Evening News, NBC Nightly News, Newsweek, and Time* (New York: Pantheon Books, 1979), 50.

11. Such advertising appeals continued through the 1990s as well; see Oren Meyers, "The Engine's in the Front, But its Heart's in the Same Place: Advertising, Nostalgia, and the Construction of Commodities as Realms of Memory," *Journal of Popular Culture* 42, no. 4 (2009): 733–55.

12. Susan G. Davis, "'Set Your Mood to Patriotic': History as Televised Special Event," *Radical History Review* 42 (Fall 1988): 128.

13. Mary Hufford, "Introduction: Rethinking the Cultural Mission," in *Conserving Culture: A New Discourse on Heritage*, ed. Mary Hufford (Urbana: University of Illinois Press, 1994), 1.

14. For authority in representation, see, for instance, Naimah Moore and Yvonne Whelan, eds., *Heritage, Memory, and the Politics of Identity: New Perspectives on the Cultural Landscape* (Burlington, Vt.: Ashgate, 2007). For implications of globalization and recent political change, see, for instance, G. J. Ashworth and P. J. Larkham, eds., *Building a New Heritage: Tourism, Culture, and Identity* (London: Routledge, 1994); and David Boswell and Jessica Evans, eds., *Representing the Nation: A Reader: Histories, Heritage, and Museums* (London: Routledge, 1999). For the nature, forms, and practices of museums, see, for instance, Gerard Corsane, ed., *Heritage, Museums, and Galleries: An Introductory Reader* (London: Routledge, 2005); Eileen Hooper-Greenhill, *Museums and the Shaping of Knowledge* (London: Routledge, 1992); Roger Silverstone, "Museums and the Media: A Theoretical and Methodological Exploration," *International Journal of Museum Management and Curatorship* 7, no. 3 (1988): 231–41; Mike Wallace, *Mickey Mouse History and Other Essays on American Memory* (Philadelphia: Temple University Press, 1996); and Sheila Watson, ed., *Museums and Their Communities* (London: Routledge, 2007).

15. Robert Hewison, *The Heritage Industry: Britain in a Climate of Decline* (London: Methuen, 1987), 9, 10, 144.

16. Robert Hewison, "Commerce and Culture," in *Enterprise and Heritage: Crosscurrents of National Culture*, ed. John Corner and Sylvia Harvey (London: Routledge, 1991), 175.

17. Kevin Walsh, *The Representation of the Past: Museums and Heritage in the Post-Modern World* (London: Routledge, 1992), 103, 104.

18. John Corner and Sylvia Harvey, "Mediating Tradition and Modernity: The Heritage/Enterprise Couplet," in *Enterprise and Heritage*, 55–57.

19. David Lowenthal, *The Heritage Crusade and the Spoils of History* (Cambridge: Cambridge University Press, 1998), 12.

20. Michael Wallace, "The Politics of Public History," in *Past Meets Present: Essays About Historic Interpretation and Public Audiences*, ed. Jo Blatti (Washington: Smithsonian Institution Press, 1987), 38, 39.

21. Wallace, *Mickey Mouse History*, 154–55.

22. Wilbur Zelinsky, *The Cultural Geography of the United States*, rev. ed. (Englewood Cliffs, NJ: Prentice Hall, 1992; originally published in 1973), 177.

23. Jim Weeks, *Gettysburg: Memory, Market, and an American Shrine* (Princeton: Princeton University Press, 2003), 175.

24. Linda Shopes, "Oral History and Community Involvement: The Baltimore Neighborhood Heritage Project," in *Presenting the Past: Essays on History and the Public*, ed. Susan Porter Benson, Stephen Brier, and Roy Rosenzweig (Philadelphia: Temple University Press, 1986), 253.

25. Chris Rojek and John Urry, "Transformations of Travel and Theory," in *Touring Cultures: Transformations of Travel and Theory*, ed. Chris Rojek and John Urry (London: Routledge, 1997), 14.

26. Michael H. Frisch and Dwight Pitcaithley, "Audience Expectations as Resource and Challenge: Ellis Island as a Case Study," in *Past Meets Present*, 155. In another refreshingly nonelite essay in this vein about Liverpool's Albert Dock, Adrian Mellor argues that "real people" bring their own capable understandings to heritage areas ("Enterprise and Heritage in the Dock," in *Enterprise and Heritage*, 45–75).

27. Jo Blatti, "Introduction: Past Meets Present: Field Notes on Historical Sites, Programs, Professionalism, and Visitors," in *Past Meets Present*, 6.

28. "Purvey misinformation" is used by Mike Wallace in *Mickey Mouse History*, 154. Hayden White, *The Content of the Form: Narrative Discourse and Historical Representation* (Baltimore: Johns Hopkins University Press, 1987). White asked, "What wish is enacted, what desire is gratified, by the fantasy that real events are properly represented when they can be shown to display the formal coherency of a story? In the enigma of this wish, this desire, we catch a glimpse of the cultural function of narrativizing discourse in general, an intimation of the psychological impulse behind the apparently universal need not only to narrate but to give to events an aspect of narrativity" (4).

29. Richard Handler and Eric Gable, *The New History in an Old Museum: Creating the Past at Colonial Williamsburg* (Durham: Duke University Press, 1997), 223.

30. Tok Thompson, "Heritage Versus the Past," in *The Past in the Present: A Multidisciplinary Approach*, ed. Fabio Mugnaini, Padraig O Healai, and Tok Thompson (Brussels: Edit Press, 2006), 204–5.

31. Maurice Halbwachs, *The Collective Memory*, trans. Francis J. Ditter Jr. and Vida Yazdi Ditter (New York: Harper and Row, 1950), 72.

32. David Glassberg, *American Historical Pageantry: The Uses of Tradition in the Early Twentieth Century* (Chapel Hill: University of North Carolina Press, 1990), 1.

33. Freeman Tilden, *Interpreting Our Heritage* (Chapel Hill: University of North Carolina Press, 1957), 9, 15, 69, 77. The continuing usefulness of Tilden's principles is indicated in their expansion and restatement more than forty years later by Larry Beck and Ted Cable in *Interpretation for the Twenty-First Century: Fifteen Guiding Principles for Interpreting Nature and Culture* (Champaign, IL: Sagamore Publishing, 1998).

34. Robert R. Archibald, *The New Town Square: Museums and Communities in Transition* (Walnut Creek, CA: AltaMira Press, 2004), 212; David Glassberg, *Sense of History: The Place of the Past in American Life* (Amherst: University of Massachusetts Press, 2001), 6.

35. Glassberg, *Sense of History*, 207–9.

36. Bella Dicks, *Heritage, Place, and Community* (Cardiff: University of Wales Press, 2000), 212. Setha M. Low uses the term "place attachment," defining this phenomenon as a "symbolic relationship formed by people giving culturally shared emotional/affective meanings to a particular space or piece of land" ("Symbolic Ties That Bind: Place Attachment in the Plaza," in *Place Attachment*, ed. Irwin Altman and Setha M. Low [New York: Plenum Press, 1992], 165).

37. Roy Rosenzweig and David Thelen, *The Presence of the Past: Popular Uses of History in American Life* (New York: Columbia University Press, 1998), 178.

38. Author's telephone interview with Edie Shean-Hammond, superintendent, Hopewell Iron Furnace, Elverson, on January 4, 2008.

39. Author's telephone interview with Harold "Kip" Hagan, superintendent, Steamtown National Historic Site, Scranton, on January 14, 2008.

40. Ronald J. Grele, "Whose Public? Whose History? What Is the Goal of the Public Historian?" *Public Historian* 3, no. 1 (Winter 1981): 47, 48.

41. Mary Hufford, "Introduction: Rethinking the Cultural Mission," in *Conserving Culture: A New Discourse on Heritage*, ed. Mary Hufford (Urbana: University of Illinois Press, 1994), 1. This book was an outcome of the 1990 American Folklife Center conference.

42. Amy K. Levin, "Why Local Museums Matter," in *Defining Memory: Local Museums and the Construction of History in America's Changing Communities*, ed. Amy K. Levin (Lanham, MD: AltaMira Press, 2007), 25.

43. This remark is from a published "conversation" between historians Michael Kammen and Carol Kammen, "Uses and Abuses of the Past: A Bifocal Perspective," in *Selvages and Biases: The Fabric of History in American Culture*, ed. Michael Kammen (Ithaca: Cornell University Press, 1987), 283; originally published in *Minnesota History* 48 (Spring 1982): 2–12.

44. Southwestern Pennsylvania Heritage Preservation Commission website, accessed September 18, 2006, http://www.sphpc.org/itsallabout.htm.

45. *Danville, Pennsylvania,* video (Danville, PA, 2002; no other production information given); purchased by the author at the 2007 Iron Heritage Festival in Danville on July 19, 2007.

46. Excerpts from e-mail text sent by Sis Hause in response to the author's questions on January 8, 2008.

47. Author's telephone interview with Kip Hagan on January 14, 2008.

48. Tamara K. Hareven and Randolph Langenbach, "Living Places, Work Places, and Historical Identity," in *Our Past Before Us: Why Do We Save It?* ed. David Lowenthal and Marcus Binney (London: Temple Smith, 1981), 114, 116, 118.

49. John A. Jakle and David Wilson, *Derelict Landscapes: The Wasting of America's Built Environment* (Savage, MD: Rowman and Littlefield, 1992), 86.

50. Barbara Kirschenblatt-Gimblett, *Destination Culture: Tourism, Museums, and Heritage* (Berkeley and Los Angeles: University of California Press, 1998), 150, 151.

51. Richard V. Francaviglia, *Hard Places: Reading the Landscape of America's Historic Mining Districts* (Iowa City: University of Iowa Press, 1991), 166, 167, 172.

52. John Bryant, "Unemployment: The Theme Park," *New York Times,* January 28, 1996, sec. 6, p. 46.

53. William Serrin, *Homestead: The Glory and Tragedy of an American Steel Town* (New York: Times Books, 1992), 404.

54. Marilyn Halter, *Shopping for Identity: The Marketing of Ethnicity* (New York: Schocken Books, 2000), 17.

55. Michael Frisch, "De- , Re- , and Post-Industrialization: Industrial Heritage as Contested Memorial Terrain," *Journal of Folklore Research* 35, no. 3 (1998): 241–49.

56. Author's in-person interview with Lenwood Sloan, director of cultural and heritage tourism, Pennsylvania Tourism Office, Harrisburg, on January 26, 2009.

57. Bella Dicks, *Culture on Display: The Production of Contemporary Visitability* (Maidenhead: Open University Press, 2003), 119.

58. Diane Barthel, *Historic Preservation: Collective Memory and Historical Identity* (New Brunswick: Rutgers University Press, 1996), 76–77.

59. Cathy Stanton, *The Lowell Experiment: Public History in a Postindustrial City* (Amherst: University of Massachusetts Press, 2006), 22, 26.

60. See Robert Weible, "Lowell: Building a New Appreciation for Historical Place," *Public Historian* 6, no. 3 (Summer 1984): 27–38; also, author's in-person interview with Weible (who now is the chief historian for the State of New York) when he was director of public history for the Pennsylvania Historical and Museum Commission, Harrisburg, on February 15, 2008.

61. See, for instance, Stanton, *The Lowell Experiment;* and Robert Weible and Francis R. Walsh, eds., *The Popular Perception of Industrial History* (Lanham, MD: American Association for State and Local History Library, 1989).

62. Author's telephone interview with August Carlino, executive director, Rivers of Steel Heritage Area, Homestead, on February 27, 2008.

63. *Northeast Pennsylvania Visitors Guide,* February–March 2007, inside back cover (no publication information given); obtained by the author in Scranton. While presumably not appreciated by the New England states, where textile mills arose in the 1820s, the "birthplace" claim is repeatedly justified by references to Pennsylvania's eighteenth- and early nineteenth-century iron furnaces.

64. Michael Blood, "History's Mother Lode," *Philadelphia Inquirer,* October 15, 1991, p. B2.

65. D. K. Shifflet and Associates, *Pennsylvania Heritage Tourism Study* (McLean, VA, May 1999), 4, 28. Prepared for the Pennsylvania Department of Conservation and Natural Resources in partnership with the Pennsylvania Department of Community and Economic

Development, the Pennsylvania Historical and Museum Commission, Preservation Pennsylvania, and the Federation of Museums and Historical Organizations; in the Library of the Pennsylvania Historical and Museum Commission, Harrisburg, Pa.

66. "Economic Impact of Pennsylvania's Heritage Areas, 2008," report dated February 11, 2010, available on the website of the Alliance of National Heritage Areas, accessed January 6, 2011, http://www.nationalheritageareas.com/documents/. I calculated these percentages myself based on the raw data in the report; its own analysis focused more on whether or not respondents were first-time visitors and stayed overnight.

67. Daniel Stynes and Ya-Yen Sun, *Lackawanna Valley National Heritage Area Visitors Survey and Economic Impact Analysis* (East Lansing: Michigan State University Department of Community, Agriculture, Recreation, and Resource Studies, 2004), 5; and Yen Le, Margaret Littlejohn, and Michael A. Schuett, *Hopewell Furnace National Historic Site: Visitor Study, Summer 2002* (Washington, DC: National Park Service Visitor Services Project, 2002), 18.

68. This is the case with regard to most of the surveys cited above, as well as a national heritage area survey that included the Delaware and Lehigh National Heritage Corridor in Pennsylvania titled "Economic Impact of Five National Heritage Areas, 2008," report dated May 11, 2010, available on the website of the Alliance of National Heritage Areas, accessed January 6, 2011, http://www.nationalheritageareas.com/documents/.

69. "The Destination That Will Follow You Home" (Harrisburg: Pennsylvania Office of Travel, Tourism, and Film, 2000]), no pagination, in Pennsylvania Documents Collection, State Library of Pennsylvania.

70. Howard Harris and Mark McCollough, introduction to *Keystone of Democracy: A History of Pennsylvania Workers*, ed. Howard Harris and Perry K. Blatz (Harrisburg: Pennsylvania Historical and Museum Commission, 1999), xi.

CHAPTER 1

The epigraph to this chapter is drawn from Peter Glick, "Industrial Pennsylvania," in *Pennsylvania Highways* (Harrisburg: Pennsylvania Department of Highways, 1930), 9, in PA Documents Collection, State Library of Pennsylvania.

1. *Pennsylvania Has Everything: Your Travel Guide to Penn's "Land of the Forest,"* 6th ed. (Harrisburg: Department of Commerce, Commonwealth of Pennsylvania, 1940), in PA Documents Collection, State Library of Pennsylvania; *All in Pennsylvania* (Harrisburg: Pennsylvania Department of Commerce, Commonwealth of Pennsylvania, no year given, but apparently 1940s), in PA Documents Collection, State Library of Pennsylvania.

2. "Pennsylvania at Your Fingertips: Your Picture Guide Book to the Keystone State" (Harrisburg: Department of Commerce, Commonwealth of Pennsylvania, 1940), n.p., in PA Documents Collection, State Library of Pennsylvania.

3. John F. Sears, *Sacred Places: American Tourist Attractions in the Nineteenth Century* (New York: Oxford University Press, 1989), 191.

4. Foundational scholarship on this much explored theme includes Leo Marx, *The Machine in the Garden: Technology and the Pastoral Ideal in America* (New York: Oxford University Press, 1964); and Henry Nash Smith, *Virgin Land: The American West as Symbol and Myth* (Cambridge: Harvard University Press, 1950).

5. *First Report of the Historical Commission of Pennsylvania: To the Governor of Pennsylvania and the General Assembly* (Lancaster: New Era, 1915), 11–12, 14–15, 32, 34, in PA Documents Collection, State Library of Pennsylvania.

6. Daniel B. Reibel, *Old Economy Village* (Harrisburg: Pennsylvania Historical and Museum Commission/Stackpole Books, 2002).

7. The surrounding town, Ambridge, is named for the American Bridge Company, one of the iron and steel manufacturers whose fortunes fueled the area's prosperity in the early twentieth century. This is no longer the case. Less than a quarter of a mile from the Old Economy Village historic site is the New Economy Business Park, but—as suggested by the Family Dollar store and shuttered Foodland just across the street—Ambridge is economically depressed (author's visit to Old Economy Village in Ambridge on July 11, 2008).

8. John T. Faris, *Seeing Pennsylvania* (Philadelphia: J. B. Lippincott, 1919), 4–5.

9. "Historical Map of Pennsylvania" (Harrisburg: State Publicity Bureau, Pennsylvania State Chamber of Commerce, 1925), n.p. It is especially interesting that Drake Well, which was the site of the first successful oil well in 1859 and would soon become the second state historical site, was not mentioned at all; Johnstown, by then a huge steelmaking city, was mentioned only as the site of the 1889 Johnstown Flood.

10. *Pennsylvania: Forty Thousand Square Miles: Beautiful Modern Highways and Historic Byways* (Harrisburg: State Publicity Bureau, Pennsylvania State Chamber of Commerce, 1925), n.p.

11. *Pennsylvania: Official Tourist Guide* (Harrisburg: State Publicity Bureau, Pennsylvania State Chamber of Commerce, 1926), and "Main Roads in Pennsylvania," *Pennsylvania: Facts Motorists Should Know* (Harrisburg: Department of Highways, 1926), 6–9, both in PA Documents Collection, State Library of Pennsylvania.

12. "Points of Interest in Pennsylvania," in *Pennsylvania: Facts Motorists Should Know* (Harrisburg: Department of Highways, 1926), 32, in PA Documents Collection, State Library of Pennsylvania.

13. "Scranton: The Heart of Northeastern Pennsylvania," advertisement in *Pennsylvania: Official Tourist Guide* (Harrisburg: State Publicity Bureau, Pennsylvania State Chamber of Commerce, 1926), 47.

14. Angus K. Gillespie, *Folklorist of the Coal Fields: George Korson's Life and Work* (University Park: Penn State University Press, 1980). In 1935 Korson founded the Pennsylvania Folk Festival, and in 1957 he succeeded Henry Shoemaker as president of the Pennsylvania Folklore Society.

15. Simon J. Bronner, *Killing Tradition: Inside Hunting and Animal Rights Controversies* (Lexington: University Press of Kentucky, 2008), 112–13.

16. Henry W. Shoemaker, "Off the Beaten Path on Pennsylvania State Highways," *Pennsylvania: Facts Motorists Should Know* (Harrisburg: Department of Highways, 1926), 11, in PA Documents Collection, State Library of Pennsylvania. The capitalization of the entire word "Pennsylvania" is from the original.

17. Simon J. Bronner, *Popularizing Pennsylvania: Henry W. Shoemaker and the Progressive Uses of Folklore and History* (University Park: Penn State University Press, 1996), xii–xiv.

18. David Glassberg, *American Historical Pageantry: The Uses of Tradition in the Early Twentieth Century* (Chapel Hill: University of North Carolina Press, 1990), 289.

19. Bronner, *Popularizing Pennsylvania*, 119. Bronner cites the "Henry W. Shoemaker scrapbook, 1929, Juniata College, Archives, Huntingdon, Pennsylvania."

20. Joseph M. Speakman, *At Work in Penn's Woods: The Civilian Conservation Corps in Pennsylvania* (University Park: Penn State University Press, 2006), 6.

21. *In Penn's Woods: A Handy and Helpful Pocket Manual of the Natural Wonders and Recreational Facilities of the State Forests of Pennsylvania*, Bulletin 31 (Harrisburg: Pennsylvania Department of Forests and Waters, 1925), 4, 6, in PA Industries File, Library of the Pennsylvania Historical and Museum Commission (PHMC), Harrisburg.

22. "Seeing Pennsylvania from the Forest Fire Observation Towers," *Pennsylvania: Facts Motorists Should Know* (Harrisburg: Department of Highways, 1926), 36, in PA Documents Collection, State Library of Pennsylvania.

23. Francis R. Cope Jr., "New Objectives in Forestry," *Forest Leaves* 26, no. 4 (October 1936), 27, in PA Industries File, Library of the PHMC, Harrisburg.

24. "History of Parks and Forests," Pennsylvania Parks and Forests Foundation website, accessed January 16, 2010, http://www.paparksandforests.org/history.html.

25. *The State Forests of Pennsylvania* (Harrisburg: Department of Forests and Waters, Commonwealth of Pennsylvania, 1946), in PA Industries File, Library of the PHMC, Harrisburg.

26. For a history of the work of the Civilian Conservation Corps in Pennsylvania, see Speakman, *At Work in Penn's Woods*. Another study of the environmental conservation work of the corps, including Gifford Pinchot's philosophical contributions to debates about its work, is Neil M. Maher, *Nature's New Deal: The Civilian Conservation Corps and the Roots of the American Environmental Movement* (New York: Oxford University Press, 2008).

27. Many books and exhibitions have documented this work, which is archived in "America from the Great Depression to World War II: Black-and-White Photographs from the FSA-OWI, 1935–1945," a part of the "American Memory" digital collection, Prints and Photographs Division, Library of Congress, accessed January 16, 2010, http://memory.loc.gov/ammem/fsahtml/fahome.html.

28. These murals were the subject of "A Common Canvas: Pennsylvania's New Deal Post Office Murals," exhibit at the State Museum of Pennsylvania, Harrisburg, November 22, 2008, to May 17, 2009, curated by Curt Miner and Dave Lembeck.

29. Pennsylvania Writers Program (Works Progress Administration), *Pennsylvania: A Guide to the Keystone State* (New York: Oxford University Press, 1940), vii, ix.

30. Pennsylvania Writers Program, *Pennsylvania*, 3, 4, 5, 295, 323.

31. Steven D. Reschly and Katherine Jellison, "Shifting Images of Lancaster County Amish in the 1930s and 1940s," paper presented at "The Amish in America" conference, Elizabethtown College, June 2007.

32. Author's visit to the Mercer Museum in Doylestown on August 26, 2008.

33. Author's visit to the Landis Valley Museum (during "Harvest Days"), Lancaster, on October 7, 2007. The quote is from the on-site, thirteen-minute orientation film, *Crossroads at Landis Valley*. Also see the Landis Valley Museum website, http://www.landisvalleymuseum .org/history.php (accessed on January 16, 2010). The state took over running the museum in 1953; by 1958 a newspaper travel writer declared it "America's Greatest Farm Museum" (A. Aubrey Bodine, "America's Greatest Farm Museum," *Baltimore Sunday Sun Magazine*, November 9, 1958, 15–18, in PHMC Sites File, Library of the PHMC, Harrisburg).

34. *Vacation Pleasures in Pennsylvania* (Harrisburg: Department of Commerce, Commonwealth of Pennsylvania, ca. 1940s), n.p., in PA Documents Collection, State Library of Pennsylvania.

35. *Hopewell Village National Historic Site,* National Park Service Historical Handbook Series No. 8 (Washington, DC: U.S. Department of the Interior, 1950), 1, in PA Industries File, Library of the PHMC, Harrisburg.

36. Author's telephone interview with Edie Shean-Hammond on January 4, 2008. For more on Hopewell's interpretation, see Cathy Stanton, "'The Past as a Public Good: The U.S. National Park Service and 'Cultural Repair' in Post-Industrial Places," in *People and Their Pasts: Public History Today,* ed. Paul Ashton and Hilda Kean (London: Palgrave Macmillan, 2009), 57–73.

37. R. Hadly Waters, "Analysis of the Tourist Industry in Pennsylvania," *Bulletin of The Pennsylvania State College Bureau of Business Research* 33 (State College: The Pennsylvania State College, 1947). This report also identified what now is called "cultural tourism" (see chapter 4) as one area for growth of the tourist industry in Pennsylvania, referring briefly to "the state's cultural inheritance—its varied people, its interesting communities, its historical monuments and landmarks. In most cases, these features are chiefly in need of publicity." (7)

38. *The Story of the Old Company* (Lansford, PA: Lehigh Navigation Coal Company, 1941), n.p., in PA Industries File, Library of the PHMC, Harrisburg. Earlier in the nineteenth century, the company was called the Lehigh Coal and Navigation Company.

39. *Pennsylvania* (Harrisburg: Commonwealth of Pennsylvania, 1944), 49.

40. Edward Martin, "My Pennsylvania," in *My Pennsylvania: A Brief History of the Commonwealth's Sixty-Seven Counties* (Harrisburg: Commonwealth of Pennsylvania, Department of Property and Supplies, Bureau of Publications, 1946), 1, in PA Documents Collection, State Library of Pennsylvania.

41. "There's More in Pennsylvania" (Harrisburg: Department of Commerce, Commonwealth of Pennsylvania, 1947?), n.p., in PA Documents Collection, State Library of Pennsylvania. The governor is listed as James H. Duff (1947–1951).

42. *Pennsylvania Panorama* (Harrisburg: Pennsylvania Department of Commerce, 194?), n.p., in PA Documents Collection, State Library of Pennsylvania. Here, too, the governor is listed as James H. Duff (1947–1951).

43. *Drake Well Memorial Park: Birthplace of the Petroleum Industry* (Harrisburg: PHMC, 1946); *Cornwall Furnace: Historic Charcoal Iron Furnace* (Harrisburg: PHMC, 1946). The Pennsylvania Historical Commission had acquired both of these sites during the early 1930s.

44. *Guide to the Historical Markers of Pennsylvania*, 2nd ed. (Harrisburg: PHMC, 1952).

45. *The Pennsylvania Historical and Museum Commission, 1945–1950* (Harrisburg: PHMC, 1950), 6.

46. *Plans for Pennsylvania Week* (Harrisburg: Commonwealth of Pennsylvania, Department of Commerce, 1949), n.p., in PA Documents Collection, State Library of Pennsylvania.

47. "Your Pennsylvania" (Harrisburg: Department of Commerce, Commonwealth of Pennsylvania, 1948), 8, in PA Documents Collection, State Library of Pennsylvania.

48. These were recounted in the 1949 guide *Plans for Pennsylvania Week* (October 17–24, 1949), n.p.

49. Martin, "My Pennsylvania," 1.

50. "Nine Decades of Oil" (New York: Esso Standard Oil Company, ca. 1950), 22, in PA Industries File, Library of the PHMC, Harrisburg.

51. *The Pennsylvania Historical and Museum Commission, 1945–1950,* 1; "the first duty of citizenship" is from p. 24.

52. "Ten Memorable Days in Pennsylvania" (Harrisburg: Department of Commerce, Commonwealth of Pennsylvania, 1952), reprinted from *Better Homes and Gardens* (April 1952) (no pagination in reprint), in PA Documents Collection, State Library of Pennsylvania.

53. PHMC, "Operation Heritage: Preserving Our Past: An Investment in Our Future" (Harrisburg: 1959?), in PA Documents Collection, State Library of Pennsylvania.

54. Esso (Standard Oil), "Pennsylvania" (Convent Station, NJ: General Drafting Company, 1958).

55. "C-Day at Titusville," *Orange Disk* (September–October 1959): 5, in PA Industries File, Library of the PHMC, Harrisburg.

56. "Oil Centennial, 1859–1959, August 23–29, Titusville, Pennsylvania: Official Program," n.p., in PA Industries File, Library of the PHMC, Harrisburg.

57. "Oil City Centennial Celebration, Oil City, Pennsylvania, 1871–1971" (pamphlet), August 12–22, 1971, no pagination; purchased by author in the "festival store" during the Oil Heritage Festival in Oil City, on July 20, 2007.

58. Charlene Mires, *Independence Hall in American Memory* (Philadelphia: University of Pennsylvania Press, 2002), 216–17.

59. *Discover the New Pennsylvania* (Harrisburg: Pennsylvania Department of Commerce, 1964), 2, 43.

60. See Thomas Dublin, *When the Mines Closed: Stories of Struggles in Hard Times* (Ithaca: Cornell University Press, 1998), and Thomas Dublin and Walter Licht, *The Face of Decline:*

The Pennsylvania Anthracite Region in the Twentieth Century (Ithaca: Cornell University Press, 2005).

61. Rose DeWolf, "What Happened Here? Coal Happened Here," *Sunday Bulletin Magazine* (August 3, 1969): 6, in PA Industries File, Library of the PHMC, Harrisburg.

62. John Bodnar, *Remaking America: Public Memory, Commemoration, and Patriotism in the Twentieth Century* (Princeton: Princeton University Press, 1992), 328.

63. "Steel-History Exhibit Featured in Museum," *Patriot Evening News,* August 19, 1976, n.p., in State Museum file, Library of the PHMC, Harrisburg.

64. Author's visit to Codorus State Park near York on June 20, 2008.

65. Author's travels along the National Road on July 25, 2008.

66. *Come to Pennsylvania and Get to Know America* (Harrisburg: Pennsylvania Bureau of Travel Development, 1976), n.p., in PA Documents Collection, State Library of Pennsylvania.

67. Jim Ruth, "Landis Valley: Window on the Past," *Lancaster Sunday News,* September 30, 1979, p. F1, in PHMC Sites File, Library of the PHMC, Harrisburg. Steve Miller went on to become the director of the Landis Valley Museum and later the director of the PHMC Bureau of Historic Sites and Museums; he was interviewed for this book in both capacities and is quoted in the following chapters.

68. *You've Got a Friend in Pennsylvania* (Harrisburg: Pennsylvania Department of Commerce, 1980), in PA Documents Collection, State Library of Pennsylvania.

69. *Task Force Report: Tourism and Travel* (Harrisburg: Pennsylvania Economic Development Partnership, Office of the Governor, January 1988), in PA Documents Collection, State Library of Pennsylvania.

70. Mary Klaus, "Memories of Coal, Rail Eras Still Much Alive in Scranton," *Sunday Patriot-News,* January 15, 1989, p. G8, in PHMC Sites file, Library of the PHMC, Harrisburg.

71. "Two Pennsylvania Towns Recall Days When Coal Was King," *New York Times,* March 22, 1981, Travel sec., p. 3, in PHMC Sites File, Library of the PHMC, Harrisburg. The other town featured in this article was Jim Thorpe.

72. *Pennsylvania: 1989–90 Fall/Winter Travel Guide* (Harrisburg: Pennsylvania Department of Commerce, Bureau of Travel Marketing, 1989), 2–3, in PA Documents Collection, State Library of Pennsylvania.

73. "Family Heritage Day: May 25, 1991" (Scranton: Anthracite Heritage Museum, 1991), n.p., in PHMC Sites File, Library of the PHMC, Harrisburg.

74. Mary Klaus, "Landis Valley Fair Trip to Past," *Harrisburg Patriot-News,* June 3, 1994, p. C5, in "PHMC Sites" File, Library of the PHMC, Harrisburg.

75. "Pennsylvania Historical Marker Program: A Preliminary Analysis of Geographic and Categorical Trends, 1946–2001" (Harrisburg: PHMC Division of History, 2001). These terms are from the PHMC's definitions of marker theme categories. These figures do not reflect the themes of markers installed after 2001.

76. "Pennsylvania: America's Industrial Heritage Starts Here," press release dated April 9, 1990(Harrisburg: Pennsylvania Department of Commerce), in PA Documents Collection, State Library of Pennsylvania. This title was a play on the state's marketing phrase at the time, "America Starts Here."

77. *Heritage Areas Program Manual* (Harrisburg: Pennsylvania Department of Conservation and Natural Resources, Bureau of Recreation and Conservation, 2006), 1.

78. Ibid., 1, 20.

CHAPTER 2

The epigraph to this chapter is drawn from "Navigating . . . Delaware and Lehigh National Heritage Corridor" (Easton: Delaware and Lehigh National Heritage Corridor, 2007), n.p.

1. Less charitably, Diane Barthel calls such groups "heritage machines," coalitions of "unlikely bedfellows, including academics, preservationists, developers, and politicians" hoping to "profit from the exploitation—and sometimes the invention—of local heritage" (*Historic Preservation: Collective Memory and Historical Identity* [New Brunswick: Rutgers University Press, 1996], 121).

2. This time frame was true of at least two of the Pennsylvania heritage areas whose directors I interviewed.

3. Author's telephone interview with Mark Platts, president, Susquehanna Gateway Heritage Area (then called the Lancaster-York Heritage Region), Wrightsville, on January 28, 2008.

4. "Industry in the Delaware and Lehigh National Heritage Corridor," Delaware and Lehigh National Heritage Corridor website, accessed January 2, 2010, http://www.delaware andlehigh.org/index.php/heritage/industry/.

5. Author's telephone interview with Allen Sachse, executive director, Delaware and Lehigh Valley National Heritage Corridor, Easton, on January 28, 2008.

6. Tom Shealey, *The Stone Coal Way: A Guide to Navigating Delaware and Lehigh National Heritage Corridor Through Eastern Pennsylvania*, ed. Elissa G. Marsden (Easton: Delaware and Lehigh National Heritage Corridor, 2004). This spiral-bound book, which unfortunately is now out of print, is one of several nicely designed and historically informative publications from this heritage group; others include "historical tours" of specific towns, such as Slatington and Slatedale (where, as you might guess, slate was mined), and Palmerton, whose industry was zinc.

7. Author's telephone interview with Allen Sachse on January 28, 2008.

8. The state tourism office also markets destinations through a rubric of regions—ten rather than twelve—some of which, confusingly, have similar names. For instance, the Endless Mountains Heritage Area is called the "Pennsylvania Wilds" in state tourism literature, while the Delaware and Lehigh Heritage Area is merely the "Lehigh Valley" in state tourism.

9. Author's telephone interview with Dan Perry, chief operating officer, Lackawanna Heritage Valley Authority, Scranton, on January 17, 2008. Actually, there is one coal breaker: the Huber Breaker, near Wilkes-Barre, which was shut down in 1976. A local group continues a campaign to preserve it and turn it into a museum and park. See the Huber Breaker Preservation Society website at http://www.huberbreaker.org/ (accessed on May 21, 2010).

10. Author's telephone interview with Brenda Barrett, director, Bureau of Recreation and Conservation, Department of Conservation and Natural Resources, Commonwealth of Pennsylvania, Harrisburg, on January 4, 2008. For more on the early years of the program, see also Shalom Staub, "Cultural Conservation and Economic Recovery Planning: The Pennsylvania Heritage Parks Program," in *Conserving Culture: A New Discourse on Heritage*, ed. Mary Hufford (Urbana: University of Illinois Press, 1994), 229–44. During this formational period, the areas were called "heritage parks," and their complicated mission was overseen by an organizational coalition impenetrably called SHPITF, the State Heritage Park Interagency Task Force (Staub, *Conserving Culture*, 233).

11. Author's telephone interview with Kurt Zwikl, executive director, Schuylkill River Heritage Area, Pottstown, on January 17, 2008.

12. Ibid.

13. Schuylkill River Heritage Area website, accessed January 2, 2010, http://www.schuyl killriver.org/Revolutionary_River.aspx.

14. Author's telephone interview with Mark Platts on January 28, 2008.

15. *Stories of the Land Along Dutch Country Roads* (Lancaster-York Heritage Region, 2006), DVD. I first saw this at the Pennsylvania Dutch Country Visitors Center in Lancaster in September 2007, which receives a great deal of tourist traffic, but when I went back in July

2010 they were no longer showing it. In mid-2010, it was still being shown at the York Visitor Center and the heritage area's own visitor center in Wrightsville.

16. Author's telephone interview with Phil Swank, executive director, Endless Mountains Heritage Region, Towanda, on February 15, 2008.

17. "Mission and Vision of the EMHR," Endless Mountain Heritage Region website, accessed January 8, 2011, http://www.endlessmountainsheritage.org/about_Mission.php.

18. "Take the Scenic Pennsylvania Route 6" (Harrisburg: Pennsylvania Tourism Office, n.d.); *Pennsylvania Route 6: Take the High Road! Pennsylvania's Heritage Route* (Galeton: Pennsylvania Route 6 Tourist Association, n.d.; obtained by author in the region in summer 2007).

19. Author's telephone interview with Terri Dennison, executive director, PA Route 6 Heritage Corridor, Galeton, on January 17, 2008.

20. Robert Bruce, *The Lincoln Highway in Pennsylvania* (Washington, DC: American Automobile Association/National Highways Association, 1920), n.p.

21. Author's visit to Caledonia Furnace in Caledonia State Park, near Chambersburg, on July 8, 2008.

22. Author's correspondence with Olga A. Herbert, executive director, Lincoln Highway Heritage Corridor, Ligonier, letter dated January 13, 2008. These are also described in a pamphlet published by this heritage group and titled "Along the Highway Guide" (n.d.)

23. "Building the Highway," interpretive wayside at the intersection of Lincolnway (U.S. Route 30) and Hanover Street in New Oxford, visited by author on July 17, 2010. New Oxford is the eastern end of the Lincoln Highway Heritage Corridor, which, despite its name, includes only six counties and thus represents only a portion of this route, from here to a point just south of Pittsburgh; the highway's passage through the eastern half of the state is not included (although a stretch between York and Lancaster lies within the Susquehanna Gateway Heritage Area).

24. See, for instance, Brian Butko, *The Lincoln Highway: Pennsylvania Traveler's Guide*, 2nd ed. (Mechanicsburg, PA: Stackpole Books, 2002), and Drake Hokanson, *The Lincoln Highway: Main Street Across America* (Iowa City: University of Iowa Press, 1988).

25. Author's correspondence with Olga A. Herbert on January 13, 2008.

26. John Brinckerhoff Jackson, *Discovering the Vernacular Landscape* (New Haven: Yale University Press, 1984), 21.

27. "Pennsylvania Trails of History," Pennsylvania Historical and Museum Commission website, accessed January 2, 2010, http://www.portal.state.pa.us/portal/server.pt/community/trails_of_history/1800.

28. "2007 PA Route 6 Artisan Trail," published jointly by several Route 6–area tourism bureaus, n.d., n.p.; and *Your Guide to Pennsylvania's Laurel Highlands, 2008* (Ligonier: Laurel Highlands Visitors Bureau, 2008), n.p.

29. "Williamsport Lycoming County Visitors Guide 2008" (Williamsport: Lycoming County Visitors Bureau, 2008), n.p.

30. "Lower Susquehanna River Valley," n.d., n.p.

31. Mary Tarkowski, "Artisan Paradise on Route 45," *Pennsylvania: Travel Guide*, n.d., n.p.; "Art Thrives on 45," n.d., n.p.; and Farron D. Brougher, "The Purple Heart Highway: 100 Miles of Whatever You Want It to Be," *Susquehanna Life* (Spring 2007): 34, 51.

32. "Come Visit 'The Road That Built the Nation': 35th Annual National Road Festival, May 16–18, 2008"; "90 Miles of American Heritage," National Road Heritage Corridor website, accessed June 21, 2007, http://www.nationalroadpa.org/.

33. Author's visit to the Madonna of the Trail near Beallsville on July 25, 2008; *Washington County Pennsylvania: 2008 Travel Planner and Calendar of Events* (Harrisburg: Pennsylvania State Tourism Office, n.d.).

34. Author's telephone interview with Donna Holdorf, executive director, National Road Heritage Corridor, Uniontown, on January 25, 2008.

35. "Come Visit 'The Road That Built the Nation.'"

36. Brochure obtained during author's visit to the Petersburg Toll House in Addison on July 25, 2008.

37. Author's visit to the Flatiron Building in Brownsville on July 25, 2008.

38. Author's telephone interview with Norma Ryan, managing director, Brownsville Area Revitalization Corporation, on January 19, 2009.

39. James T. Yenckel, "Two Pennsylvania Paths: A Scenic Drive Through the Past in the Alleghenies," *Washington Post,* April 30, 1995, p. E1.

40. Diane Barthel, "Getting in Touch with History: The Role of Historic Preservation in Shaping Collective Memories," *Qualitative Sociology* 19, no. 3 (1996): 349.

41. Author's telephone interview with David Dunn, former director, Railroad Museum of Pennsylvania, Strasburg, on March 5, 2008, and author's in-person interview with Steve Miller, director, Bureau of Historic Sites and Museums, PHMC, Harrisburg, on September 18, 2009.

42. Author's telephone interview with Harold "Kip" Hagan, superintendent, Steamtown National Historic Site, Scranton, on January 14, 2008.

43. Author's visit to the Railroaders Memorial Museum in Altoona on July 7, 2007.

44. Author's interview with Kip Hagan on January 14, 2008, and visit to Steamtown, Scranton, on June 24, 2007.

45. For instance, "Phoebe says and Phoebe knows / That smoke and cinders spoil good clothes / 'Tis thus a pleasure and delight/To take the Road of Anthracite."

46. Between 1901 and 1917 she became a national celebrity; the railroad even employed an actress, Marion Murray, to "play" her, making public appearances in her all-white outfit, posing for photographs, and giving interviews to newspapers. This advertising campaign was the focus of research I did while I as a PHMC scholar-in-residence at the Railroad Museum of Pennsylvania in Strasburg during the summer of 2004, with the help of archivist Kurt Bell, using the Thomas T. Taber Collection. Further sources of information on Phoebe Snow are cited in the article that resulted from that study: Carolyn Kitch, "'A Genuine, Vivid Personality': Newspaper Coverage and the Construction of a 'Real' Advertising Celebrity in a Pioneering Publicity Campaign," *Journalism History* 31, no. 3 (Fall 2005): 122–37.

47. She also went to Buffalo. Phoebe Snow Road is located at mile marker 350 off the eastbound side of PA Route 940. I found this accidentally on August 28, 2009.

48. This phrase ended every one of her seventy-two jingles. Today the phrase appears on the front of the engines of the Reading and Northern Railroad, a freight railroad still in operation.

49. I visited these sites on, respectively, June 7, 2008, May 2, 2009, and July 12, 2008. There is an entire body of literature, historical as well as enthusiast in nature, on this subject. One, which details not only on the history of railroads that once ran throughout Pennsylvania but also what is left visible on the landscape and what groups still preserve the history, is Lorett Treese, *Railroads of Pennsylvania: Fragments of the Past in the Keystone Landscape* (Mechanicsburg, PA: Stackpole Books, 2003).

50. For examples of these and other reuses, see *Pennsylvania Train Stations: Restored and Revitalized* (University Park: Penn State Public Broadcasting, 2007), DVD.

51. Author's visits to and meals at the Tarentum Station Grille in Tarentum on July 13, 2007, and The Restaurant at the Station in Tamaqua on June 23, 2007.

52. "Historic Menu: Front Street Station: A Railroad Eatery," obtained on site by author on September 2, 2007.

53. The trains I personally experienced are listed here, in alphabetical order, with the towns where they are based and dates I rode them in parentheses: Bellefonte Historical Railroad

(Bellefonte, June 14, 2008); East Broad Top Railroad (Orbisonia, July 22, 2007); Kiski Junction Railroad (Schenley, July 14, 2007); Lehigh Gorge Scenic Railway (Jim Thorpe, November 4, 2007); "Ma & Pa" (Maryland and Pennsylvania) Railroad (Muddy Creek Forks, June 29, 2008); Middletown and Hummelstown Railroad (Middletown, July 17, 2007); New Hope and Ivyland Railroad (New Hope, August 24, 2007); Oil Creek and Titusville Railroad (Titusville, July 21, 2007); Pioneer Scenic Lines Railroad (Gettysburg, August 25, 2007); Steamtown (a steam train ride and a caboose ride) (Scranton, June 24, 2007); Strasburg Railroad (Strasburg, September 3, 2007, and July 8, 2010); Stourbridge Railroad (Honesdale, October 6, 2007); Tioga Railroad (Wellsboro, July 8, 2007); and Wanamaker, Kempton, and Southern Railroad (Kempton, August 26, 2007). In addition, there is the West Chester Railroad in West Chester, which I did not get to ride. It's possible that I have missed one or two others.

The trolley rides I took are those that go out of the Electric City Trolley Museum in Scranton (which I rode on June 24, 2007), the Pennsylvania Trolley Museum in the town of Washington (July 15, 2007), and the Rockhill Trolley Museum, which runs in conjunction with the East Broad Top Railroad, near Orbisonia (July 22, 2007). These cars run on rails. Here I am not counting the "trolley" rides, such as those in Williamsport and Hershey, aboard buses designed to look like trolley cars (although I rode them, too).

54. J. Geraint Jenkins, *Getting Yesterday Right: Interpreting the Heritage of Wales* (Cardiff: University of Wales Press, 1992), 57. This excellent book is among the few models I had for my own project. It assesses heritage interpretation of several different industries within one geographic area, and they are pretty much the same industries (mainly coal, but also slate, textiles, and iron and steel). There are a number of similarities between his points about Wales and mine about Pennsylvania. Among them are the past reason for and current nature of steam trains; the fact that, despite each region's former fame as a kingdom of coal, farming was and still is the main industry; and, as further discussed in chapter 8, the conclusion that labor history is actually obscured by heritage celebrations of the nobility and bravery of the common worker.

55. These phrases are from, respectively, promotional pamphlets obtained on board the East Broad Top Railroad near Orbisonia and the New Hope and Ivyland Railroad in Easton.

56. Author's rides on these railroads on July 8, 2007, November 4, 2007, and August 26, 2007, respectively.

57. Author's ride on the Middletown and Hummelstown Railroad on July 17, 2007.

58. The same year the Railroad Museum of Pennsylvania also held a "Swing Train" dance featuring Big Band music and inviting visitors to "come in uniform or '40s clothing (Friends of the Railroad Museum, "Railroad Museum of Pennsylvania Announces Special Events for 30th Anniversary Year," January 31, 2005).

59. These phrases are from a promotional brochure the Strasburg Rail Road published in the 1990s: "The Road to Paradise" (Lancaster: Strasburg Railroad, 1994), in the PHMC Sites File, Library of the PHMC, Harrisburg.

60. Author's rides on the Strasburg Railroad on September 3, 2007, and July 8, 2010. York and Berks Counties also claim to have been the manufacturing site of Conestoga wagons.

61. "America Is Beautiful: See for Yourself on Amtrak" (promotional brochure in use in 2007), 7.

62. "Application for Special Fund License Plate," Pennsylvania Bureau of Motor Vehicles, Department of Transportation (Harrisburg, n.d.). This is plate #906. The fee in 2010 was $35.

CHAPTER 3

The epigraph to this chapter is drawn from "Growing Traditions: Lancaster-York Heritage Region Discovery Guide," accessed April 25, 2011, http://www.growingtraditions.org/.

1. Wilbur Zelinsky, *The Cultural Geography of the United States,* rev. ed. (Englewood Cliffs, NJ: Prentice Hall, 1992; originally published in 1973), 64.

2. John F. Sears, *Sacred Places: American Tourist Attractions in the Nineteenth Century* (New York: Oxford University Press, 1989), 191.

3. "Everything Amish—Buggies, Mules, Scooters, and More!" *Lancaster County: The Heart of Pennsylvania Dutch Country* (Lancaster: Pennsylvania Dutch Convention and Visitors Bureau, 2008), 4.

4. Sasha Issenberg, "The Simplest Life: Why Americans Romanticize the Amish," *Washington Monthly* (October 2004): 39–40.

5. David Walbert, *Garden Spot: Lancaster County, the Old Order Amish, and the Selling of Rural America* (New York: Oxford University Press, 2002), 100.

6. Author's in-person interview with Steve Miller, director, Bureau of Historic Sites and Museums, PHMC, Harrisburg, on September 18, 2009. Miller was also the farm interpreter featured in the 1979 newspaper article that is quoted in chapter 1.

7. Tim Kelsey, *The Joy of Farm Watching: A Roadside Guide to Pennsylvania Agriculture* (University Park: Penn State College of Agricultural Sciences, 2006), 2.

8. This figure comes from the pamphlet "Pennsylvania's Dairy Farmers Bring More Than Just Milk to the Table" (Harrisburg: Center for Dairy Excellence, 2006), n.p., which is given out at the annual Pennsylvania Farm Show.

9. Christine Layne, "It's a Farmer's Life," *Pennsylvania Pursuits* (Spring 2007): 62, 63.

10. Ann Witmer, "Who Says Camp Is for Kids? Adults Can Milk Cows, Canoe," *Harrisburg Sunday Patriot-News,* September 13, 2009, p. B4.

11. Cherry Crest Farm website, accessed July 31, 2009, http://www.cherrycrestfarm.com; also Cherry Crest Farm tourism brochure, n.d., n.p.

12. "Family Adventures. Country Fun," advertisement for Stoners Dairy Farm in Mercersburg; "Franklin County, PA" (2009), 61.

13. Author's tour of the Kreider Farm in Manheim on September 10, 2007.

14. WGAL-TV News at 11, York-Lancaster-Harrisburg, aired on January 7, 2011; "Pennsylvania Farm Show: 95 Reasons to Go!" *Harrisburg Patriot-News,* January 6, 2001, overwrap.

15. Author's attendance at and review of press coverage, print and online schedules, and promotional materials for the 2007, 2008, and 2009 Pennsylvania Farm Shows.

16. Mary Klaus, "State Fairs Offer Visitors a Glimpse of Nation's Agrarian Traditions," *Harrisburg Patriot-News,* July 9, 2009, pp. E1, E10.

17. "Rural History Confederation," pamphlet (no publication information) obtained by author at the state Welcome Center on I-83 at the Maryland border on June 6, 2010.

18. Author's visits to Mascot Roller Mills and Homestead in Ronks on June 21, 2008; Wallace-Cross Mill in Felton on June 20, 2008; Haines Mill in Cetronia on August 30, 2008; McConnell's Mill in McConnell's Mill State Park near Porterville on July 11, 2008; The Mill at Anselma in Chester Springs on July 20, 2008; and the Pennsylvania State Farm Show in Harrisburg on January 13, 2009.

19. Saint Vincent Gristmill website, accessed October 3, 2009, http://www.saintvincent gristmill.com/.

20. Kelly Ann Butterbaugh, "Farming the Past: A View of Daily Life on an 1800s Farm," *Pennsylvania Magazine* (September/October 2007): 14, 16.

21. Quiet Valley Living Historical Farm website, accessed July 31, 2009, http://www.quiet valley.org/about/directions.htm.

22. Author's visits to the Pennsylvania Heritage Festival at the Bradford County Heritage Association and Farm Museum, Troy, on September 16, 2007, and the Meadowcroft Rockshelter and Museum of Rural Life, near Avella, on August 21, 2009. The phrase "step back in time" (while used elsewhere as well) is used in the promotional brochure of the Meadowcroft Museum, obtained by the author on site.

23. Author's visit to the Somerset Historical Center, near Somerset, on September 29, 2007. The fifteen-minute film, not available for sale, is titled *Patterns on the Land.*

24. Somerset Historical Center website, accessed July 31, 2009, http://www.somersethistoricalcenter.org/calendar_of_events.htm.

25. Author's visit to the Landis Valley Museum (during "Harvest Days"), Lancaster, on October 7, 2007. The thirteen-minute orientation film is titled *Crossroads at Landis Valley.*

26. Landis Valley Museum website, accessed July 31, 2009, http://www.landisvalleymuseum.org/classes.php.

27. Author's telephone interview with Steve Miller, former director, Landis Valley Museum, PHMC, Lancaster, on January 4, 2008.

28. Kelly Ann Butterbaugh, "Celebrating the Horse, Buggy, and Whip," *Pennsylvania Magazine* (May/June 2009): 13.

29. Union County Historical Society website, accessed June 24, 2008, http://www.unioncountyhistoricalsociety.org/RHD08SCHEDULE.html.

30. Author's visit to the Williams Grove Historical Steam Engine Association Annual Show in Williams Grove, on September 5, 2009; also: Roger Quigley, "Down on the Farm," *Harrisburg Patriot-News*, September 5, 2009, p. A4.

31. J. Mickey Rowley, "From the PA Tourism Office," *Pennsylvania Pursuits* (Winter 2007): 2.

32. Diane Barthel, "Getting in Touch with History: The Role of Historic Preservation in Shaping Collective Memories," *Qualitative Sociology* 19, no. 3 (1996): 355.

33. Barthel, *Historic Preservation: Collective Memory and Historical Identity* (New Brunswick: Rutgers University Press, 1996), 36, 37. She calls such historic sites "staged symbolic communities" (36).

34. John Corner and Sylvia Harvey, "Mediating Tradition and Modernity: The Heritage/Enterprise Couplet," in *Enterprise and Heritage: Crosscurrents of National Culture*, ed. John Corner and Sylvia Harvey (London: Routledge, 1991), 53.

35. Patricia West, "Uncovering and Interpreting Women's History at Historic House Museums," in *Restoring Women's History Through Historic Preservation*, ed. Gail Lee Dubrow and Jennifer B. Goodman (Baltimore: Johns Hopkins University Press, 2003), 85.

36. Ian McKay, *The Quest of the Folk: Antimodernism and Cultural Selection in Twentieth-Century Nova Scotia* (Montreal: McGill-Queen's University Press, 1994), xvi.

37. Tony Bennett, "Museums and 'The People,'" in *The Museum Time-Machine: Putting Cultures on Display*, ed. Robert Lumley (London: Routledge, 1988), 68. Both Barthel and Bennett are writing about open-air, re-created historic "villages" in the United Kingdom.

38. David Lowenthal, "Pioneer Museums," in *History Museums in the United States: A Critical Assessment*, ed. Warren Leon and Roy Rosenzweig (Urbana: University of Illinois Press, 1989), 116.

39. "You Touch the History. The History Touches You," advertisement in *Pennsylvania Pursuits* (Spring 2008): 56.

40. Lowenthal, "Pioneer Musuems," 122.

41. Author's visit to the Meadowcroft Rockshelter and Museum of Rural Life near Avella on August 21, 2009.

42. Author's attendance at Drake Well Extravaganza/Oil 150 Celebration in Titusville on August 27, 2009.

43. Author's visit to Harvest Time at Hopewell Furnace, Elverson, on September 15, 2007.

44. Author's visit to the Hay Creek Festival, Joanna Furnace, near Geigertown, on September 8, 2007; also "Festivals," Hay Creek Valley Historical Association website, accessed May 27, 2010, http://www.haycreek.org/festivals.htm.

45. These towns include Wrightsville, Chambersburg, Hanover, Carlisle, and York, all of which were briefly occupied by the Confederacy in late June 1863, prior to the Battle of

Gettysburg on the first three days of July. The state tourism office tells their stories with a series of waysides and small museums promoted as a driving route called the "Civil War Trails"; see "Civil War Trails," visitPA website, accessed July 15, 2010, http://www.pacivilwartrails .com/.

46. Author's visits to Eckley Miners Village near Hazleton on August 15, 2009, and the Pennsylvania Heritage Festival at the Bradford County Heritage Association and Farm Museum in Troy on September 16, 2007.

47. These numbers are from the author's conversation with an Old Bedford Village employee during a visit there on July 18, 2008. A full list of this site's weekend events, which also include Murder Mystery Weekends, can be seen on the "Events" page of the Old Bedford Village website, accessed August 1, 2009, http://www.oldbedfordvillage.com/events.php.

48. A similar but less well-developed site is Old Mill Village in New Milford, a town in northeastern Pennsylvania, which also has weekend events based on themes, including Frontier Days: Eighteenth-Century Living History, World War II Living History, Civil War Living History, and Westward Ho! (featuring a "cowboy action troop" with "shoot-out excitement"); see the "Events Calendar" on the Old Mill Village Museum website, accessed May 27, 2010, http://www.oldmillvillage.org/eventsCalender.htm.

49. "Crafts," Old Bedford Village website, accessed August 1, 2009, http://www.oldbedford village.com/crafts.php. The author also visited this site and saw the crafts demonstrations on July 18, 2008.

50. Lowenthal, "Pioneer Museums," 120, 121.

51. Penn State College of Agricultural Sciences, "Timber 2007" (brochure distributed at the 2007 Pennsylvania Farm Show).

52. *The Hiawatha Paddlewheeler* (CD; Williamsport: Hiawatha/Williamsport Bureau of Transportation, 1997); author's ride on the Hiawatha Riverboat in Williamsport, on August 29, 2007. The Susquehanna Boom is also explained in Williamsport's Thomas T. Taber Museum (Lycoming County Historical Society).

53. "Schedule of Events," Woodmen's Show website, accessed August 1, 2009, http://www .woodsmenshow.com/schedule_of_events.htm.

54. Author's attendance at the Bark Peelers' Convention, Lumber Museum of Pennsylvania, PHMC, between Wellsboro and Galeton, on July 8, 2007; also, "Welcome to the 33rd Annual Bark Peelers' Convention" (2007 program listing events, distributed on site).

55. "Parker Dam Events," Pennsylvania State Parks website, accessed September 7, 2009, http://www.dcnr.state.pa.us/stateparks/parks/parkerdam.aspx#events.

56. Product tag on blanket purchased by the author at the Woolrich Company Store in August 2007. This company's history—which thematically is very similar to the stories told at the factory tours described in chapter 6—also is told in a company-sponsored book: Doug Traux, *Woolrich: 175 Years of Excellence* (South Boardman, MI: Crofton Creek Press, 2005).

57. Traux, *Woolrich*, 18.

58. Ibid., 28.

59. Cindy Ross, "A Showplace of a Town," *Pennsylvania Magazine* (September/October 2009): 10.

60. "Calendar of Events," Grey Towers website, accessed June 8, 2011, http://greytowers .org/calendarofevents.html.

61. Author's tour of Grey Towers National Landmark in Milford on September 15, 2007.

62. Author's visits to the Lumber Museum of Pennsylvania, between Wellsboro and Galeton, on July 8, 2007; the Lou and Helen Adams Civilian Conservation Corps Museum in Parker Dam State Forest, near Penfield, on July 13, 2008; the visitor center in Laurel Hill State Park, near Somerset, on August 22, 2009; and the Masker Museum in Promised Land State Park, northeast of Scranton, on August 28, 2009.

63. Author's visit to the Lou and Helen Adams Civilian Conservation Corps Museum on July 13, 2008.

64. Author's visit to Laurel Hill State Park on August 22, 2009. The word "monument" is used in signage on the site. Other parks containing CCC worker statues include Promised Land State Park and Leonard Harrison State Park, near Wellsboro, overlooking Pine Creek Gorge; author visited the latter on July 8, 2007, and August 26, 2009.

65. Author's telephone interview with Edie Shean-Hammond, superintendent, Hopewell Iron Furnace, Elverson, on January 4, 2008. For more on Hopewell's interpretation as a heritage site, see Stanton, "The Past as a Public Good: The U.S. National Park Service and 'Cultural Repair' in Post-Industrial Places," in *People and Their Pasts: Public History Today*, ed. Paul Ashton and Hilda Kean (London: Palgrave Macmillan, 2009), 57–73.

66. Author's telephone interview with Sarah Hopkins, chief, Division of Environmental Education, Department of Conservation and Natural Resources, Commonwealth of Pennsylvania, Harrisburg, on January 4, 2008.

67. *A Public Use Map for Pine Creek Rail Trail* (Harrisburg: Pennsylvania Department of Conservation and Natural Resources, 2007), n.p., obtained by the author in Leonard Harrison State Park on August 26, 2009.

68. Author's visits to Greenwood Furnace State Park, Greenwood Furnace, on July 19, 2008; Pine Grove Furnace State Park, Gardner (near Carlisle), on July 8, 2008; and Caledonia State Park, Fayetteville (near Chambersburg), on July 8, 2008. The story of Caledonia State Furnace is part of military history as well; owned by abolitionist and political Thaddeus Stevens, it was destroyed in 1863 by Confederate soldiers on their way to nearby Gettysburg.

69. Author's visit to Canoe Creek State Park in Hollidaysburg (near Altoona) on July 19, 2008.

70. Author's visit to Keystone State Park near Derry on August 22, 2009.

71. Bob West, "The Making of the English Working Past: A Critical View of the Ironbridge Gorge Museum," in *The Museum Time-Machine: Putting Cultures on Display*, ed. Robert Lumley (London: Routledge, 1988), 54, 56.

72. "A Buried Story," interpretive exhibit panel erected by the Lancaster-York Heritage Region along its Susquehanna River Trail in Marietta.

73. Author's visit to Canoe Creek State Park on July 19, 2008.

74. Author's visits to Oil Creek State Park and Pithole, near Titusville, on July 20 and 21, 2007, and August 27, 2009.

75. Guy V. Thayer Jr., *Born in Freedom: The Story of Colonel Drake* (film shown and sold at Drake Well) (Washington, DC: American Petroleum Institute, 1954).

76. Iris Samson and Pierina Morrelli, *The Valley that Changed the World* (Pittsburgh: WQED Multimedia/Oil Region Alliance, 2009).

77. Author's visit to the Venango Museum of Art and Science in Oil City on August 14, 2008.

78. *Oil Creek State Park: A Contrast in Time* (Harrisburg: Pennsylvania Department of Conservation and Natural Resources, 2005).

79. *A Journey Through the Valley that Changed the World* (CD; Oil City: Oil Creek Railway Historical Society, 2002); author's ride on the Oil Creek and Titusville Railroad in Oil Creek State Park on July 21, 2007.

80. "Rivers of Oil" promotional poster, Drake Well Museum website, accessed August 25, 2009, http://www.oarsontheallegheny.com/news_etc/Rivers%202009%20poster.pdf.

81. Chris A. Courogen, "Walking 'Exhibit' to Share Trail Tales," *Harrisburg Patriot-News*, November 1, 2009, p. A6; see also Appalachian Trail Museum Society website, accessed January 8, 2011, http://www.atmuseum.org/intro.htm.

82. Dan White, "Biking Coal Country's Tracks and Tunnels," *New York Times*, October 23, 2009, p. C30.

83. "Allegheny Portage Railroad," National Park Service website, accessed August 25, 2009, http://www.nps.gov/alpo/index.htm.

84. Author's visit to the Allegheny Portage Railroad National Historic Site in Gallitzin on July 22, 2007; Erik N. von Spaeth, *The Allegheny Portage Railroad* (Washington, DC: National Park Service, U.S. Department of the Interior, n.d.).

85. Linda K. Delaney, *The Gamble for Glory in the World's First Billion Dollar Oilfield* (Bradford: Forest Press, 2007), 12. Delaney notes that this is actually the Cline Oil No. 1 Well and that "the restaurant was built around the well" (12).

86. Author's trips to these regions in July 2007, September 2007, July 2008, August 2008, and August 2009.

87. Neil King Jr., "As Oil Prices Soar, Prospectors Return to Pennsylvania," *Wall Street Journal* (eastern edition), February 19, 2008, p. A1 (accessed via Proquest database on September 26, 2009); Ryan Talbott, "Oil Wells Drain Beauty from State Forests," *Harrisburg Sunday Patriot-News*, April 27, 2008, pp. F1, F4.

88. Author's visit to the Penn-Brad Oil Museum in Custer City on August 15, 2008.

89. Author's attendance at Drake Well Extravaganza/Oil 150 Celebration in Titusville on August 27, 2009. See, for instance, Don Hopey, "Drilling Stalled in Allegheny National Forest," *Pittsburgh Post-Gazette*, March 16, 2009, accessed on September 26, 2009, http://www.post-gazette.com/pg/09075/955874-85.stm.

90. Erik N. von Spaeth, *The Allegheny Portage Railroad* (Washington, DC: National Park Service, U.S. Department of the Interior, n.d.).

CHAPTER 4

The epigraph to this chapter is drawn from a promotional pamphlet obtained by the author at the Frank and Sylvia Pasquerilla Heritage Discovery Center in Johnstown during visits there on July 29, 2005, July 27, 2007, and July 11, 2009. At the time it closed, and for most of the twentieth century, this plant was owned by Bethlehem Steel.

1. "History of Steelmaking in Johnstown," Johnstown Area Heritage Association Frank and Sylvia Pasquerilla Heritage Discovery Center website, accessed October 3, 2009, http://www.jaha.org/DiscoveryCenter/steel.html.

2. Author's telephone interview with Richard Burkert, executive director, Johnstown Area Heritage Association, on January 4, 2008.

3. Johnstown Heritage Discovery Center promotional pamphlet.

4. Scott D. Camp notes that the balance between eastern and western European immigrant residents of Johnstown shifted dramatically between 1900 and 1910, after which eastern Europeans constituted two-thirds of the city's immigrants (*Worker Response to Plant Closings: Steelworkers in Johnstown and Youngstown* [New York: Garland Publishing, 1995], 151–52). German ancestry also is acknowledged in the Wagner-Ritter House, located across the street from the Heritage Discovery Center, which itself occupies a building that once was the Germania Brewing Company; see "Virtual Tour—America: Through Immigrant Eyes," Johnstown Area Heritage Association Frank and Sylvia Pasquerilla Heritage Discovery Center website, accessed October 3, 2009, http://www.jaha.org/DiscoveryCenter/virtualtour.html. Josef can be seen on the home page of "Virtual Tour—America: Through Immigrant Eyes."

5. Given this museum's focus on eastern European immigrants, this fond and almost wistful treatment of the "old days" in Johnstown's ethnic (largely Slavic) neighborhoods

stands as a modern-day reversal of public communication about workers a century earlier. In his study of turn-of-the-(twentieth)-century Pittsburgh media and civic rhetoric, Edward Slavishak detects a "nostalgia of the city's work iconography [that] was devoted to a bygone era," with an emphasis on the bodies of skilled, native-born workers, an idealized image of "white manliness" marketed to a population "inundated with perceived threats from foreign arrivals" (Edward Slavishak, *Bodies of Work: Civic Display and Labor in Industrial Pittsburgh* [Durham: Duke University Press, 2008], 147, 148).

6. This term was used by, among others, Lenwood Sloan (author's in-person interview in Harrisburg on January 26, 2009).

7. Tok Thompson, "Heritage Versus the Past," in *The Past in the Present: A Multidisciplinary Approach*, ed. Fabio Mugnaini, Padraig O Healai, and Tok Thompson (Brussels: Edit Press, 2006), 203.

8. Bella Dicks, *Culture on Display: The Production of Contemporary Visitability* (Maidenhead: Open University Press, 2003), 121, 139.

9. E-mail correspondence (sent to list subscribers) from August R. Carlino, "Season's Greetings from Rivers of Steel National Heritage Area," December 18, 2008.

10. "Honor Thy Father and Mother," booklet obtained by the author at the Senator John Heinz History Center in Pittsburgh on July 15, 2007.

11. Author's visits to the Railroad Museum of Pennsylvania on July 8, 2010 (and many times previously) and to the Horseshoe Curve National Historic Site and the Railroaders Memorial Museum, both in Altoona and both on July 7, 2007; see also "Railroaders Memorial Museum and Horseshoe Curve National Historic Landmark Guide" (Altoona: Railroaders Memorial Museum, 2007), 16.

12. Author's visit to the Atlas Cement Company Memorial Museum in Northampton and on-site discussion with founder Ed Pany on August 24, 2008. This company also contributed cement to the building of Rockefeller Center, thus accounting for the Atlas figure that stands at its base.

13. Author's visit to the Old Jail in Jim Thorpe on August 17, 2007. Critical of the "romantic" heritage story told today in that upscale, Victorian town, historian Philip Jenkins writes of tourists in search of the lore, "If there is a real Molly Maguire landscape, it is to be found in the decaying patch towns that they drive through on the way to the sumptuous glories of old Mauch Chunk" ("Mis-Remembering America's Industrial Heritage: The Molly Maguires," paper presented to the American Historical Association, Pacific Coast Branch, Vancouver, Canada, August 2001).

14. Author's visits to Eckley Miners Village near Hazleton on June 23, 2007, and August 15, 2009.

15. Author's visit to the Slate Belt Heritage Center in Bangor on August 19, 2007.

16. Author's visit to the Old Line Museum and Welsh Cottages in Delta on June 29, 2008.

17. Author's visits to the Pennsylvania Anthracite Heritage Museum in Scranton on June 25, 2007, and September 15, 2007.

18. Philip Ruth, prod., dir., and writer, *Silver Cinders: The Legacy of Coal and Coke in Southwestern Pennsylvania* (North Wales, PA: Cultural Heritage Research Services, 2005).

19. Jayne Clark, "Pittsburgh Forges Ahead," *USA Today*, July 18, 2008, p. 2D.

20. "Babushkas and Hard Hats" tour, Rivers of Steel National Heritage Area, live tour narration by Communications Director Jan Dofner, Pittsburgh; tour taken by author on August 22, 2009.

21. Dan Karaczun, ed., *Out of This Kitchen: A History of the Ethnic Groups and Their Foods in the Steel Valley* (Pittsburgh: Publassist, 1998).

22. Rick Sebak, prod. and narr., *What Makes Pittsburgh Pittsburgh?* (Pittsburgh: WQED Multimedia, 2006).

23. "Up in Oil Country: Where Country Roads Lead to Oil Booms, Simpler Times and Skydiving Aussies," "4,466 Miles from Naples: The Pizza Capital of the World," and "Pittsburgh's South Side Renaissance: One Funky Neighborhood and Five Meals a Day," all from visitPA.com website, accessed October 31, 2009, http://ww.visitpa.com/trip-ideas/shunpikers-guides/index.aspx.

24. Author's in-person interview with Lenwood Sloan on January 26, 2009.

25. Herbert J. Gans, "Symbolic Ethnicity: The Future of Ethnic Groups and Cultures in America," *Ethnic and Racial Studies* 2, no. 1 (January 1979): 1.

26. Marilyn Halter, *Shopping for Identity: The Marketing of Ethnicity* (New York: Schocken Books, 2000), 79.

27. Barbara Kirschenblatt-Gimblett, *Destination Culture: Tourism, Museums, and Heritage* (Berkeley and Los Angeles: University of California Press, 1998), 200.

28. Robert Archibald, *The New Town Square: Museums and Communities in Transition* (Walnut Creek, CA: AltaMira Press, 2004), 13, 212; see also Archibald, "A Personal History of Memory," in *Social Memory and History: Anthropological Perspectives*, ed. Jacob J. Climo and Maria G. Cattell (Walnut Creek, CA: AltaMira Press, 2002), 72.

29. Author's in-person interview with Lenwood Sloan on January 26, 2009. See also PA Artisan Trails website, accessed January 8, 2011, http://www.paartisantrails.com/.

30. Michael Frisch, *A Shared Authority: Essays on the Craft and Meaning of Oral and Public History* (Albany: State University of New York Press, 1990).

31. Donald L. Miller and Richard E. Sharpless, *The Kingdom of Coal: Work, Enterprise, and Ethnic Communities in the Mine Fields* (Philadelphia: University of Pennsylvania Press, 1985), 203.

32. "Voices from the Ridge: Songs and Stories of Working People and Their Participation in America's Industrial History," audiotape (Folklife Division, America's Industrial Heritage Project, no date or place of production given).

33. "Tradition Bearers," Rivers of Steel website, accessed November 1, 2009, http://www.riversofsteel.com/traditionbearers/index.html; "Tradition Bearers Radio Series," Rivers of Steel website, accessed June 27, 2007, but no longer available as of the writing of this chapter in 2010, http://www.riversofsteel.com/radioseries/index.html.

34. "Rivers of Steel Regional Folklife Center," undated pamphlet; "Regional Folklife Directory," Rivers of Steel website, accessed November 1, 2009, http://www.riversofsteel.com/folklife-directory/.

35. John Corner and Sylvia Harvey, "Mediating Tradition and Modernity: The Heritage/Enterprise Couplet," in *Crosscurrents of National Culture*, ed. John Corner and Sylvia Harvey (London: Routledge, 1991), 49, 51. Emphases are in the original text.

36. Author's in-person interview with Kenneth Wolensky, historian, Bureau for Historic Preservation, PHMC, Harrisburg, on January 26, 2009.

37. "New Steelton," *Harrisburg Patriot-News*, January 7, 2009, p. A8.

38. John Bodnar, *Immigration and Industrialization: Ethnicity in an American Mill Town, 1870–1940* (Pittsburgh: University of Pittsburgh Press, 1977), 102.

39. Author's participation in "Babushkas and Hard Hats" tour.

40. Peter Miller, "Pittsburgh: Stronger Than Steel," *National Geographic* (December 1991): 131.

41. Randy Griffith, "Resurrection Church Rises from Cambria City Parishes," *Johnstown Tribune-Democrat*, July 27, 2009 (plus subsequent reader commentary), accessed November 1, 2009, http://www.tribune-democrat.com/multimedia/local_story_207225744.html.

42. Author's visit to the Railroaders Memorial Museum in Altoona on July 7, 2007.

43. I would note among these exceptions the tour interpretation I heard or read at the No. 9 Mine in Lansford on June 23, 2007, and at the Heritage Discovery Center in Johnstown on July 27, 2007, and July 11, 2009.

44. Regina Medina, "Town Torn Apart: Shenandoah's Ethnic Strife and Violence Bring America's Immigration Issue into Sharp Focus," *Philadelphia Daily News*, September 17, 2008, p. 1.

45. Antonio Olivo, "Immigrant's Death Splits Blue-Collar Town," *Chicago Tribune*, August 12, 2008, accessed November 7, 2009, http://www.chicagotribune.com/news/nationalworld/chi-hatecrimeaug12,0,47994865.story.

46. The same kinds of headlines were used when, in December 2009, the accused young men were re-indicted in federal court, amid charges of local police corruption after a federal investigation of the incident. See, for instance, Ford Turner, "A Town Divided," *Harrisburg Patriot-News*, December 22, 2009, pp. A1, A18.

47. Sean D. Hamill, "Mexican's Death Bares a Town's Ethnic Tension," *New York Times*, August 5, 2008, p. A12.

CHAPTER 5

The epigraph to this chapter is drawn from National Broadcasting Company, "Miners in Somerset County, Pennsylvania, Say They Try Not to Think About Potential Hazards of Coal Mining," *NBC Nightly News*, July 27, 2002. Transcript accessed via Lexis-Nexis academic database on October 25, 2005.

1. Tom Gibb, "Crying Time Again: All Through Somerset County, Mine Families Maintain a Vigil," *Pittsburgh Post-Gazette*, July 26, 2002, p. A12.

2. Elisabeth Bumiller, "Bush Meets Rescued Miners, Saying They Represent Spirit of America," *New York Times*, August 6, 2002, p. A10.

3. "Pennsylvania Miners' Survival, Rescue Renews Faith in America," *USA Today*, July 31, 2002, p. 11A. These letter writers were identified as, respectively, Chris Fyfe of Laurel Fork, Va., and Carol Carey Leblique of Lake City, Fla.

4. Columbia Broadcasting System, "Rescue of Nine Trapped Miners Giving Americans a Happy Story to Focus on Amidst Market Scandals and Terrorism," *CBS Morning News*, July 30, 2007. Transcript accessed via Lexis-Nexis Academic database on October 25, 2005.

5. Author's visit to Dormel Farms (site of the Quecreek rescue) in Sipesville on September 29, 2007.

6. Author's in-person interview with Christopher Barkley, director, Windber Coal Heritage Center in Windber, on July 11, 2009.

7. I was struck by the similarity between this interpretive language and the story I heard at the nearby Flight 93 crash site, where a temporary memorial sits in the middle of a windy field that once was a strip mine and now is maintained by the National Park Service. There, along with a large group of bikers (motorcycle riders), I listened to a "Flight 93 ambassador," one of dozens of local volunteers who have been trained by the National Park Service to give talks to the 150,000 people who visit each year. The story we heard was a patriotic one told by the volunteer with considerable passion, even as he provided great logistical detail, and with admiration for the individual passengers whose lives and character he described. He concluded by asking us to imagine being aboard the airplane. *What would we do in their circumstances?* (Author's visit to Flight 93 Memorial near Shanksville on September 28, 2007.)

8. Author's visit to Windber Coal Heritage Center in Windber on July 18, 2008.

9. Jack Lule, *Daily News, Eternal Stories: The Mythological Role of Journalism* (New York: Guilford Press, 2001), 15.

10. Betty Houchin Winfield, "The Press Response to the Corps of Discovery: The Making of Heroes in an Egalitarian Age," *Journalism and Mass Communication Quarterly* 80, no. 4 (Winter 2003): 877.

11. Janice Hume, "Changing Characteristics of Heroic Women in Midcentury Mainstream Media," *Journal of Popular Culture* 34, no. 1 (Summer 2000): 10.

12. Susan J. Drucker and Robert S. Cathcart, "The Hero as a Communication Phenomenon," in *American Heroes in a Media Age,* ed. Susan J. Drucker and Robert S. Cathcart (Cresskill, NJ: Hampton Press, 1994), 2.

13. John Bodnar, *Remaking America: Public Memory, Commemoration, and Patriotism in the Twentieth Century* (Princeton: Princeton University Press, 1992), 18.

14. According to Barkley (July 11, 2009, interview), in 1952 a large, stone miner figure was erected outdoors; he now stands at the entryway to the museum, after a smaller statue was put in his place in the park in 1990.

15. Inside the museum is a large board, placed outside on display during the annual Windber Miners' Memorial Day Weekend every June (on Father's Day weekend), containing more than three hundred additional names that didn't make it onto the wall.

16. Author's visits to Windber on July 30, 2005, and July 18, 2008. For more on Windber's history, see Margaret M. Mulrooney, *A Legacy of Coal: The Coal Company Towns of Southwestern Pennsylvania* (Washington, DC: National Park Service, 1989).

17. Based on the author's travel across the state over various dates between 2007 and 2009. The latter were the subject of the exhibit titled "A Common Canvas."

18. Kenneth C. Wolensky, "Coal," in *Modern Ruins: Portraits of Place in the Mid-Atlantic Region,* photography by Shaun O'Boyle and introduction by Geoff Managh (University Park: Penn State University Press, 2010), 67.

19. Bodnar, *Remaking America,* 238.

20. Author's visit to Pittston on September 15, 2007.

21. The same company is celebrated on another historical marker in nearby Summit Hill, noting the discovery of coal there in 1791. Author's visits to Lansford on August 19, 2007, and October 7, 2007, and to Summit Hill on October 7, 2007.

22. Linda Shopes, "Building Bridges Between Academic and Public History," *Public Historian* 19, no. 2 (Spring 1997): 53–56.

23. On the monument, this text is attributed to author Roseann Hall; author's visit to Shenandoah on June 23, 2007.

24. Author's visit to Forest City on June 24, 2007.

25. This verse is attributed, on the stone, to Kathryn D. Teagarden; author's visit to the Fredericktown area on September 28, 2007.

26. Dolores Hayden, *The Power of Place: Urban Landscapes as Public History* (Cambridge: MIT Press, 1995), 245–46.

27. Author's visit to Harwick on July 13, 2007.

28. The Portage Station Museum, in a former Pennsylvania railroad station, also sells a DVD about the Sonman Mine Explosion, which ends with this written text: "This work is dedicated to the miners, their families, and the citizens of Portage, whose spirit and courage enables them to stand strong in the face of adversity" (Barbara Yetsko, prod., *63 Men Down: The Story of the Sonman Mine Explosion* [Portage, PA: Portage Area Historical Society, n.d.], funded partly by the Folklife Division of the America's Industrial Heritage Project).

29. Greg McDonnell, "The Portage Coal Heritage Auto Tour," ed. Ginny McDonnell (Portage, PA: Mainline Heritage Association, n.d.), obtained by the author, who took the auto tour; author's visit to Portage on July 18, 2008.

30. Author's visit to I-79 Welcome Center near Kirby on September 28, 2007.

31. Author's visit to Lattimer on August 17, 2007. There also is a state historical marker on this site, dedicated in 1987.

32. Author's visit to Scranton on September 15, 2007.

33. Author's visits to Coaldale on June 23, 2007, and October 7, 2007.

34. Author's visit to Minersville, August 17, 2007.

35. "'Black Diamonds': Experience Pennsylvania's Anthracite Mining Heritage" website, accessed multiple times between 2007 and 2009, http://www.pacoalhistory.com/; author's visit to Frackville on August 17, 2007.

36. Joseph W. Leonard III, *Anthracite Roots: Generations of Coal Mining in Schuylkill County, Pennsylvania* (Charleston, SC: History Press, 2005), 18, 20.

37. Author's visits to the Tour-Ed Mine in Tarentum on July 12, 2009, and the Seldom Seen Mine near St. Boniface on July 27, 2007.

38. Joe Sharkey, "Resurrecting the Miner's World," *New York Times,* June 9, 2000, sec. E-2, p. 25.

39. Author's visit to the Lackawanna Coal Mine in Scranton on June 24, 2007.

40. Author's visit to the Pioneer Tunnel and Coal Mine in Ashland on June 25, 2007; Lorett Treese, *Railroads of Pennsylvania: Fragments of the Past in the Keystone Landscape* (Mechanicsburg, PA: Stackpole Books, 2003), 108; Edward Slavishak, "Photo Ops: Centralia and the Flattening of History," paper presented at the Pennsylvania Historical Association Conference, Bethlehem, Pa., October 18, 2008.

41. Author's visit to the No. 9 Mine and Museum in Lansford on June 23, 2007.

42. Author's visits to the Pennsylvania Anthracite Heritage Museum and Courthouse Square, both in Scranton, on June 25, 2007, and September 15, 2007. The phrase "Champion of Labor" is on the Mitchell statue.

43. Author's visit to Eckley Miners Village near Hazleton on June 23, 2007.

44. In all, I visited a total of fifteen mining museums and coal mining historical displays. I am counting the displays inside the main buildings of four of the mine tour destinations since they are "museums" and two of them in particular—the No. 9 Mine and the Tour-Ed museum—contain a great number of artifacts. I am not counting two museums whose interpretation I was unable to see: the Coal Miners Memorial in St. Michael, Pa., which I have not been able to find open, and the mine history exhibit in the Luzerne County Historical Society in Wilkes-Barre, Pa., which was under renovation during the years I was working on this project. I also am aware that there are coal mining history displays in several other county and town historical societies that I did not have the chance to visit.

45. Author's visit to the Anthracite Mining Museum in Knoebels Amusement Park, near Elysburg, on July 9, 2008.

46. Author's visit to Coalport Area Coal Museum in Coalport on September 27, 2007.

47. Author's visit to the Museum of Anthracite Mining in Ashland on July 9, 2008.

48. Even though its displays are meant for visitors, this is more of a research center than a museum. Author's visit to the Coal and Coke Heritage Center, Penn State Fayette, between Uniontown and Connellsville, on September 28, 2007.

49. Author's visit to the Williamstown-Williams Township Historical Society in Williamstown on June 16, 2008.

50. Author's visits to the Broad Top Area Coal Miners Museum in Robertsdale on July 18, 2008 and July 11, 2009.

51. Richard Francaviglia, *Hard Places: Reading the Landscape of America's Historic Mining Districts* (Iowa City: University of Iowa Press, 1991), 204.

52. Thomas Dublin and Walter Licht, *The Face of Decline: The Pennsylvania Anthracite Region in the Twentieth Century* (Ithaca: Cornell University Press, 2005), 198. Another excellent history of work and life in Pennsylvania's anthracite region is Donald L. Miller and Richard E. Sharpless, *The Kingdom of Coal: Work, Enterprise, and Ethnic Communities in the Mine Fields* (Philadelphia: University of Pennsylvania Press, 1985).

53. "Shunpiker's Guide: Coal County," Pennsylvania State Tourism Office advertisement, *Harrisburg Patriot-News,* February 10, 2008, p. G10.

54. Dublin and Licht's study of residents in one part of the region, known as the Panther Valley, revealed that 65 percent of high school graduates between 1945 and 1960, "the most intense period of anthracite's decline" in that area, left the valley (*The Face of Decline*, 214). According to Dublin, by 1992, the Pennsylvania anthracite industry employed only 1,400 workers, compared to 175,000 during World War I, the peak period of anthracite production (Dublin, *When the Mines Closed: Stories of Struggles in Hard Times* [Ithaca: Cornell University Press, 1998], 1).

55. Ian Urbina, "King Coal Country Debates a Sacrilege, Gas Heat," *New York Times*, June 10, 2008, p. A1.

56. Jim Lewis, "Switch from Coal to Gas?" *Harrisburg Patriot-News*, June 23, 2008, p. A1.

57. Stuart Elliott, "They're Looking for a Few Good Coal Miners," *New York Times*, March 23, 2007, p. C3.

58. These words are from the *NBC Nightly News* report that began this chapter.

59. Wolensky, "Coal," 69.

CHAPTER 6

The epigraph to this chapter is drawn from the author's in-person interview with Lenwood Sloan in Harrisburg on January 26, 2009.

1. "Made in PA," exhibit at the State Museum of Pennsylvania, Harrisburg, PA, November 10, 2007, to May 18, 2008, curated by Curt Miner; visited by author on January 11, 2008.

2. Robert C. Alberts, *The Good Provider: H. J. Heinz and His 57 Varieties* (Boston: Houghton Mifflin, 1973), 124–25. Alberts claims that Heinz was the first U.S. company to offer a factory tour.

3. Roland Marchand, *Creating the Corporate Soul: The Rise of Public Relations and Corporate Imagery in American Big Business* (Berkeley and Los Angeles: University of California Press, 1998), 258. There are no more tours at Heinz, which no longer has manufacturing plants in Pennsylvania, even though corporate headquarters remain in Pittsburgh (confirmed by author's phone call to Heinz Customer Service on February 20, 2009).

4. Alberts, *The Good Provider*, 124.

5. For more, in general, on this shift in corporate public relations strategies during the first half of the twentieth century, see Marchand, *Creating the Corporate Soul*.

6. Wm. F. B. Murrie, president, Hershey Chocolate Corporation, in a letter dated January 5, 1938, and printed on the letterhead of the Hershey Chocolate Corporation, on display at the Hershey-Derry Township Historical Society, visited by the author on August 18, 2008.

7. *Historic Pennsylvania: America's Cradle of Democracy* (Harrisburg: Pennsylvania Department of Commerce, 195? [date is recorded as such]), in PA Documents Collection, State Library of Pennsylvania.

8. *Plant Tours* (Harrisburg: Pennsylvania Department of Commerce, three editions, no dates), all in PA Documents Collection, State Library of Pennsylvania. Date ranges can be determined, however, based on who was listed as the governor on the back of each booklet: for the first one, George M. Leader (1955–1959), and for the second two, William W. Scranton (1963–1967).

9. Stephen V. Ward, *Selling Places: The Marketing and Promotion of Towns and Cities, 1850–2000* (New York: Routledge, 1998), 256.

10. Ellen Perlman, "Keep on Noshin': Pennsylvania's Junk Food Trail," *Washington Post*, March 8, 2006, p. C02.

11. "York County Pennsylvania 2008 Visitors Guide" (York County Convention and Visitors Bureau, 2008), p. 13. This is a play on the former Pennsylvania state tourism slogan "You've Got a Friend in Pennsylvania."

12. "Made in America Tours, June 17–20, 2009," promotional brochure (York County Convention and Visitors Bureau, 2008).

13. For instance, see Patricia Harris and David Lyon, "Snack-Food Factory Tours Are Worth Savoring," *Boston Globe*, June 29, 2005, p. F11; Dave Hoekstra, "'Making It' in York—That's York, Pa.," *Chicago Sun-Times*, May 18, 2003, travel sec., p. 4; Laura Stassi Jeffrey, "Vroom, Vroom: Pa. Harley Tour Gets Motors Running," *Washington Post*, September 24, 2008, p. C02; Liz Johnston, "Crunch Time in Snack HQ," *Queensland (Australia) Sunday Mail*, May 8, 2005, p. E18; Matt Nesvisky, "Touring Plants, Not Mansions," *New York Times*, March 25, 2001, sec. 5, p. 1; Jill Sell, "Thousands of Harley Lovers Head to Pennsylvania Shrine," *Cleveland Plain Dealer*, September 22, 2002, p. L5; "Tours of Factories Produce Made-in-America Vacations," *Arkansas Democrat-Gazette*, May 6, 2001, p. H2; "York, Pa., Factory Fest Has It Made," *Boston Herald*, June 17, 2001, p. A28.

14. From text on a historic plaque at the Milton S. Hershey fountain inside Hersheypark; author's visit to Hersheypark in Hershey on August 4, 2007.

15. This claim is made in the worker's talk given as part of the "tour" of the Intercourse Pretzel Factory in Intercourse, visited by the author on November 17, 2007. What this statement probably really means is that the great majority of America's pretzels are made in adjacent *York* County.

16. Author's tour of Snyder's in Hanover on August 28, 2007.

17. Author's tours of the Harley-Davidson motorcycle plant in York on November 3, 2007, and June 17, 2009.

18. Author's tour of the Mack Truck assembly plant in Macungie on August 14, 2009.

19. Author's tour of the Tröegs Brewery in Harrisburg on July 24, 2010.

20. Author's visit to Wilbur Chocolate in Lititz on November 17, 2007. The Hershey figures are from a recipe and trivia book sold in the huge retail store at Chocolate World, Marilyn Odesser-Torpey, *The Hershey, Pennsylvania Cookbook: Fun Treats and Trivia from the Chocolate Capital of the World* (Guilford, CT: Morris Book Publishing, 2007), 6.

21. The exhibit brochure is available on the Children's Museum of Pittsburgh website, accessed May 29, 2010, http://www.pittsburghkids.org/hpmt/. After this exhibit closed in Pittsburgh, it toured other Pennsylvania cities; see, for instance, David Dunkle, "Whitaker Center Exhibit Gives Sense of Factory Work," *Harrisburg Patriot-News*, January 17, 2009, p. B2.

22. Despite its name, this is a private, local museum.

23. Author's visit to the Crayola Factory and the National Canal Museum in Easton on June 14, 2007.

24. Author's visits to Hershey's Chocolate World in Hershey on July 10, 2007, August 4, 2007, and January 5, 2011. This facility used to be primarily a public relations tool, but now it is a revenue generator in and of itself. While the "Great American Chocolate Tour" (the ride) is still free, parents must pay $8.95 for the "factory gear" box their children assemble, plus $14.95 per person for admission to the "Create Your Own Candy Bar" area.

25. Author's tour of the Sturgis Pretzel House in Lititz on November 17, 2007.

26. Author's visit to the Intercourse Pretzel Factory on November 17, 2007.

27. Author's tour of the Revonah Pretzel Factory in Hanover on June 20, 2008.

28. Author's tours of the Martin's Potato Chip Factory in Thomasville on November 6, 2007, and June 17, 2009.

29. "Made in America Tours, June 17–20, 2009."

30. *Stories of the Land Along Dutch Country Roads* (Lancaster-York Heritage Region, 2006), DVD.

31. Author's tour of the Tröegs Brewery in Harrisburg on July 24, 2010. In mid-2010, however, Tröegs announced plans to expand its operations (and its public tours) by moving, in late 2011, into a new plant in Hershey that once was used by the Hershey Chocolate Company

(Dan Miller and Robyn Sidersky, "Growth Is Brewing," *Harrisburg Patriot-News*, June 26, 2010, pp. A1, A12). This plan was confirmed by the tour guide as well.

32. Author's tour of Straub's Brewery in St. Mary's on August 15, 2008.

33. Author's visit to Utz Potato Chips in Hanover on August 28, 2007.

34. Author's visit to Wilbur Chocolate on November 17, 2007; author's visit to the Wolfgang Candy Company in York on November 3, 2007.

35. Author's tour of the Susquehanna Glass Factory in Columbia on June 18, 2008; promotional brochures obtained in 2008 and 2010, the latter being the company's centennial.

36. Author's tour of Bluett Bros. Violins in York on June 24, 2010.

37. Author's in-person interview with Lenwood Sloan on January 26, 2009.

38. Author's tour of George's Woodcrafts near Marietta on June 18, 2008.

39. Author's tour of York Wallcoverings in York on June 17, 2009.

40. Tour brochure and tour narration, Wilton Armetale Factory in Mount Joy, visited by the author on August 18, 2008.

41. Author's viewing of the "video tour" of Seltzer's Lebanon Bologna Store in Palmyra on November 17, 2007. Interestingly, this narration also references the initial reason for factory tours—proof of cleanliness—by noting that Seltzer's is the "oldest inspected plant in Pennsylvania" (1907), linking its own history with that of the Pure Food and Drug Act (1906) and concluding, "Just look for USDA stamp #474 and you can be sure you're getting Seltzer's."

42. "Yuengling: America's Oldest Brewery," tour brochure (Pottsville, PA: Yuengling, 2007); author's tour of the Yuengling Brewery in Pottsville on August 17, 2007.

43. Display inside museum, Martin Guitar factory in Nazareth, seen on author's visit on June 12, 2009.

44. Author's tours of the Yuengling Brewery, Straub's Brewery, and the Martin Guitar factory.

45. See "Our Story" on the C. F. Martin Guitar and Co. website, accessed June 20, 2009, http://www.martinguitar.com/history/ourstory.php.

46. Author's tour of the Yuengling Brewery on August 17, 2007; also tour brochure, "Yuengling: America's Oldest Brewery."

47. Author's tour of the Wolfgang Candy Company on November 3, 2007.

48. Tour brochure, wall text, and video narration at Asher's Chocolates in Souderton, visited by the author on November 19, 2009.

49. Author's visit to Wilbur Chocolate on November 17, 2007.

50. Jennifer Bobbin, "Art Meets Metal: The Story of Wilton Armetale," *Susquehanna Life* (Fall 2007): 26.

51. Author's tour of the Harley-Davidson plant on June 17, 2009.

52. Author's visit to Utz Potato Chips on August 28, 2007.

53. Author's tour of the Martin's Potato Chip Factory on November 6, 2007.

54. Tour brochure and narration at Herr's in Nottingham, visited by the author on August 30, 2007; Phillip R. Bellury and Gail Guterl, *The History of Herr's* (Nottingham, PA: Herr Foods Inc., 1995), 3–4.

55. Author's visits to Hershey's Chocolate World; trolley tours taken on July 17, 2007 (the 45-minute "Trolley Summer Adventure"), and July 25, 2007 (the hour-long "Chocolate-Tasting and Historical Tour"); and visit to The Hershey Story (museum) on January 11, 2009.

56. Author's visit to the Hershey Museum in Hershey on January 2, 2007.

57. Author's tour of the Yuengling Brewery on August 17, 2007; "Yuengling: America's Oldest Brewery," tour brochure; John Luciew, "Business is Brewing," *Harrisburg Patriot-News*, March 29, 2009, pp. A1, A14–15.

58. Author's tours of the Harley-Davidson motorcycle plant on November 3, 2007, and June 17, 2009.

59. Author's tours of the Harley-Davidson motorcycle plant on November 3, 2007, and June 17, 2009; author's tour of the Martin Guitar factory on June 12, 2009.

60. These figures are based on, respectively, the tour narration at Martin Guitar and a statement by a representative of the York County Convention and Visitors Bureau in Diana Fishlock, "State Hopes to Keep Economic Engine," *Harrisburg Patriot-News,* November 30, 2009, pp. A1, A2.

61. Jill Sell, "Thousands of Harley Lovers Head to Pennsylvania Shrine," *Cleveland Plain Dealer,* September 22, 2002, p. L5.

62. Peter Gerstenzang, "A Journey Shaped by a Guitar," *New York Times,* February 22, 2008, p. F-1.

63. Author's visit to the Martin Guitar factory on June 12, 2009.

64. Zippo/Case Museum website, accessed on June 20, 2009, http://www.zippo.com/ZippoCaseMuseum/index.aspx.

65. This is from the recollection of his daughter, Sarah Zorn, on the company's website, accessed on June 20, 2009, http://www.zippo.com/corporateInfo/index.aspx.

66. Tour brochures, film, and museum at the Zippo/Case Museum in Bradford, visited by the author on August 15, 2008; see also Zippo/Case Museum website, accessed June 20, 2009, http://www.zippo.com/ZippoCaseMuseum/index.aspx. In the store, the woman in front of me in the checkout line, having just spent more than $150 for items her teenage sons had picked out, asked if they had an online catalog. The clerk paused awkwardly and then said, "Well, we're not allowed to sell knives on the Internet"—a startling reminder that these made-in-Pennsylvania gifts are deadly weapons. Another product for sale in the gift shop was a DVD set of the first season of *Mad Men* (a television show about the advertising industry in the 1960s, which features much smoking) packaged inside a box designed as a Zippo lighter; when you open the hinged top of the box, the round, red DVDs appear to create a flame.

67. "Walk the Line," advertisement, *Pennsylvania Pursuits* (Winter 2009): 3.

68. Cara Williams Crammer, exec. prod., *Explore PA: Fairs and Festivals: York* (Harrisburg: WITF, 2006).

69. Author's tour of the Mack Truck assembly plant on August 14, 2009.

70. Author's tour of the Martin Guitar factory on June 12, 2009.

71. See, for instance, "Harley-Davidson Hits Bump," and Dan Strumph, "Stumping for Jobs," both in *Harrisburg Patriot-News,* January 24, 2009, p. A6, and May 14, 2009, p. A17, respectively.

72. Author's tour of the Harley-Davidson factory on June 17, 2009.

73. Lara Brenckle, "Soggy Day Doesn't Slow Harley Celebration," *Harrisburg Patriot-News,* June 21, 2009, p. A5.

74. Mary Klaus, "A Huge Kiss," *Harrisburg Patriot-News,* July 8, 2007, p. B1; "Hershey Pays Homage to Founder," *Harrisburg Patriot-News,* September 13, 2007, p. A2.

75. Gene Sloan, "Hershey Honors Its Past, Looks to the Future," *USA Today,* May 17, 2007, accessed May 18, 2007, http://www.usatoday.com/travel/destinations/2007-05-17-hersheypark-anniversary_N.htm.

76. "A Lot of Fear," *Harrisburg Patriot-News,* March 27, 2007, pp. A1, A5; "Kiss Jobs Goodbye," *Harrisburg Patriot-News,* February 16, 2007, pp. C1, C4; Daniel Victor, "What Would Milton Do?" *Harrisburg Patriot-News,* March16, 2007, pp. A1, A12.

77. Sharon Smith, "Founder's Family Saddened by Price of Globalization," *Harrisburg Patriot-News,* April 4, 2007, p. C4.

78. "Cheers and Jeers," *Harrisburg Patriot-News,* July 7, 2007, p. A7.

79. Sherry Christian, reporter, "Special Report: The Future of Hershey," WHP-TV, November 26, 2007.

CHAPTER 7

The epigraph to this chapter is drawn from Nancy Polinsky Johnson, "Letters: Forge a Steel Museum," *Pittsburgh Post-Gazette,* November 19, 2002, p. C14.

1. Sandy Trozzo, "A Future in the Past: Group Hoping Historic Sites Will Generate Tourism," *Pittsburgh Post-Gazette,* March 17, 1991, p. V1.

2. William Serrin, *Homestead: The Glory and Tragedy of an American Steel Town* (New York: Times Books, 1992), 405.

3. Ibid., 404.

4. "Welcome to Pittsburgh and Its Countryside," in *Pittsburgh and Its Countryside: Official Visitors Guide* (Harrisburg: Pennsylvania Tourism Office, n.d.; obtained by author in 2007), 2.

5. Heather Boynton, "A City Recast," *Pennsylvania Travel Guide* (Harrisburg: Pennsylvania Tourism Office, 2006/7), 30.

6. Ilona Biro, "The Comeback Kid," *Toronto Globe and Mail,* February 21, 1998, p. F1.

7. Jeff Schlegel, "36 Hours in Pittsburgh," *New York Times,* July 6, 2008, p. TR10; Jennifer C. Yates (Associated Press), "City Celebrates 250th with Year of Activities," *Harrisburg Patriot-News,* December 30, 2007, p. G1.

8. Jayne Clark, "Pittsburgh Forges Ahead," *USA Today,* July 18, 2008, p. 2D.

9. Ramit Plushnick-Masti (Associated Press), "Pittsburgh: City Celebrates Its Past, Future After 250 Years," *Harrisburg Patriot-News,* November 30, 2008, p. G10.

10. Ian Urbina, "For Host City, G-20 Is a Shot at Image Repair," *New York Times,* September 24, 2009, p. A26.

11. John Luciew, "From Ashes of Steel, a Future Is Forged," *Harrisburg Patriot-News,* September 20, 2009, p. A26.

12. Jeff Sewald, prod. and dir., *Gridiron and Steel* (Pittsburgh: Real As Steel Media Ventures, 2001), DVD.

13. Kirk Savage, "Monuments of a Lost Cause: The Postindustrial Campaign to Commemorate Steel," in *Beyond the Ruins: The Meanings of Deindustrialization,* ed. Jefferson Cowie and Joseph Heathcott (Ithaca, NY: ILR Press, 2003), 249–50.

14. Janet Marstine, "William Gropper's 'Joe Magarac': Icon of American Industry," in *The Gimbel Pennsylvania Art Collection from the Collection of the University of Pittsburgh,* ed. Paul Chew (Greensburg, PA: Westmoreland Museum of Art, 1986). Marstine's essay is about a 1946 painting of Magarac by artist William Gropper showing "a giant, grinning in triumph while bending a molten rod of steel with his bare hands," a figure with "huge forearms, swelling chest, and massive thighs. . . . An American demi-god of industry" (n.p.) For more on the Magarac legend, see also Roy Kahn, "Just an Average Joe," *Pittsburgh* (November 1985): 17–18.

15. Cowie and Heathcott, "Introduction: The Meanings of Deindustrialization," in *Beyond the Ruins: The Meanings of Deindustrialization,* ed. Jefferson Cowie and Joseph Heathcott (Ithaca, NY: ILR Press, 2003), 2–3.

16. Ibid., 15.

17. Author's visit to The Waterfront complex in Homestead on July 13, 2007; I also visited this complex on July 26, 2008, and August 22, 2009.

18. Quotes are from Dolores Hayden, *The Power of Place: Urban Landscapes as Public History* (Cambridge: MIT Press, 1995), 245, 246.

19. Mark Roth, "Homestead Works: Steel Lives in Its Stories," *Pittsburgh Post-Gazette,* July 30, 2006, accessed January 21, 2010, http://www.post-gazette.com/pg/06211/709449-85.stm.

20. Kathryn Marie Dudley, *The End of the Line: Lost Jobs, New Lives in Postindustrial America* (Chicago: University of Chicago Press, 1994), xxv.

21. Margaret Smykla, "Steelworkers Asked Back to Carrie Furnace for Tour," *Pittsburgh-Post Gazette,* August 10, 2006, accessed June 21, 2007, http://www.post-gazette.com.

22. All of this description, unless otherwise noted, comes from my own tour of the Carrie Furnaces in Braddock on July 14, 2007.

23. Steven High and David W. Lewis, *Corporate Wasteland: The Landscape and Memory of Deindustrialization* (Ithaca: ILR Press/Cornell University Press, 2007), 8; see also Tim Edensor, *Industrial Ruins: Spaces, Aesthetics, and Materiality* (Oxford: Berg, 2005), and John A. Jakle and David Wilson, *Derelict Landscapes: The Wasting of America's Built Environment* (Savage, MD: Rowman and Littlefield, 1992). In addition to academic treatments of such topics, the "deindustrial sublime" and the shared stories of workers' feelings of loss have inspired books of photographic tribute; see, for instance, Steve Mellon, *After the Smoke Clears: Struggling to Get By in Rustbelt America* (Pittsburgh: University of Pittsburgh Press, 2002); Judith Modell and Charlee Brodsky, *Envisioning Homestead: A Town Without Steel* (Pittsburgh: University of Pittsburgh Press, 1998); Shaun O'Boyle (photographer) and Geoff Managh (introduction), *Modern Ruins: Portraits of Place in the Mid-Atlantic Region* (University Park: Penn State University Press, 2010); and Mark Perrot (photographer) and John R. Lane (introduction), *Eliza: Remembering a Pittsburgh Steel Mill* (Charlottesville, VA: Howell Press, 1989).

24. High and Lewis, *Corporate Wasteland*, 9.

25. This plan is explained in *Carrie Furnaces* (Pittsburgh: Rivers of Steel National Heritage Area, n.d.), DVD, on sale at the Pump House and the Bost Building.

26. Rivers of Steel's "Lords of the Mon" cruise and "Babushkas and Hard Hats" tour, both in Pittsburgh, taken by the author on July 26, 2008, and August 22, 2009, respectively.

27. Author's visits to the Bost Building in Homestead on August 22, 2009, and July 14, 2007.

28. Barbara L. Jones, with Edward K. Muller and Joel A. Tarr, *Born of Fire: The Valley of Work: Industrial Scenes of Southwestern Pennsylvania* (Westmoreland, PA: Westmoreland Museum of American Art, 2006); Bill Mosher, exec. prod., *Born of Fire: How Pittsburgh Built a Nation* (Westmoreland, PA: Westmoreland Museum of American Art, 2006). Another excellent permanent exhibit of artwork depicting Pennsylvania industries is in the Earth and Mineral Sciences Building on the University Park campus of Penn State, near State College, PA (visited by the author on July 14, 2008). Its collection is the subject of a book as well, Betsy Fahlman and Eric Schruers, *Wonders of Work and Labor: The Steidle Collection of American Industrial Art* (University Park: Penn State University Press, 2008).

29. This effort was led in part by the foundation's then-president, Charles McCollester, an Indiana University of Pennsylvania history professor who also is the author of an excellent history of Pittsburgh labor history, *The Point of Pittsburgh: Production and Struggle at the Forks of the Ohio* (Pittsburgh, PA: Battle of Homestead Foundation, 2008).

30. "A Century of Steelworkers: Pump House Banners" (Pittsburgh: Battle of Homestead Foundation and the United Steelworkers of America, 2004). This narrative individualization is even more ironic given who the second sponsor of this booklet is—the union. The descriptions in this paragraph are from the author's visits to the Pump House on July 14, 2007, and August 22, 2009, and from emails received by the author from Rivers of Steel publicizing various events there.

31. Angel Hernandez, exec. prod., *Explore PA: Pittsburgh* (Harrisburg, PA: WITF, 2005).

32. Author's telephone interview with Andy Masich, executive president and CEO, John Heinz Regional History Center in Pittsburgh, on January 10, 2008.

33. Author's visits to the Heinz History Center in Pittsburgh on July 15, 2007, and July 12, 2009.

34. High and Lewis, *Corporate Wasteland*, 86.

35. Rick Sebak, prod. and narr., *Invented Engineered and Pioneered in Pittsburgh* (Pittsburgh: WQED Multimedia, 2008).

36. High and Lewis, *Corporate Wasteland*, 85.

37. Ron Scherer, "Forging a Future Beyond Steel," *Christian Science Monitor,* February 11, 1998, p. 10.

38. Mayor John Callahan, State of the City Address, February 19, 2009, published on the website of the City of Bethlehem, PA, accessed January 26, 2010, http://www.bethlehem-pa .gov/about/state_of_city/index.htm.

39. All of these are part of an architect's model on display inside the casino. Unless otherwise noted, all of this information is from the author's visit to the Sands Casino Resort Bethlehem on July 26, 2009.

40. Sherry Lee Linkon and John Russo, *Steeltown U.S.A.: Work and Memory in Youngstown* (Lawrence: University Press of Kansas, 2002), 240. This work was one model for my own book, in that it considers public representations of the city's image and its meaning in memory from sources including newspaper and magazine articles, art, and film.

41. See the National Museum of Industrial History, accessed multiple times between 2006 and 2010 and still accessible as of May 29, 2010, http://www.nmih.org/.

42. All information and quotations about the plans for the National Museum of Industrial History, up to this point, are from the author's telephone interview with Steve Donches, executive director of the (planned) National Museum of Industrial History, on March 28, 2008.

43. Nicole Radzievich, "Valley to Get a Peek at Industrial History," *Allentown Morning Call,* August 7, 2006, p. B1.

44. Author's telephone interview with Allen Sachse executive director, Delaware and Lehigh Valley National Heritage Corridor, Easton, on January 28, 2008.

45. Amy Burkett, exec. prod., *Bethlehem Steel: The People Who Built America* (Allentown, Bethlehem, and Easton, PA: Lehigh Valley PBS/WLVT-TV, 2003). Ironically, this is sold in the Sands Bethlehem Resort Casino's gift shop.

46. For more information about this group, see the Steelworkers Archives website, accessed multiple times between 2006 and 2010 and still accessible as of May 29, 2010, http:// www.steelworkersarchives.com/About.htm.

47. "Designing Interpretation for the Bethlehem Steel Site . . . and Beyond," working document prepared by the Mid-Atlantic Regional Center for the Humanities, September 11, 2007, p. 2.

48. Author's visit to the Steelworker Memorial in Bethlehem on July 26, 2009.

49. Christian D. Berg, "Memorial Would Honor Steel Workers," *Allentown Morning Call,* April 28, 1998, n.p.

50. John Bodnar, *Immigration and Industrialization: Ethnicity in an American Mill Town, 1870–1940* (Pittsburgh: University of Pittsburgh Press, 1977); Michael Barton and Simon J. Bronner, introduction to *Images of America: Steelton* (Charleston, SC: Arcadia Publishing, 2008), 7–10.

51. Emily Opilo, "Steelton Factory to Add 200 Jobs," *Harrisburg Patriot-News,* February 19, 2009, p. A8; "KOZ," *Harrisburg Patriot-News,* March 22, 2009, p. F2.

52. Jim Lewis, "Costly Renewal," *Harrisburg Patriot-News,* October 2, 2006, pp. A1, A12; and Janet Pickel, "'The New Steelton' Sees Small Gains," *Harrisburg Patriot-News,* January 2, 2009, accessed on January 28, 2010, http://www.pennlive.com/midstate/index.ssf/2009/01/ the_new_steelton_sees_small_ga.html.

53. Steelton Borough website, accessed January 26, 2010, http://steeltonpa.com/index.asp.

54. See Explore PA website, http://explorepahistory.com/. One "interpretive exhibit panel" erected by a regional heritage organization, the Susquehanna Gateway Heritage Region (formerly the Lancaster-York Heritage Region) along its Susquehanna River Trail, does recognize Steelton's industrial history. Titled "Foundations of Steel," it notes the town's once-thriving population and the plant's use of "an innovative steel-making process called the Bessemer Method to produce large quantities of steel inexpensively," adding, "The Steel molded

in Steelton built the American railroad system, U.S. military battleships, skyscrapers, and bridges." This marker is not in Steelton, however; it is on the other side of the Susquehanna River, in the town of New Market, which is within this heritage area (Steelton is not, being in Dauphin County, which is part of no heritage area).

55. Mike Newall and Doron Taussig, "Coatesville Is Burning," *Philadelphia City Paper,* February 12–19, 2009, pp. 16–21.

56. All of the quotations in this section are from the author's in-person interview with Scott Huston, president, and Eugene DiOrio, vice president and director, Graystone Society, in Coatesville on January 24, 2008.

57. "The World Trade Center Trees" page on the Lukens National Historic District website, accessed July 27, 2010, http://www.lukenshistoricdistrict.org/trees.htm

58. All of the quotations in this section so far are from the author's telephone interview with Richard Burkert, executive director, Johnstown Area Heritage Association, on January 4, 2008.

59. Johnstown Area Heritage Association, prod., *The Mystery of Steel* (Pittsburgh, PA: The Magic Lantern, 2009), viewed by the author at the Johnstown Heritage Discovery Center on July 11, 2009.

60. Don Giles (photographer) and Robert Weible (exhibit coordinator), "Steel: Made in Pennsylvania," exhibit seen by the author at the State Museum of Pennsylvania in Harrisburg in 2007 (date not recorded) and at the Johnstown Heritage Discovery Center on July 11, 2009. For a fuller description of this exhibit, see Charles Kupfer, "Exhibit Review: Steel: Made in Pennsylvania," *Pennsylvania History: A Journal of Mid-Atlantic Studies* 75, no. 1 (2008): 120.

61. Author's telephone interview with Richard Burkert on January 4, 2008.

62. *Black Friday,* film first shown for the flood centennial on May 31, 1989, at the Johns-town Flood National Memorial (a National Park Service site) in St. Michael; viewed by author on site on July 28, 2007, and July 30, 2005.

63. Author's telephone interview with August Carlino on February 27, 2008.

64. Thomas E. Leary and Elizabeth C. Sholes, "Authenticity of Place and Voice: Exam-ples of Industrial Heritage Preservation and Interpretation in the U.S. and Europe," *Public Historian* 22, no. 3 (Summer 2000): 57. They cite Debra S. Moffitt, "Boon or Boondoggle?" *Johnstown Tribune-Democrat,* June 23, 1996; "Path of Progress at Crossroad," *Johnstown Tribune-Democrat,* June 24, 1996; and Urban Design Associates architects et al., "Rivers of Steel: Management Action Plan," March 17, 1995.

65. Angel Hernandez, exec. prod., *Explore PA: Bethlehem* (Harrisburg: WITF, 2005).

66. Menu obtained by author at the Bethlehem Brew Works in Bethlehem on October 17, 2008.

67. Bernard Fernandez, "Lehigh Valley is High on Its Hogs, the IronPigs," *Philadelphia Daily News,* March 28, 2008, p. 118.

68. Kirk Savage, "Monuments of a Lost Cause," 247.

69. Author's visit to the Steelworkers Monument in Pittsburgh (South Side) on July 2, 2008.

70. Author's participation in the "Lords of the Mon" cruise on July 26, 2008. Its narration implies that the "lords" are both the industries—steel, coke, river transportation, and rail-roading—and the men who worked in them.

71. Author's participation in the "Babushkas and Hard Hats" tour on August 22, 2009.

CHAPTER 8

The epigraph to this chapter is drawn from Robin Van Auken and Louis E. Hunsinger Jr., *Images of America: Lycoming County's Industrial Heritage* (Charleston, SC: Arcadia, 2005), 6.

1. James F. Abrams, "Lost Frames of Reference: Sightings of History and Memory in Pennsylvania's Documentary Landscape," in *Conserving Culture: A New Discourse on Heritage*, ed. Mary Hufford (Urbana: University of Illinois Press, 1994), 25.

2. Raymond Williams, *The Long Revolution* (London: Chatto and Windus, 1961), 53.

3. Lonna M. Malmsheimer, "Three Mile Island: Fact, Frame, and Fiction," *American Quarterly* 38, no. 1 (Spring 1986): 35.

4. Author's visit to the State Museum of Pennsylvania in Harrisburg on June 19, 2010. In her book about the river, *Susquehanna: River of Dreams* (Baltimore: Johns Hopkins University Press, 1993), Susan Q. Stranahan includes a chapter about the role of nuclear power in its history and identity. See also J. Samuel Walker, *Three Mile Island: A Nuclear Crisis in Historical Perspective* (Berkeley and Los Angeles: University of California Press, 2004).

5. Schulkill River Heritage Area, "Schuylkill River Heritage Area Receives More Than $300,000 in Grants to Improve the Watershed," press release dated August 30, 2010, accessed December 29, 2010, http://www.schuylkillriver.org/press_releases/2010_SR_Restoration_Fund_pressrelease.pdf

6. Robert L. Thayer Jr., "Pragmatism in Paradise: Technology and the American Landscape," *Landscape* 30, no. 3 (1990): 6.

7. Mike Wallace, *Mickey Mouse History and Other Essays on American Memory* (Philadelphia: Temple University Press, 1996), 89.

8. Lizabeth Cohen, "What Kind of World Have We Lost? Workers' Lives and Deindustrialization in the Museum," *American Quarterly* 41 (December 1989): 680. This is an exhibition review of the Hagley Museum in Delaware, Eckley Miners Village in Hazleton, and an exhibit titled "Homestead: The Story of a Steel Town, 1860–1945" at the Historical Society of Western Pennsylvania (now Heinz History Center) in Pittsburgh, February 1989 to June 1990.

9. "Made in PA," exhibit at the State Museum of Pennsylvania, Harrisburg, PA, November 10, 2007, to May 18, 2008, curated by Curt Miner; visited by author on January 11, 2008.

10. "Native Lands County Park" (Wrightsville: Susquehanna Gateway Heritage Area, n.d.), n.p., obtained at the Susquehanna Gateway Heritage Area offices on July 23, 2010.

11. Iris Samson and Pierina Morrelli, *The Valley that Changed the World* (Pittsburgh: WQED Multimedia/Oil Region Alliance, 2009).

12. *Stories of the Land Along Dutch Country Roads* (Lancaster-York Heritage Region, 2006), DVD.

13. Author's visit to Caledonia Furnace in Caledonia State Park, between Chambersburg and Gettysburg, on July 8, 2008.

14. "Underground Railroad Tour," on the Amish Experience website, accessed on May 29, 2010, http://www.amishexperience.com/tours/undergroundrailroadtour.html.

15. Author's ride on the New Hope and Ivyland Railroad on August 24, 2007.

16. Author's ride on the Williamsport Trolley Tour in Williamsport on August 29, 2007.

17. Angel Hernandez, exec. prod., *Explore PA: Crawford County* (Harrisburg: WITF, 2005).

18. Cara Williams Crammer, exec. prod., *Explore PA: Spirit of Independence: The Underground Railroad in Northeast PA* (Harrisburg: WITF, 2007); author's visit to the Pennsylvania Heritage Festival at the Bradford County Heritage Association and Farm Museum.

19. Author's visit to the Railroaders Memorial Museum in Altoona on July 7, 2007.

20. The full publication is Kurt R. Bell, "Tears, Trains, and Triumphs: The Historical Legacy of African Americans and Pennsylvania's Railroad," at the Railroad Museum of Pennsylvania website, accessed May 19, 2010, http://www.rrmuseumpa.org/about/rrpeopleandsociety/africanamericans.shtml.

21. National Park Service, "Steamtown NHS to Premiere 'Rising from the Rails: The Story of the Pullman Porter,'" press release dated April 10, 2007, accessed February 21, 2010,

http://www.nps.gov/stea/parknews/movie-premiere-at-steamtown-nhs.htm; author's visit to Steamtown on June 24, 2007. The film was made from a book: Larry Tye, *Rising from the Rails: The Story of the Pullman Porter* (New York: Henry Holt, 2004). The quotation is attributed, on the wall, to H. N. Hall, "The Art of the Pullman Porter," *American Mercury* (July 1931).

22. See Amy G. Richter, *Home on the Rails: Women, the Railroad, and the Rise of Public Domesticity* (Chapel Hill: University of North Carolina Press, 2005).

23. Carolyn Kitch, "'A Genuine, Vivid Personality: Newspaper Coverage and the Construction of a 'Real' Advertising Celebrity in a Pioneering Publicity Campaign," *Journalism History* 31, no. 3 (Fall 2005): 122–37.

24. The Utz company sells doll versions of her and of "Grandma Utz." See Utz's website, accessed April 26, 2010, http://www.utzsnacks.com/store/p-128-utz-dolls.aspx. The Little Utz Girl also now has a blog, accessed on April 26, 2010, at http://www.utzsnackcentral.com/. The phrase "spotlessly clean girls" is from Robert C. Alberts, *The Good Provider: H. J. Heinz and His 57 Varieties* (Boston: Houghton Mifflin, 1973), 124.

25. Author's visit to 150th Anniversary Drake Well Extravaganza in Titusville on August 27, 2009.

26. Phillip R. Bellury and Gail Guterl, *The History of Herr's* (Nottingham, PA: Herr Foods Inc., 1995), 14.

27. Among the many venues in which these stories are told are the tourism trolleys that travel throughout the town, departing from Hershey's Chocolate World (taken by the author on July 17, 2007, and July 25, 2007), and an authorized company history, sold in Hersheypark gift shops: James D. McMahon Jr., *Built on Chocolate: The Story of the Hershey Chocolate Company* (Los Angeles: General Publishing Group, 1998).

28. "Legendary Ladies: A Guide to Where Women Made History in Pennsylvania: Greater Pittsburgh" (Harrisburg: Pennsylvania Commission for Women, n.d.), n.p. There are two other publications with the same title and publication information but different regional subtitles: "Greater Philadelphia" and "Northeast Mountains Region." It is also worth noting that many iron or steel furnaces had female names, often that of the owner's daughter or wife. Among those noted in industrial heritage literature and/or marked on the Pennsylvania landscape include Carrie, Eliza, Mary Ann, Sarah Ann, Sharon, Rebecca, Lucy, and Joanna.

29. Author's visit to the Heinz History Center in Pittsburgh on July 12, 2009.

30. Evelyn A. Hovanec, *Common Lives of Uncommon Strength: The Women of the Coal and Coke Area of Southwestern Pennsylvania, 1880–1970* (Dunbar, PA: Patch/Work Voices Publishing, 2001).

31. For its own Harvest Days weekend, the Hopewell Furnace National Historic Site provides a one-sheet flyer explaining "women's work" (obtained on site by author in 2007).

32. Author's visit to Eckley Miners Village near Hazleton on June 23, 2007.

33. Author's visit to the Railroaders Memorial Museum in Altoona on July 7, 2007. Many women's history scholars have noted "the feminization of place," especially through the symbols of home and motherhood, and especially when that imagined, idealized mother is working-class. Such female symbols "represent the values of others, including their sense of belonging to a place," writes Gillian Rose (*Feminism and Geography: The Limits of Geographical Knowledge* [Minneapolis: University of Minnesota Press, 1993], 56, 57, 59.)

34. Author's visit to the Railroaders Memorial Museum in Altoona on July 7, 2007.

35. Author's ride on the Bellefonte Historical Railroad on June 14, 2008.

36. Author's visit to the Heinz History Center in Pittsburgh on July 12, 2009. This is here because its creator was an artist for the Pittsburgh-based Westinghouse company.

37. Author's visit to the Piper Aviation Museum in Lock Haven on July 14, 2008.

38. Author's visit to the Franklin Institute in Philadelphia on October 15, 2007. The museum's small display on Lukens is on a side wall in the room containing the museum's huge

stream locomotive; her story is told alongside that of Elijah McCoy, an African American scientist who invented a train lubricant.

39. *Rebecca Webb Lukens Bicentennial, 1794–1994* (Coatesville, PA: The Graystone Society, 1994), 9. Historian Judith Scheffler argues that Lukens's life should be understood not as "the anomaly of a woman who dared to step outside her place and succeeded," but rather "as a fascinating example of the complexity of women's roles and the extent of a woman's possible achievement in antebellum America" (Judith Scheffler, "'. . . there was difficulty and danger on every side': The Family and Business Leadership of Rebecca Lukens," *Pennsylvania History* 66, no. 3 [Summer 1999]: 276, 277). For more about Lukens, see also Lynn Y. Wiener, "Women and Work," in *Reclaiming the Past: Landmarks of Women's History,* ed. Page Putnam Miller, 199–223 (Bloomington: Indiana University Press, 1992).

40. Email correspondence to the author from Barbara Zolli, director, Drake Well Museum, dated January 3, 2008.

41. Author's visits to Drake Well in Titusville as recently as August 27, 2009.

42. Author's visit to the Venango Museum of Art and Science in Oil City on August 14, 2008.

43. In this instance, worker history is not just conflated with generalized patriotism but made an illogical footnote to it. There also is a state historical marker in the town of Arnold, where Sellins is buried beneath a gravestone that was erected by the United Mine Workers of America and declares that she was "killed by the enemies of organized labor." Author's visits to Natrona and Arnold, both on July 14, 2007.

44. "The Penn Salt National Historic District/Fannie Sellins Labor Heritage Site (Harrison Township/Natrona, PA: Allegheny-Kiski Valley Historical Society, n.d.), n.p.

45. Author's visit to the Heinz History Center in Pittsburgh on November 12, 2009.

46. Maurine Greenwald, "Women and Pennsylvania Working-Class History," *Pennsylvania History* 63, no. 1 (Winter 1996): 9.

47. Author's visit to the Railroaders Memorial Museum in Altoona on July 7, 2007.

48. Kenneth C. Wolensky, Nicole H. Wolensky, and Robert P. Wolensky, *Fighting for the Union Label: The Women's Garment Industry and the ILGWU in Pennsylvania* (University Park: Penn State University Press, 2002), 203. See also Marion W. Roydhouse, *Women of Industry and Reform: Shaping the History of Pennsylvania, 1865–1940* (Mansfield, PA: Pennsylvania Historical Association, 2007), and the Explore PA website, accessed May 29, 2010, at http://www.explorepahistory.com/hmarker.php?markerId=403. As the Wolenskys note, garment manufacturing also experienced deindustrialization in the 1960s and 70s, with statewide employment peaking in 1968 and falling to thirty-three thousand in 1999.

49. Author's visit to the Lehigh Valley Heritage Center on June 22, 2008.

50. Author's visit to the Pennsylvania Anthracite Museum in Scranton on June 25, 2007.

51. Author's telephone interview with Dan Perry, chief operating officer, Lackawanna Heritage Valley Authority, Scranton, on January 17, 2008.

52. Author's visit to the Electric City Trolley Museum in Scranton on June 24, 2007.

53. Diane Barthel, *Historic Preservation: Collective Memory and Historical Identity* (New Brunswick: Rutgers University Press, 1996), 70.

54. David Thelen, introduction to *History as a Catalyst for Civic Dialogue: Case Studies from Animating Democracy,* ed. Pam Korza and Barbara Schaffer Bacon (Washington, DC: Americans for the Arts, 2005), v.

55. Kenneth E. Foote, *Shadowed Ground: America's Landscapes of Violence and Tragedy* (Austin: University of Texas Press, 1997), 295.

56. Philip Jenkins, "Mis-Remembering America's Industrial Heritage: The Molly Maguires," paper presented to the American Historical Association, Pacific Coast Branch, Vancouver, Canada, August 2001.

57. Kathryn Marie Dudley, *The End of the Line: Lost Jobs, New Lives in Postindustrial America* (Chicago: University of Chicago Press, 1994), 26, 171.

58. Author's visit to the Pumping Jack Museum and Oil Heritage Region Visitors Center on August 14, 2008.

59. Author's visit to the Venango Museum of Art and Science on August 14, 2008.

EPILOGUE

The epigraph to this chapter is drawn from "1997 Bristol Borough Delaware Canal Lagoon Restoration Project: A Tribute to Volunteerism," park sign in Bristol, visited by the author on August 26, 2008. Unless otherwise noted, all description comes from notes and photographs taken by the author on this date.

1. Rich Henson, "Borough Seeks a Future in its Past: With Factories Idle, Bristol Has Been Learning to Market its Centuries-Old Charm," *Philadelphia Inquirer*, February 8, 1993, p. B1.

2. See also the National Park Service National Register of Historic Places website, accessed May 31, 2010, http://www.nps.gov/nr/travel/delaware/gru.htm.

3. Website for the Power House at Grundy Mills condominiums, accessed May 31, 2010, but no longer available, http://www.thepowerhouseatgrundymills.com/.

4. Gema Maria Duarte, "Borough Council Upset over Change in Developer's Plans," *Bucks County Courier Times*, November 19, 2009, accessed via Newsbank database on May 24, 2010, http://infoweb.newsbank.com/.

5. Kimra McPherson, "Erie Shakes off Ashes of Industry, Attempts to Dress for Company," *Erie Times-News*, August 25, 2002, p. L1.

6. "Highlights of Erie," *Erie Area Visitor Guide, 2007–2008* (Erie: Erie Area Convention and Visitors Bureau, 2007), p. 8.

7. Pennsylvania Department of Conservation and Natural Resources interpretive panels at Presque Isle State Park in Erie.

8. Author's visit to the Erie Maritime Museum and the brig *Niagara* in Erie on July 12, 2008.

9. Author's visits to the Independence Seaport Museum and the Franklin Institute, both in Philadelphia, on October 14, 2007. Philadelphia contains another museum that does interpret the city's industrial past, the Atwater-Kent Museum, but it was closed during the years I spent researching this book. It is set to reopen in 2011 as the Philadelphia History Museum. For more information on its collections and development, see the Philadelphia History Museum website, http://www.philadelphiahistory.org/.

10. Bailey Pryor, writer, prod., and dir., *Our National Heritage: The Story of America: Episode 1: The Revolutionary River* (Telemark Films, 2010), DVD. This is the first of a six-part series, eventually to be broadcast on PBS, about *national* heritage areas, a designation that the Schuylkill River Heritage Area has in addition to its state heritage area status.

11. Charlene Mires, *Independence Hall in American Memory* (Philadelphia: University of Pennsylvania Press, 2002), 121.

12. Federal Writers' Project, Works Progress Administration for the Commonwealth of Pennsylvania, *Philadelphia: A Guide to the Nation's Birthplace* (Philadelphia: William Penn Association of Philadelphia, Inc./Pennsylvania Historical Museum, 1937), 9, 513–33.

13. Mires, *Independence Hall in American Memory*, 215.

14. This is noted in the "About Historical Manayunk" section of the area's promotional website, accessed May 2010, http://www.manayunk.com/. The brewery quote is from the Manayunk Brewery and Restaurant website, accessed May 2010, http://www.manayunkbrewery.com/about.php.

15. Kenneth Warren, "Steel," in *Modern Ruins: Portraits of Place in the Mid-Atlantic Region*, Shaun O'Boyle (photographer) and Geoff Managh (introduction) (University Park: Penn State University Press, 2010), 40.

16. Author's in-person interview with Robert Weible, former director of public history, State Museum of Pennsylvania, Pennsylvania Historical and Museum Commission, Harrisburg, on February 15, 2008. Weible is now chief historian for the State of New York.

17. Ron Scherer, "Forging a Future Beyond Steel," *Christian Science Monitor*, February 11, 1998, p. 10.

18. Allison Garvey and Barbara Miller, "A Star Reborn," *Harrisburg Patriot-News*, July 1, 2008, pp. B1, B12.

19. At any rate, these are the circumstances as of the author's most recent visits to the state museum and Drake Well on, respectively, June 19, 2010, and August 27, 2009.

20. "Rock and Roll" (Scranton: Lackawanna County Convention and Visitors Bureau, n.d.); see also The Office Convention website, accessed January 8, 2011, http://www.the officeconvention.com/newmail.

21. Pennsylvania Historical and Museum Commission Railroad Museum of Pennsylvania promotional brochure dated September 2008.

22. "Pennsylvania's Energy Trail of History," advertisement in *Pennsylvania Pursuits* (Summer 2009), 62–65.

23. Author's telephone interview with August Carlino on February 27, 2008.

24. Author's in-person interview with Kenneth Wolensky on January 26, 2009.

25. Bella Dicks, *Culture on Display: The Production of Contemporary Visitability* (Maidenhead: Open University Press, 2003), 119.

26. See The Haunted Mine website, accessed June 8, 2011, http://www.thehauntedmine. com/ the West Chester Railroad website, accessed December 30, 2010, http://www.westches terr.com/index.html.

27. "Having a Chilling Experience: Haunted Excursions at Eckley Miners Village," *Happenings Magazine: In and Around Northeast Pennsylvania* (October 2007): 58.

28. "Halloween Ghost Tours at the Old Jail Museum in Jim Thorpe, PA," October 29, 2009, Examiner.com, accessed December 30, 2010, http://www.examiner.com/ poconos-travel-in-allentown/halloween-ghost-tours-at-the-old-jail-museum-jim-thorpe-pa.

29. There is, accordingly, a growing scholarly literature on this phenomenon, including Kenneth E. Foote, *Shadowed Ground: America's Landscapes of Violence and Tragedy* (Austin: University of Texas Press, 1997); John Lennon and Malcolm Foley, *Dark Tourism: The Attraction of Death and Disaster* (London: Continuum, 2000); William Logan and Keir Reeves, eds., *Places of Pain and Shame: Dealing with "Difficult Heritage"* (London: Routledge, 2009); and Paul Harvey Williams, *Memorial Museums: The Global Rush to Commemorate Atrocities* (New York: Berg, 2007).

30. "Artisan Trail in the Pennsylvania Wilds" (Harrisburg: Pennsylvania State Tourism Office, n.d.).

31. Author's visit to Cabela's in Hamburg on June 21, 2008. This store is part of a chain.

32. Simon J. Bronner, *Killing Tradition: Inside Hunting and Animal Rights Controversies* (Lexington: University Press of Kentucky, 2008), 239–40; Cabela's store brochure (n.d.).

33. "You're Invited: Holiday Heritage Market at the Pump House Dec. 4," email correspondence received by the author on December 2, 2010, from riversofsteel.com.

34. Author's visits to Eckley Miners Village on August 15, 2009, and the Drake Well Extravaganza/Oil 150 Celebration.

35. Author's visit to "Civil War Day" at the Landis Valley Museum in Lancaster on July 24, 2010.

36. "Pennsylvania Civil War Trails: Passport to History" (no publication information given, n.d.), front cover; visitPA Civil War Trails web page, accessed May 31, 2010, http://

pacivilwartrails.com/index.aspx/; "Civil War Connection," *Hershey Harrisburg 2009 Regional Visitors Guide* (Harrisburg: Hershey Harrisburg Regional Visitors Bureau, 2009).

37. For instance, "Harrisburg: Crossroads of the Union" story stop sign in Harrisburg, seen by author on June 24, 2010; "Pennsylvania's Iron Industry Fuels Progress and Victory" and "Railroads During the Civil War" story stop signs in Columbia, both seen on June 20, 2010; and "Mills and Manufacturing—Fueling the Cause" story stop sign, seen on June 24, 2010. I should add that the interpretation of the "Pennsylvania 150 Civil War Road Show," a portable museum that in spring 2011 began traveling around the state in a tractor-trailer, is explicit about the state's industrial contributions to the war, quantifying its provisions of oil, coal, lumber, iron, clothing, food, and ammunition. I saw the exhibit for the first time in Gettysburg on June 12, 2011, as this book was in its final editing stage.

38. "Pennsylvania Civil War Trails: Road to Gettysburg: Defending the Commonwealth/Road to Harrisburg: The Pennsylvania Breadbasket" (Harrisburg: PA Tourism Office, n.d., obtained by author in summer 2008); "Gettysburg: 2010 Attractions and Dining Guide" (Gettysburg: Gettysburg Convention and Visitors Bureau, 2010), 27.

39. "Civil War Trails," *Hershey Harrisburg Regional Visitors Guide* (Harrisburg: Hershey Harrisburg Regional Visitors Bureau, 2010), 26.

40. National Civil War Museum website, accessed July 26, 2010, http://www.nationalcivilwarmuseum.org/node/298.

41. visitPA Civil War Trails website, accessed on May 31, 2010, http://www.pacivilwartrails.com/index.aspx.

42. Robert M. Archibald, *A Place to Remember: Using History to Build Community* (Walnut Creek, CA: AltaMira Press, 1999), 66.

43. Author's telephone interview with Edie Shean-Hammond on January 4, 2008.

Bibliography

PRIMARY SOURCES

Press Coverage

ABC News/*USA Today. 50 States in 50 Days.* Special edition DVD included in *America Speaks: The Historic 2008 Election.* Chicago: Triumph Books, 2008.

Bachko, Katia. "Talking Shop: Dennis Roddy: *Pittsburgh Post-Gazette* Reporter Talks About the Recession's Effects in Western Pennsylvania." *Columbia Journalism Review,* May 28, 2009. Accessed May 30, 2009. http://www.cjr.org.campaign_desk-talking_shop_Dennis_Roddy_1.php.

Berg, Christian D. "Memorial Would Honor Steel Workers." *Allentown Morning Call,* April 28, 1998.

Biro, Ilona. "The Comeback Kid." *Toronto Globe and Mail,* February 21, 1998, F1.

Blood, Michael (Associated Press). "History's Mother Lode." *Philadelphia Inquirer,* October 15, 1991, B2.

Bobbin, Jennifer. "Art Meets Metal: The Story of Wilton Armetale." *Susquehanna Life* (Fall 2007): 26–29.

Bodine, A. Aubrey. "America's Greatest Farm Museum." *Sunday Baltimore Sun Magazine,* November 9, 1958, 15–18.

Brenckle, Lara. "Soggy Day Doesn't Slow Harley Celebration." *Harrisburg Patriot-News,* June 21, 2009, A5.

Brougher, Farron D. "The Purple Heart Highway: 100 Miles of Whatever You Want It to Be." *Susquehanna Life* (Spring 2007): 34–35, 50–51.

Bryant, John. "Unemployment: The Theme Park." *New York Times,* January 28, 1996, sec. 6, 46.

Bumiller, Elisabeth. "Bush Meets Rescued Miners, Saying They Represent Spirit of America." *New York Times,* August 6, 2002, A10.

Butterbaugh, Kelly Ann. "Celebrating the Horse, Buggy, and Whip." *Pennsylvania Magazine* (May/June 2009): 12–13.

———. "Farming the Past: A View of Daily Life on an 1800s Farm." *Pennsylvania Magazine* (September/October 2007): 14–16.

CBS Morning News. "Rescue of Nine Trapped Miners Giving Americans a Happy Story to Focus on Amidst Market Scandals and Terrorism." Columbia Broadcasting System, July 30, 2007. Transcript accessed via LexisNexis academic database on October 25, 2005.

"Cheers and Jeers." *Harrisburg Patriot-News,* July 7, 2007, A7.

Christian, Sherry, reporter. "Special Report: The Future of Hershey." WHP-TV (Channel 21), November 26, 2007.

Clark, Jayne. "Pittsburgh Forges Ahead." *USA Today,* July 18, 2008, 1D, 2D.

Courogen, Chris A. "Walking 'Exhibit' to Share Trail Tales." *Harrisburg Patriot-News,* November 1, 2009, A6.

DeWolf, Rose. "What Happened Here? Coal Happened Here." *Sunday Bulletin Magazine* (August 3, 1969): 6–9.

Duarte, Gema Maria. "Borough Council Upset over Change in Developer's Plans." *Bucks County Courier Times*, November 19, 2009. Accessed May 24, 2010. http://infoweb .newsbank.com.

Dunkle, David. "Delicious Days." *Harrisburg Patriot-News*, October 5, 2006, *Go!* weekend sec., 3.

———. "Whitaker Center Exhibit Gives Sense of Factory Work." *Harrisburg Patriot-News*, January 17, 2009, B2.

Elliott, Stuart. "They're Looking for a Few Good Coal Miners." *New York Times*, March 23, 2007, C3.

"Ethnic Food, Music at Heritage Fest." *Harrisburg Patriot-News*, September 13, 2009, B8.

Fernandez, Bernard. "Lehigh Valley is High on Its Hogs, the IronPigs." *Philadelphia Daily News*, March 28, 2008, 118.

Fishlock, Diana. "State Hopes to Keep Economic Engine." *Harrisburg Patriot-News*, November 30, 2009, A1, A2.

Frederick, Don. "Hillary Clinton Returns to Her Roots in Scranton." *Los Angeles Times*, March 10, 2008. Accessed February 16, 2010. http://latimesblogs.latimes.com/washing ton/2008/03/clinton-in-scra.html.

Garvey, Allison, and Barbara Miller. "A Star Reborn." *Harrisburg Patriot-News*, July 1, 2008, B1, B12.

Gerstenzang, Peter. "A Journey Shaped by a Guitar." *New York Times*, February 22, 2008, F-1.

Gibb, Tom. "Crying Time Again: All Through Somerset County, Mine Families Maintain a Vigil." *Pittsburgh Post-Gazette*, July 26, 2002, A12.

Griffith, Randy. "Resurrection Church Rises from Cambria City Parishes." *Johnstown Tribune-Democrat*, July 27, 2009. Accessed November 1, 2009. http://www.tribune-democrat .com/multimedia/local_story_207225744.html.

Guydish, Mark. "Bishop's Plan Will Close 39 Churches in County." *Wilkes-Barre Times Leader*, April 12, 2009. Accessed November 1, 2009. http://www.timesleader.com/news/hot topics/churchclosings/.

Hamill, Sean D. "Mexican's Death Bares a Town's Ethnic Tension." *New York Times*, August 5, 2008, A12.

"Harley-Davidson Hits Bump." *Harrisburg Patriot-News*, January 24, 2009, A6.

Harris, Patricia, and David Lyon. "Snack-Food Factory Tours Are Worth Savoring." *Boston Globe*, June 29, 2005, F11.

Henson, Rich. "Borough Seeks a Future in its Past: With Factories Idle, Bristol Has Been Learning to Market its Centuries-Old Charm." *Philadelphia Inquirer*, February 8, 1993, B1.

"Hershey Pays Homage to Founder." *Harrisburg Patriot-News*, September 13, 2007, A2.

Hoekstra, Dave. "'Making It' in York—That's York, Pa." *Chicago Sun-Times*, May 18, 2003, travel sec.

Hopey, Don. "Drilling Stalled in Allegheny National Forest." *Pittsburgh Post-Gazette*, March 16, 2009. Accessed September 26, 2009. http://www.post-gazette.com/pg/09075/955 874–85.stm.

Horsley, Scott, reporter, and Steve Inskeep, host. "GOP Ticket in Hershey, Pennsylvania." *Morning Edition*. National Public Radio, October 29, 2008. Transcript accessed via LexisNexis academic database on October 31, 2008.

Hunsinger, Lou Jr. "Ten Hours or No Sawdust." *Williamsport Sun-Gazette*, n.d., 1976. Accessed February 21, 2010. http://www.historicwilliamsport.com/Features/Sawdust%20 War.htm.

Issenberg, Sasha. "The Simplest Life: Why Americans Romanticize the Amish." *Washington Monthly* (October 2004): 39–40.

Jeffrey, Laura Stassi. "Vroom, Vroom: Pa. Harley Tour Gets Motors Running." *Washington Post,* September 24, 2008, C02.

Johnson, Nancy Polinsky. "Letters: Forge a Steel Museum." *Pittsburgh Post-Gazette,* November 19, 2002, C14.

Johnston, Liz. "Crunch Time in Snack HQ." *Queensland Sunday Mail,* May 8, 2005, E18.

Kahn, Roy. "Just an Average Joe." *Pittsburgh* (November 1985): 17–18.

King, Neil Jr. "As Oil Prices Soar, Prospectors Return to Pennsylvania." *Wall Street Journal* (eastern edition), February 19, 2008, A1. Accessed via Proquest database on September 26, 2009.

"Kiss Jobs Goodbye." *Harrisburg Patriot-News,* February 16, 2007, C1, C4.

Klaus, Mary. "A Huge Kiss." *Harrisburg Patriot-News,* July 8, 2007, B1, B4.

———. "Landis Valley Fair Trip to Past." *Harrisburg Patriot-News,* June 3, 1994, C5.

———. "Memories of Coal, Rail Eras Still Much Alive in Scranton." *Harrisburg Sunday Patriot-News,* January 15, 1989, G8.

———. "State Fairs Offer Visitors a Glimpse of Nation's Agrarian Traditions." *Harrisburg Patriot-News,* July 9, 2009, E1, E10.

"KOZ." *Harrisburg Patriot-News,* March 22, 2009, F2.

Lewis, Jim. "Costly Renewal." *Harrisburg Patriot-News,* October 2, 2006, A1, A12.

———. "Switch from Coal to Gas?" *Harrisburg Patriot-News,* June 23, 2008, A1, A10.

Longman, Jere. "A Link Forged by Tragedy." *New York Times,* February 3, 2006, C1, C17.

"A Lot of Fear." *Harrisburg Patriot-News,* March 27, 2007, A1, A5.

Luciew, John. "Business is Brewing." *Harrisburg Patriot-News,* March 29, 2009, A1, A14–15.

———. "From Ashes of Steel, a Future is Forged," *Harrisburg Patriot-News,* September 20, 2009, A26.

———. "Welcome to Steelers Country." *Harrisburg Patriot-News,* February 1, 2009, C1, C3.

Marchese, John. "Scranton Embraces the 'Office' Infamy." *New York Times,* October 21, 2007, "Television" sec., 1.

McPherson, Kimra. "Erie Shakes off Ashes of Industry, Attempts to Dress for Company." *Erie Times-News,* August 25, 2002, L1.

Medina, Regina. "Town Torn Apart: Shenandoah's Ethnic Strife and Violence Bring America's Immigration Issue into Sharp Focus." *Philadelphia Daily News,* September 17, 2008, 3–4, 24, 31.

Miller, Dan, and Robyn Sidersky. "Growth is Brewing." *Harrisburg Patriot-News,* June 26, 2010, A1, A12.

Miller, Peter. "Pittsburgh: Stronger than Steel." *National Geographic* (December 1991): 125–45.

NBC Nightly News. "Miners in Somerset County, Pennsylvania, Say They Try Not to Think About Potential Hazards of Coal Mining." National Broadcasting Company, July 27, 2002. Transcript accessed via LexisNexis academic database on October 25, 2005.

Nesvisky, Matt. "Touring Plants, Not Mansions." *New York Times,* March 25, 2001, sec. 5, 1 (International).

Newall, Mike, and Doron Taussig. "Coatesville is Burning." *Philadelphia City Paper,* February 12–19, 2009, 16–21.

"New Steelton." *Harrisburg Patriot-News,* January 7, 2009, A8.

Olivo, Antonio. "Immigrant's Death Splits Blue-Collar Town." *Chicago Tribune,* August 12, 2008. Accessed November 7, 2009. http://www.chicagotribune.com/news/national world/chi-hatecrimeaug12,0,47994865.story.

Opilo, Emily. "Steelton Factory to Add 200 Jobs." *Harrisburg Patriot-News,* February 19, 2009, A8.

Osgood, George. "Coal Festival 'A Uniting Force' in Pennsylvania." *Elmira Star-Gazette*, May 20, 2008. Accessed July 7, 2008. http://stargazette.com.

"Pennsylvania Farm Show: 95 Reasons to Go!" *Harrisburg Patriot-News*, January 6, 2001, overwrap.

"Pennsylvania Miners' Survival, Rescue Renews Faith in America." *USA Today*, July 31, 2002, 11A.

Perlman, Ellen. "Keep on Noshin': Pennsylvania's Junk Food Trail." *Washington Post*, March 8, 2006, C02.

Pickel, Janet. "'The New Steelton' See Small Gains." *Harrisburg Patriot-News*, January 2, 2009. Accessed January 28, 2010. http://www.pennlive.com/midstate/index.ssf/2009/01/the_new_steelton_sees_small_ga.html.

Plushnick-Masti, Ramit (Associated Press). "Pittsburgh: City Celebrates Its Past, Future After 250 Years." *Harrisburg Patriot-News*, November 30, 2008, G10.

Powell, Michael. "Democrats in Steel Country See Skin Color, and Beyond It." *New York Times*, October 27, 2008, A1, A18.

Quigley, Roger. "Down on the Farm." *Harrisburg Patriot-News*, September 5, 2009, A4.

Radzievich, Nicole. "Valley to Get a Peek at Industrial History." *Allentown Morning Call*, August 7, 2006, B1.

Roberts, Robin. "Whistle-Stop America: Voices from the Train." In *America Speaks: The Historic 2008 Election*. Chicago: Triumph Books, 2008.

Robinson, Constance. "Discover Our History at the Seventh Annual Juneteenth Celebration." *Williamsport Guardian*, May 2006. Accessed February 21, 2010. http://www.williamsportguardian.com/?article=200605011502.

Ross, Cindy. "A Showplace of a Town." *Pennsylvania Magazine* (September/October 2009): 9–11.

Roth, Mark. "Homestead Works: Steel Lives in Its Stories." *Pittsburgh Post-Gazette*, July 30, 2006. Accessed January 21, 2010. http://www.post-gazette.com/pg/06211/709449-85.stm.

Ruth, Jim. "Landis Valley: Window on the Past." *Lancaster Sunday News*, September 30, 1979, F1, F3.

Scherer, Ron. "Forging a Future Beyond Steel." *Christian Science Monitor*, February 11, 1998, 10.

Schlegel, Jeff. "36 Hours in Pittsburgh." *New York Times*, July 6, 2008, TR10.

Seelye, Katherine. "One Clinton Hometown Sees Her in Images Befitting a '50s Movie." *New York Times*, March 10, 2008, A13.

Sell, Jill. "Thousands of Harley Lovers Head to Pennsylvania Shrine." *Cleveland Plain Dealer*, September 22, 2002, L5.

Sharkey, Joe. "Resurrecting the Miner's World." *New York Times*, June 9, 2000, sec. E-2, 25.

Simonich, Milan. "After Year, Tourists Still Dig Site of Miners' Rescue in Quecreek, Pa." *Pittsburgh Post-Gazette*, July 25, 2003.

Sloan, Gene. "Hershey Honors its Past, Looks to the Future." *USA Today*, May 17, 2007. Accessed May 18, 2007. http://www.usatoday.com/travel/destinations/2007-05-07-hersheypark-anniversary_N.htm.

Smith, Sharon. "Founder's Family Saddened by Price of Globalization." *Harrisburg Patriot-News*, April 4, 2007, C1, C4.

Smykla, Margaret. "Steelworkers Asked Back to Carrie Furnace for Tour." *Pittsburgh-Post Gazette*, August 10, 2006. Accessed June 21, 2007. http://www.post-gazette.com.

Sojak, Frank. "Celebrating Somerset." *Johnstown Tribune-Democrat* (Somerset edition), July 29, 2005, A1, A4.

"Steel-History Exhibit Featured in Museum." *Harrisburg Patriot Evening News*, August 19, 1976.

Streitfeld, David. "Rock Bottom for Decades, but Showing Signs of Life." *New York Times*, February 1, 2009, sec. 1, 14.

Strumph, Dan. "Stumping for Jobs." *Harrisburg Patriot-News*, May 14, 2009, A17.

Talbott, Ryan. "Oil Wells Drain Beauty from State Forests." *Harrisburg Sunday Patriot-News*, April 27, 2008, F1, F4.

"Ten Memorable Days in Pennsylvania." Harrisburg: Department of Commerce, Commonwealth of Pennsylvania, 1952; reprinted from *Better Homes and Gardens* (April 1952).

"Tours of Factories Produce Made-in-America Vacations." *Arkansas Democrat-Gazette*, May 6, 2001, H2.

Trozzo, Sandy. "A Future in the Past; Group Hoping Historic Sites Will Generate Tourism." *Pittsburgh Post-Gazette*, March 17, 1991, V1.

Turner, Ford. "A Town Divided." *Harrisburg Patriot-News*, December 22, 2009, A1, A18.

"Two Pennsylvania Towns Recall Days When Coal Was King." *New York Times*, March 22, 1981, travel sec., 3.

Urbina, Ian. "For Host City, G-20 Is a Shot at Image Repair." *New York Times*, September 24, 2009, A26.

———. "King Coal Country Debates a Sacrilege, Gas Heat." *New York Times*, June 10, 2008, A1, A16.

Victor, Daniel. "Small Town Shrugs Off Controversy." *Harrisburg Patriot-News*, April 14, 2008, A1, A5.

———. "What Would Milton Do?" *Harrisburg Patriot-News*, March 16, 2007, A1, A12.

White, Dan. "Biking Coal Country's Tracks and Tunnels." *The New York Times*, October 23, 2009, C30, C31.

Witmer, Ann. "Who Says Camp Is for Kids? Adults Can Milk Cows, Canoe." *Harrisburg Sunday Patriot-News*, September 13, 2009, B4.

Yates, Jennifer C. (Associated Press). "City Celebrates 250th with Year of Activities." *Harrisburg Patriot-News*, December 30, 2007, G1, G12.

Yenckel, James T. "Two Pennsylvania Paths: A Scenic Drive Through the Past in the Alleghenies." *Washington Post*, April 30, 1995, E1.

"York, Pa., Factory Fest Has It Made." *Boston Herald*, June 17, 2001, A28.

Tourism and Public History Media (Including Documentaries)

All in Pennsylvania. Harrisburg: Pennsylvania Department of Commerce, Commonwealth of Pennsylvania, no year given but apparently 1940s.

"Along the Highway Guide." Ligonier, PA: Lincoln Highway Heritage Corridor, n.d.

"America is Beautiful: See for Yourself on Amtrak." Amtrak: n.d., in use in 2007.

"Artisan Trail in the Pennsylvania Wilds." Pennsylvania State Tourism Office, n.p., n.d.

"Art Thrives on 45." Advertisement. N.p., n.d.

Aurand, Harold W. *Anthracite Heritage Museum and Scranton Iron Furnaces*. Harrisburg: Pennsylvania Historical and Museum Commission/Stackpole Books, 2002.

Bellury, Phillip R., and Gail Guterl. *The History of Herr's*. Nottingham, PA: Herr Foods Inc., 1995.

Beyer, George R. *Guide to the State Historical Markers of Pennsylvania*. Harrisburg: Pennsylvania Historical and Museum Commission, 2000.

"'Black Diamonds': Experience Pennsylvania's Anthracite Mining Heritage." Accessed May 29, 2010. http://www.pacoalhistory.com.

Blatz, Perry. *Eckley Miners' Village.* Harrisburg, PA: Pennsylvania Historical and Museum Commission/Stackpole Books, 2003.

Boyd, Therese. *The Best Places You've Never Seen: Pennsylvania's Small Museums: A Traveler's Guide.* University Park: Penn State University Press, 2003.

Boynton, Heather. "A City Recast." In *Pennsylvania Travel Guide,* 30–33. Harrisburg: Pennsylvania Tourism Office, 2006/7.

Bruce, Robert. *The Lincoln Highway in Pennsylvania.* Washington, DC: American Automobile Association/National Highways Association, 1920.

Burkett, Amy, exec. prod. *Bethlehem Steel: The People Who Built America.* Bethlehem, PA: Lehigh Valley PBS/WLVT-TV, 2003.

Butko, Brian. *The Lincoln Highway: Pennsylvania Traveler's Guide.* 2nd ed. Mechanicsburg, PA: Stackpole Books, 2002.

Carrie Furnaces. DVD. Pittsburgh: Rivers of Steel National Heritage Area, n.d.

"A Century of Steelworkers: Pump House Banners." Pittsburgh: Battle of Homestead Foundation and the United Steelworkers of America, 2004.

"Civil War Connection." *Hershey Harrisburg 2009 Regional Visitors Guide.* Harrisburg: Hershey Harrisburg Regional Visitors Bureau, 2009.

"Civil War Trails." *Hershey Harrisburg Regional Visitors Guide: 2010 Edition.* Harrisburg: Hershey Harrisburg Regional Visitors Bureau, 2010.

Clark, Mabel K. "Ida Tarbell." Historic Pennsylvania Leaflet no. 22. Titusville: Pennsylvania Historical and Museum Commission, 1997.

Come to Pennsylvania and Get to Know America. Harrisburg: Pennsylvania Bureau of Travel Development, 1976.

"Come Visit 'The Road that Built the Nation': Thirty-Fifth Annual National Road Festival, May 16–18, 2008." Brochure.N.p., n.d.

Cornwall Furnace: Historic Charcoal Iron Furnace. Harrisburg: Pennsylvania Historical and Museum Commission, 1946.

Crammer, Cara Williams, exec. prod. *Explore PA: Fairs and Festivals: York.* Harrisburg: WITF, 2006.

———. *Explore PA: Pennsylvania Railroads: Altoona.* Harrisburg: WITF, 2007.

———. *Explore PA: Spirit of Independence: The Underground Railroad in Northeast PA.* Harrisburg: WITF, 2007.

Crossroads at Landis Valley. Film presented at the Landis Valley Museum. Harrisburg: Pennsylvania Historical and Museum Commission/Commonwealth Media Services, 2000.

Cupper, Dan. *Railroad Museum of Pennsylvania.* Harrisburg: Pennsylvania Historical and Museum Commission/Stackpole Books, 2002.

Currin, Robert. *Pennsylvania Lumber Museum.* Harrisburg: Pennsylvania Historical and Museum Commission/Stackpole Books, 2005.

Danville, Pennsylvania. Video. No production information given. Danville, PA, 2002.

"The Destination That Will Follow You Home." Harrisburg: Pennsylvania Office of Travel Tourism and Film, 2000?.

Dieffenbach, Sue. *Cornwall Iron Furnace.* Harrisburg: Pennsylvania Historical and Museum Commission/Stackpole Books, 2003.

Discover the New Pennsylvania. Harrisburg: Pennsylvania Department of Commerce, 1964.

Drake Well Memorial Park: Birthplace of the Petroleum Industry. Harrisburg: Pennsylvania Historical and Museum Commission, 1946.

Drake Well Museum and Park. Harrisburg: Pennsylvania Historical and Museum Commission/Stackpole Books, 2002.

English, Annette. "Sawdust War: Jim Washington." Williamsport, PA: Black Studies Center, Lycoming County Bicentennial Committee/Lycoming County Historical Museum, 1976.

"The Enola Yard: A Centennial Celebration: Official Souvenir Program." No publication place given, 2005.

Esso (Standard Oil). "Pennsylvania." Convent Station, NJ: General Drafting Company, 1958.

"Everything Amish—Buggies, Mules, Scooters, and More!" In *Lancaster County: The Heart of Pennsylvania Dutch Country,* 4. Lancaster: Pennsylvania Dutch Convention and Visitors Bureau, 2008.

"Family Adventures. Country Fun." Advertisement for Stoners Dairy Farm in Mercersburg, n.d.

"Family Heritage Day: May 25, 1991." Scranton, PA: Anthracite Heritage Museum, 1991.

Faris, John T. *Seeing Pennsylvania.* Philadelphia: J. B. Lippincott, 1919.

Federal Writers' Project (Works Progress Administration for the Commonwealth of Pennsylvania). *Philadelphia: A Guide to the Nation's Birthplace.* Philadelphia: William Penn Association of Philadelphia/Pennsylvania Historical Museum, 1937.

"Franklin County PA." Tourism promotion booklet. N.p., n.d. (obtained in 2009), 61.

Friends of the Railroad Museum. "Railroad Museum of Pennsylvania Announces Special Events for 30th Anniversary Year." Press release dated January 31, 2005.

Fry, Cara Williams, exec. prod. *Explore PA: Fairs and Festivals: Schuylkill County.* Harrisburg: WITF, 2008.

———. *Explore PA: Pennsylvania Homecomings: Pittsburgh.* Harrisburg: WITF, 2007.

"Gettysburg: 2010 Attractions and Dining Guide." Gettysburg: Gettysburg Convention and Visitors Bureau, 2010.

Glick, Peter. "Industrial Pennsylvania." In *Pennsylvania Highways,* 9. Harrisburg: Pennsylvania Department of Highways, 1930.

"Growing Traditions: Lancaster-York Heritage Region Discovery Guide." Booklet. N.p., n.d.

Guide to the Historical Markers of Pennsylvania. 2nd ed. Harrisburg: Pennsylvania Historical and Museum Commission, 1952.

"Harley-Davidson 2009." Promotional booklet given out at end of plant tour in York, PA. N.p., n.d.

"Having a Chilling Experience: Haunted Excursions at Eckley Miners' Village." *Happenings Magazine: In and Around Northeast Pennsylvania* (October 2007): 58.

Hernandez, Angel, exec. prod. *Explore PA: Bethlehem.* Harrisburg: WITF, 2005.

———. *Explore PA: Crawford County.* Harrisburg: WITF, 2005.

———. *Explore PA: Pittsburgh.* Harrisburg: WITF, 2005.

The Hiawatha Paddlewheeler. Compact disc recording played on the *Hiawatha Paddlewheeler Riverboat* tour in Williamsport, PA. Williamsport, PA: Hiawatha/Williamsport Bureau of Transportation, 1997.

"Highlights of Erie." *Erie Area Visitor Guide, 2007–2008.* Erie: Erie Area Convention and Visitors Bureau, 2007.

Historic Pennsylvania: America's Cradle of Democracy. Harrisburg: Pennsylvania Department of Commerce, 195?.

"History and Heritage Adventures." *Butler County 2008 Official Visitors Guide,* 6–10. N.p., n.d.

"Holiday Heritage Market at the Pump House." Email communication dated December 2, 2010, received by author from Rivers of Steel National Heritage Area.

Hope, John G. *Westsylvania Heritage Trail: A Guide to Southwest Pennsylvania's Historic Places.* Harrisburg: RB Books, 2001.

"Hopewell Furnace: Calendar of Events 2007." Flyer distributed on site. N.p, n.d.

Hopewell Village National Historic Site. National Park Service Historical Handbook Series No. 8. Washington, DC: U.S. Department of the Interior, 1950.

Johnson, Elizabeth. *Landis Valley Museum.* Harrisburg: Pennsylvania Historical and Museum Commission/Stackpole Books, 2002.

Johnstown Area Heritage Association, prod. *The Mystery of Steel.* Film shown at the Johnstown Heritage Discovery Center. Pittsburgh, PA: The Magic Lantern, 2009.

Johnstown, PA Heritage Attractions. Brochure. N.p., 2007.

A Journey Through the Valley That Changed the World. Compact disc recording played on the Oil Creek and Titusville Railroad in Oil Creek State Park near Titusville, PA. Oil City: Oil Creek Railway Historical Society, 2002.

Karaczun, Dan, ed. *Out of This Kitchen: A History of the Ethnic Groups and Their Foods in the Steel Valley.* Pittsburgh: Publassist, 1998.

Kelsey, Tim. *The Joy of Farm Watching: A Roadside Guide to Pennsylvania Agriculture.* University Park: Penn State College of Agricultural Sciences, 2006.

Kyper, Frank. *A Ramble into the Past on the East Broad Top Railroad.* Rockhill Furnace, PA: East Broad Top Railroad and Coal Company, 1971.

Layne, Christine. "It's a Farmer's Life." *Pennsylvania Pursuits* (Spring 2007): 60–63.

"Legendary Ladies: A Guide to Where Women Made History in Pennsylvania: Greater Philadelphia." Harrisburg: Pennsylvania Commission for Women, n.d.

"Legendary Ladies: A Guide to Where Women Made History in Pennsylvania: Greater Pittsburgh." Harrisburg: Pennsylvania Commission for Women, n.d.

Lincoln Highway Driving Guide. Lincoln Highway Heritage Corridor, n.d.

"Lower Susquehanna River Valley." Tourism brochure. N.p., n.d.

"Made in America Tours, June 17–20, 2009." York: York County Convention and Visitors Bureau, 2008.

"Main Roads in Pennsylvania." In *Pennsylvania: Facts Motorists Should Know,* 6–9. Harrisburg: Department of Highways, 1926.

Martin, Edward. "My Pennsylvania." Introduction to *My Pennsylvania: A Brief History of the Commonwealth's Sixty-Seven Counties,* 1. Harrisburg: Bureau of Publications, Department of Property and Supplies, Commonwealth of Pennsylvania, 1946.

McDonnell, Greg. "The Portage Coal Heritage Auto Tour." Edited by Ginny McDonnell. Portage, PA: Mainline Heritage Association, n.d.

McMahon, James D. Jr. *Built on Chocolate: The Story of the Hershey Chocolate Company.* Los Angeles: General Publishing Group, 1998.

Murrie, Wm. F. B. "To People Everywhere and Especially Children." Press release dated January 5, 1938.

"Native Lands County Park." Wrightsville, PA: Susquehanna Gateway Heritage Area, n.d.

"Navigating . . . Delaware and Lehigh National Heritage Corridor." Easton, PA: Delaware and Lehigh National Heritage Corridor, 2007.

"Nine Decades of Oil." New York: Esso Standard Oil Company, ca. 1950.

"90 Miles of American Heritage." Accessed June 21, 2007. http://www.nationalroadpa.org.

Northeast Pennsylvania Visitors Guide. N.p., February–March 2007.

Nunley, Debbie, and Karen Jane Elliott. *A Taste of Pennsylvania History: A Guide to Historic Eateries and Their Recipes.* Winston-Salem, NC: John F. Blair, 2000.

Odesser-Torpey, Marilyn. *The Hershey, Pennsylvania, Cookbook: Fun Treats and Trivia from the Chocolate Capital of the World.* Guilford, CT: Morris Book Publishing, 2007.

"Oil Centennial, 1859–1959, August 23–29, Titusville, Pennsylvania." Official program. N.p., n.d.

"Oil City Centennial Celebration, Oil City, Pennsylvania, 1871–1971." Pamphlet. N.p., 1971.

Oil Creek State Park: A Contrast in Time. Video shown at the visitor center in Oil Creek State Park near Titusville, PA. Harrisburg: Pennsylvania Department of Conservation and Natural Resources, 2005.

"100 Years of Happy: Hersheypark, Spring and Summer 2007." Hershey: Hersheypark, 2007.

"The Penn Salt National Historic District/Fannie Sellins Labor Heritage Site." Harrison Township/Natrona, PA: Allegheny-Kiski Valley Historical Society, n.d.

In Penn's Woods: A Handy and Helpful Pocket Manual of the Natural Wonders and Recreational Facilities of the State Forests of Pennsylvania. Bulletin 31. Harrisburg: Pennsylvania Department of Forests and Waters, April 1925.

Pennsylvania. Harrisburg: Commonwealth of Pennsylvania, 1944.

"Pennsylvania: America's Industrial Heritage Starts Here." Press release dated April 9, 1990. Harrisburg: Pennsylvania Department of Commerce.

Pennsylvania: America's Tourist State! More Vacation Fun for Everyone in Pennsylvania. Harrisburg: Pennsylvania Department of Commerce, 1962.

Pennsylvania at Your Fingertips. Harrisburg: Bureau of Publications, Department of Property and Supplies, Commonwealth of Pennsylvania, 1940.

"Pennsylvania Civil War Trails: Passport to History." Booklet. N.p., n.d.

"Pennsylvania Civil War Trails: Road to Gettysburg: Defending the Commonwealth/ Road to Harrisburg: The Pennsylvania Breadbasket." Harrisburg: Pennsylvania Tourism Office, n.d. (obtained in summer 2008).

Pennsylvania: Forty Thousand Square Miles: Beautiful Modern Highways and Historic Byways. Harrisburg: State Publicity Bureau, Pennsylvania State Chamber of Commerce, 1925.

Pennsylvania Has Everything: Your Travel Guide to Penn's "Land of the Forest." 6th ed. Harrisburg: Department of Commerce, Commonwealth of Pennsylvania, 1940.

Pennsylvania: 1989–90 Fall/Winter Travel Guide. Harrisburg: Pennsylvania Department of Commerce, Bureau of Travel Marketing, 1989.

Pennsylvania: Official Tourist Guide. Harrisburg: State Publicity Bureau, Pennsylvania State Chamber of Commerce, 1926.

Pennsylvania Panorama. Harrisburg: Pennsylvania Department of Commerce, 194?.

Pennsylvania Route 6: Take the High Road! Pennsylvania's Heritage Route. Galeton: Pennsylvania Route 6 Tourist Association, n.d.

"Pennsylvania's Dairy Farmers Bring More than Just Milk to the Table." Harrisburg: Center for Dairy Excellence, 2006.

"Pennsylvania's Energy Trail of History." *Pennsylvania Pursuits* (Summer 2009): 62–65.

Pennsylvania Trail of History Cookbook. Mechanicsburg: Stackpole Books/Pennsylvania Historical and Museum Commission, 2004.

Pennsylvania Train Stations: Restored and Revitalized. DVD. University Park: Penn State Public Broadcasting, 2007.

"Pennsylvania Wilds Adventure Guide." Harrisburg: Pennsylvania State Tourism Office, n.d.

Pennsylvania Writers Program (Works Progress Administration). *Pennsylvania: A Guide to the Keystone State.* New York: Oxford University Press, 1940.

Perry, Daniel K. *Pennsylvania's Northeast Treasures: A Visitor's Guide to Scranton, the Lackawanna Valley, and Beyond.* Mayfield, PA: Heritage Valley Press, 2007.

Pinchot, Gifford. "The Best Highway System in America." In *Pennsylvania: Facts Motorists Should Know,* 1. Harrisburg: Department of Highways, 1926.

"Pittsburgh and its Countryside." *Pennsylvania Pursuits* (Spring 2008): 75.

Plant Tours. Harrisburg: Pennsylvania Department of Commerce, three undated editions.

"Points of Interest in Pennsylvania." In *Pennsylvania: Facts Motorists Should Know,* 31–32. Harrisburg: Department of Highways, 1926.

Pryor, Bailey, writer, prod., and dir. *Our National Heritage: The Story of America: Episode 1: The Revolutionary River.* DVD. Telemark Films, 2010.

A Public Use Map for Pine Creek Rail Trail. Harrisburg: Pennsylvania Department of Conservation and Natural Resources, 2007.

"Railroaders Memorial Museum and Horseshoe Curve National Historic Landmark Guide." Altoona: Railroaders Memorial Museum, 2007.

Rebecca Webb Lukens Bicentennial, 1794–1994. Coastesville, PA: The Graystone Society, 1994.

Reibel, Daniel B. *Old Economy Village.* Harrisburg: Pennsylvania Historical and Museum Commission/Stackpole Books, 2002.

"The Road to Paradise." Lancaster: The Strasburg Rail Road, 1994.

"Rock and Roll." Scranton: Lackawanna County Convention and Visitors Bureau, n.d.

Routes to Roots: Discover the Cultural and Industrial Heritage of Southwestern Pennsylvania. Homestead, PA: Rivers of Steel National Heritage Area/Steel Industry Heritage Corporation, 2004.

Rowley, J. Mickey. "From the PA Tourism Office." *Pennsylvania Pursuits* (Winter 2007): 2.

"Rural History Confederation." Promotional pamphlet. N.p., n.d.

Ruth, Philip, prod., dir., and writer. *Silver Cinders: The Legacy of Coal and Coke in Southwestern Pennsylvania.* DVD. North Wales, PA: Cultural Heritage Research Services, 2005.

Samson, Iris, and Pierina Morrelli, prod. *The Valley That Changed the World.* Pittsburgh, PA: WQED Multimedia/Oil Region Alliance, 2009.

"Scranton: The Heart of Northeastern Pennsylvania." Advertisement in *Pennsylvania: Official Tourist Guide.* Harrisburg: State Publicity Bureau, Pennsylvania State Chamber of Commerce, 1926.

Sebak, Rick, prod. and narr. *Invented Engineered and Pioneered in Pittsburgh.* Pittsburgh: WQED Multimedia, 2008.

———. *What Makes Pittsburgh Pittsburgh?* Pittsburgh: WQED Multimedia, 2006.

"Seeing Pennsylvania from the Forest Fire Observation Towers." In *Pennsylvania: Facts Motorists Should Know,* 6. Harrisburg: Department of Highways, 1926.

Sewald, Jeff, prod. and dir. *Gridiron and Steel.* Pittsburgh: Real As Steel Media Ventures, 2001.

Shealey, Tom. *The Stone Coal Way: A Guide to Navigating Delaware and Lehigh National Heritage Corridor Through Eastern Pennsylvania.* Edited by Elissa G. Marsden. Easton, PA: Delaware and Lehigh National Heritage Corridor, 2004.

Shoemaker, Henry W. "Off the Beaten Path on Pennsylvania State Highways." In *Pennsylvania: Facts Motorists Should Know,* 10–11. Harrisburg: Department of Highways, 1926.

"Shunpiker's Guide: Coal County." *Harrisburg Patriot-News,* February 10, 2008, G10.

"Shunpiker's Guide: PA Roadtrips: Cruising the Artisan Cheese Trail in Franklin County." *Harrisburg Patriot-News,* January 14, 2007, G15.

Simpson, Bill. *Guide to Pennsylvania's Tourist Railroads.* 2nd ed. Gretna, LA: Pelican Publishing, 2003.

The State Forests of Pennsylvania. Harrisburg: Department of Forests and Waters, Commonwealth of Pennsylvania, 1946.

Stories of the Land Along Dutch Country Roads. DVD. Wrightsville, PA: Lancaster-York Heritage Region, 2006.

"Take the Scenic Pennsylvania Route 6." Harrisburg: Pennsylvania Tourism Office, n.d.

Tarkowski, Mary. "Artisan Paradise on Route 45." In *Pennsylvania: Travel Guide.* N.p., n.d.

Thayer, Jr., Guy V., exec. prod. *Born in Freedom: The Story of Colonel Drake.* Film shown and sold at Drake Well. Washington, DC: American Petroleum Institute, 1954.

"There's More in Pennsylvania." Harrisburg: Commonwealth of Pennsylvania, Department of Commerce, 1947?.

Traux, Doug. *Woolrich: 175 Years of Excellence.* South Boardman, MI: Crofton Creek Press, 2005.

Treese, Lorett. *Somerset Historical Center.* Harrisburg: Pennsylvania Historical and Museum Commission/Stackpole Books, 2002.

"2007 PA Route 6 Artisan Trail." Published jointly by several Route 6–area tourism bureaus, 2007.

Vacation Pleasures in Pennsylvania. Harrisburg: Department of Commerce, Commonwealth of Pennsylvania, ca. 1940s.

Visit the Industries of Pennsylvania: Watch Pennsylvania Make It. Harrisburg: Travel Development Bureau, Pennsylvania Department of Commerce, 1974?.

"Voices from the Ridge: Songs and Stories of Working People and Their Participation in America's Industrial History." Driving-tour audiotape from Folklife Division, America's Industrial Heritage Project. No date or place of production given.

von Spaeth, Erik N., prod. and dir. *The Allegheny Portage Railroad.* Film shown at the Allegheny Portage Railroad National Historic Site. Washington, DC: National Park Service, U.S. Department of the Interior, n.d.

"Walk the Line." *Pennsylvania Pursuits* (Winter 2009): 3.

Washington County Pennsylvania: 2008 Travel Planner and Calendar of Events. Pennsylvania State Tourism Office, no place, n.d.

"Welcome to Pittsburgh and Its Countryside." In *Pittsburgh and Its Countryside: Official Visitors Guide,* 2–3. Harrisburg: Pennsylvania Tourism Office, n.d.

"Williamsport Lycoming County Visitors Guide 2008." Williamsport: Lycoming County Visitors Bureau, 2008.

"Yes! We've Got M-I-L-K!" In *Franklin County, PA,* 40. N.p., 2009.

Yetsko, Barbara, prod. *63 Men Down: The Story of the Sonman Mine Explosion.* DVD. Portage, PA: Portage Area Historical Society, n.d.

"York County Pennsylvania 2008 Visitors Guide." York: York County Convention and Visitors Bureau, 2008.

Your Guide to Pennsylvania's Laurel Highlands, 2008. Ligonier: Laurel Highlands Visitors Bureau, 2008.

"Your Pennsylvania." Harrisburg: Department of Commerce, Commonwealth of Pennsylvania, 1948.

"You Touch the History. The History Touches You." *Pennsylvania Pursuits* (Spring 2008): 56.

You've Got a Friend in Pennsylvania. Harrisburg: Pennsylvania Department of Commerce, 1980.

"Yuengling: America's Oldest Brewery." Pottsville, PA: Yuengling, 2007.

Other Primary Sources

"America from the Great Depression to World War II: Black-and-White Photographs from the FSA-OWI, 1935–1945." "American Memory" digital collection, Prints and Photographs Division, Library of Congress. Accessed January 16, 2010. http://memory.loc .gov/ammem/fsahtml/fahome.html.

Callahan, John. State of the City Address, February 19, 2009. Accessed January 26, 2010. http://www.bethlehem-pa.gov/about/state_of_city/index.htm.

"C-Day at Titusville." *Orange Disk* (September-October 1959): 4–7.

"A Common Canvas: Pennsylvania's New Deal Post Office Murals." Exhibit at the State Museum of Pennsylvania, Harrisburg, November 22, 2008, to May 17, 2009. Curated by Curt Miner and Dave Lembeck.

Cope, Francis R. Jr. "New Objectives in Forestry." *Forest Leaves* 26, no. 4 (October 1936): 11–14, 27–30. Wayne, PA: The Pennsylvania Forestry Association.

Cupper, Dan. *75th Farm Show: A History of Pennsylvania's Annual Agricultural Exposition.* Harrisburg: Pennsylvania Historical and Museum Commission, 1991.

"Designing Interpretation for the Bethlehem Steel Site . . . and Beyond." Working document prepared by the Mid-Atlantic Regional Center for the Humanities, September 11, 2007. Accessed May 29, 2010. http://march.rutgers.edu/bethSteelJuneconf.htm.

"Economic Impact of Pennsylvania's Heritage Areas, 2008." Report dated February 11, 2010. Available on the website of the Alliance of National Heritage Areas. Accessed January 6, 2011. http://www.nationalheritageareas.com/documents/.

First Report of the Historical Commission of Pennsylvania: To the Governor of Pennsylvania and the General Assembly. Lancaster: New Era Printing Company, 1915.

Foster, Stephen Collins. "Hard Times Come Again No More." Washington, DC: Public Broadcasting Service, n.d. Accessed February 16, 2010. http://www.pbs.org/wgbh/amex/foster/gallery/pop_ie_hardtimes_listen.html.

Giles, Don, photographer, and Robert Weible, exhibit coordinator. "Steel: Made in Pennsylvania." Exhibition sponsored by the Society of Industrial Archaeology, the State Museum of Pennsylvania, the National Museum of Industrial History, and the Rivers of Steel National Heritage Area, 2006–2008.

Heritage Areas Program Manual. Harrisburg: Bureau of Recreation and Conservation, Pennsylvania Department of Conservation and Natural Resources, 2006.

Le, Yen, Margaret Littlejohn, and Michael A. Schuett. *Hopewell Furnace National Historic Site: Visitor Study, Summer 2002.* Washington, DC: National Park Service Visitor Services Project, 2002.

Made in Pennsylvania: An Overview of the Major Historical Industries of the Commonwealth. Harrisburg: Pennsylvania Historical and Museum Commission, 1991.

"Moving Heritage Tourism Forward in Pennsylvania." Harrisburg: Pennsylvania Department of Conservation and Natural Resources, Pennsylvania Department of Community and Economic Development, Pennsylvania Historical and Museum Commission, and the Center for Rural Pennsylvania, May 2001.

"Operation Heritage: Preserving Our Past: An Investment in Our Future." Harrisburg: Pennsylvania Historical and Museum Commission, n.d.

The Pennsylvania Historical and Museum Commission, 1945–1950. Harrisburg: Pennsylvania Historical and Museum Commission, 1950.

"Pennsylvania Historical Marker Program: A Preliminary Analysis of Geographic and Categorical Trends, 1946–2001." Harrisburg: Pennsylvania Historical and Museum Commission Division of History, 2001.

Plans for Pennsylvania Week (October 17–24, 1949). Harrisburg: Department of Commerce, Commonwealth of Pennsylvania, 1949.

Shifflet, D. K., and Associates. *Pennsylvania Heritage Tourism Study.* Prepared for the Pennsylvania Department of Conservation and Natural Resources in partnership with the Pennsylvania Department of Community and Economic Development, the Pennsylvania Historical and Museum Commission, Preservation Pennsylvania, and the Federation of Museums and Historical Organizations, McLean, VA, May 1999.

The Story of the Old Company. Lansford, PA: Lehigh Navigation Coal Company Inc., 1941.

Stynes, Daniel, and Ya-Yen Sun. *Lackawanna Valley National Heritage Area Visitors Survey and Economic Impact Analysis.* East Lansing: Michigan State University Department of Community, Agriculture, Recreation, and Resource Studies, 2004.

"VP Debate." *Saturday Night Live.* First aired on October 4, 2008, on the National Broadcasting Corporation (NBC) and subsequently re-aired on several broadcasts of the

Saturday Night Live Presidential Bash, including on January 18, 2008. Accessed January 19, 2008. http://www.nbc.com/Saturday_Night_Live/video/clips/vp-debate-open-palin-biden/727421/.

Waters, R. Hadly. "Analysis of the Tourist Industry in Pennsylvania." Bulletin No. 33. State College: The Pennsylvania State College, 1947.

SECONDARY SOURCES

Abrams, James F. "Lost Frames of Reference: Sightings of History and Memory in Pennsylvania's Documentary Landscape." In *Conserving Culture: A New Discourse on Heritage,* edited by Mary Hufford, 24–38. Urbana: University of Illinois Press, 1994.

Alberts, Robert C. *The Good Provider: H. J. Heinz and His 57 Varieties.* Boston: Houghton Mifflin, 1973.

Archibald, Robert. *The New Town Square: Museums and Communities in Transition.* Walnut Creek, CA: AltaMira Press, 2004.

———. "A Personal History of Memory." In *Social Memory and History: Anthropological Perspectives,* edited by Jacob J. Climo and Maria G. Cattell, 65–80. Walnut Creek, CA: Alta Mira Press, 2002.

———. *A Place to Remember: Using History to Build Community.* Walnut Creek, CA: AltaMira Press, 1999.

Aron, Cindy S. *Working at Play: A History of Vacations in the United States.* New York: Oxford University Press, 1999.

Ashworth, G. J., and P. J. Larkham, eds. *Building a New Heritage: Tourism, Culture, and Identity.* London: Routledge, 1994.

Barthel, Diane. "Getting in Touch with History: The Role of Historic Preservation in Shaping Collective Memories." *Qualitative Sociology* 19, no. 3 (1996): 245–364.

———. *Historic Preservation: Collective Memory and Historical Identity.* New Brunswick, NJ: Rutgers University Press, 1996.

Barton, Michael, and Simon J. Bronner. "Introduction." In *Images of America: Steelton,* 7–10. Charleston, SC: Arcadia Publishing, 2008.

Beck, Larry, and Ted Cable. *Interpretation for the Twenty-First Century: Fifteen Guiding Principles for Interpreting Nature and Culture.* Champaign, IL: Sagamore Publishing, 1998.

Bennett, Tony. "Museums and 'The People.'" In *The Museum Time-Machine: Putting Cultures on Display,* edited by Robert Lumley, 63–85. London: Routledge, 1988.

Birkner, Michael J., ed. "Deindustrialization: A Panel Discussion." *Pennsylvania History* 58, no. 3 (July 1991): 181–211.

Blatti, Jo. "Introduction: Past Meets Present: Field Notes on Historical Sites, Programs, Professionalism, and Visitors." In *Past Meets Present: Essays About Historic Interpretation and Public Audiences,* edited by Jo Blatti, 1–20. Washington, DC: Smithsonian Institution Press, 1987.

Blewett, Mary H. "Machines, Workers, and Capitalists: The Interpretation of Textile Industrialization in New England Museums." In *History Museums in the United States: A Critical Assessment,* edited by Warren Leon and Roy Rosenzweig, 262–93. Urbana: University of Illinois Press, 1989.

Bluestone, Barry, and Bennett Harrison. *The Deindustrialization of America: Plant Closing, Community Abandonment, and the Dismantling of Basic Industry.* New York: Basic Books, 1982.

Bodnar, John. *Immigration and Industrialization: Ethnicity in an American Mill Town, 1870–1940.* Pittsburgh: University of Pittsburgh Press, 1977.

————. *Remaking America: Public Memory, Commemoration, and Patriotism in the Twentieth Century*. Princeton, NJ: Princeton University Press, 1992.

Boswell, David, and Jessica Evans, eds. *Representing the Nation: A Reader: Histories, Heritage and Museums*. London: Routlege, 1999.

Bronner, Simon J. *Killing Tradition: Inside Hunting and Animal Rights Controversies*. Lexington: University Press of Kentucky, 2008.

————. *Popularizing Pennsylvania: Henry W. Shoemaker and the Progressive Uses of Folklore and History*. University Park: Penn State University Press, 1996.

Camp, Scott D. *Worker Response to Plant Closings: Steelworkers in Johnstown and Youngstown*. New York: Garland Publishing, 1995.

Cohen, Lizabeth. "What Kind of World Have We Lost? Workers' Lives and Deindustrialization in the Museum." *American Quarterly* 41 (December 1989): 670–81.

Corner, John, and Sylvia Harvey. "Mediating Tradition and Modernity: The Heritage/Enterprise Couplet." In *Enterprise and Heritage: Crosscurrents of National Culture*, edited by John Corner and Sylvia Harvey, 45–75. London: Routledge, 1991.

Corsane, Gerard, ed. *Heritage, Museums and Galleries: An Introductory Reader*. London: Routledge, 2005.

Cowie, Jefferson, and Joseph Heathcott. "Introduction: The Meanings of Deindustrialization." In *Beyond the Ruins: The Meanings of Deindustrialization*, edited by Jefferson Cowie and Joseph Heathcott, 1–15. Ithaca, NY: ILR Press, 2003.

D'Antonio, Michael. *Hershey: Milton S. Hershey's Extraordinary Life of Wealth, Empire, and Utopian Dreams*. New York: Simon and Schuster, 2006.

Davis, Susan G. "'Set Your Mood to Patriotic': History as Televised Special Event." *Radical History Review* 42 (Fall 1988): 122–43.

Delaney, Linda K. *The Gamble for Glory in the World's First Billion Dollar Oilfield*. Bradford, PA: Forest Press, 2007.

Dicks, Bella. *Culture on Display: The Production of Contemporary Visitability*. Maidenhead, UK: Open University Press, 2003.

————. *Heritage, Place, and Community*. Cardiff: University of Wales Press, 2000.

Drucker, Susan J., and Robert S. Cathcart. "The Hero as a Communication Phenomenon." In *American Heroes in a Media Age*, edited by Susan J. Drucker and Robert S. Cathcart, 1–11. Cresskill, NJ: Hampton Press, 1994.

Dublin, Thomas. *When the Mines Closed: Stories of Struggles in Hard Times*. Ithaca: Cornell University Press, 1998.

Dublin, Thomas, and Walter Licht. *The Face of Decline: The Pennsylvania Anthracite Region in the Twentieth Century*. Ithaca: Cornell University Press, 2005.

Dudley, Kathryn Marie. *The End of the Line: Lost Jobs, New Lives in Postindustrial America*. Chicago: University of Chicago Press, 1994.

Durel, John, and Anita Nowery Durel. "A Golden Age for Historic Properties." *History News* (Summer 2007): 7–15.

Edensor, Tim. *Industrial Ruins: Spaces, Aesthetics, and Materiality*. Oxford: Berg, 2005.

Edwards, J. Arwel, and Joan Carles Llurdés i Coit. "Mines and Quarries: Industrial Heritage Tourism." *Annals of Tourism Research* 23, no. 2 (1996): 341–63.

Eggert, Gerald G. *The Iron Industry in Pennsylvania*. Pennsylvania Historical Studies No. 25. Harrisburg: Huggins Printing/Pennsylvania Historical Association, 1994.

Fahlman, Betsy, and Eric Schruers. *Wonders of Work and Labor: The Steidle Collection of American Industrial Art*. University Park: Penn State University Press, 2008.

Foote, Kenneth E. *Shadowed Ground: America's Landscapes of Violence and Tragedy*. Austin: University of Texas Press, 1997.

Francaviglia, Richard V. *Hard Places: Reading the Landscape of America's Historic Mining Districts.* Iowa City: University of Iowa Press, 1991.

Frisch, Michael. "De- , Re- , and Post-Industrialization: Industrial Heritage as Contested Memorial Terrain." *Journal of Folklore Research* 35, no. 3 (1998): 241–49.

———. *A Shared Authority: Essays on the Craft and Meaning of Oral and Public History.* Albany: State University of New York Press, 1990.

Frisch, Michael H., and Dwight Pitcaithley. "Audience Expectations as Resource and Challenge: Ellis Island as a Case Study." In *Past Meets Present: Essays About Historic Interpretation and Public Audiences,* edited by Jo Blatti, 153–65. Washington, DC: Smithsonian Institution Press, 1987.

Gans, Herbert J. *Deciding What's News: A Study of CBS Evening News, NBC Nightly News, Newsweek and Time.* New York: Pantheon Books, 1979.

———. "Symbolic Ethnicity: The Future of Ethnic Groups and Cultures in America." *Ethnic and Racial Studies* 2, no. 1 (January 1979): 1–20.

Gillespie, Angus. K. *Folklorist of the Coal Fields: George Korson's Life and Work.* University Park: Penn State University Press, 1980.

Gillette, Howard Jr. *Camden After the Fall: Decline and Renewal in a Post-Industrial City.* Philadelphia: University of Pennsylvania Press, 2005.

Glassberg, David. *American Historical Pageantry: The Uses of Tradition in the Early Twentieth Century.* Chapel Hill: University of North Carolina Press, 1990.

———. *Sense of History: The Place of the Past in American Life.* Amherst: University of Massachusetts Press, 2001.

Goin, Peter, and Elizabeth Raymond. "Living in Anthracite: Mining Landscape and Sense of Place in Wyoming Valley, Pennsylvania." *Public Historian* 23, no. 2 (Spring 2001): 29–45.

Gordon, Robert B. *American Iron, 1607–1900.* Baltimore: Johns Hopkins University Press, 1996.

Graham, Laurie. *Singing the City: The Bonds of Home in an Industrial Landscape.* Pittsburgh: University of Pittsburgh Press, 1998.

Greenwald, Maurine. "Women and Pennsylvania Working-Class History." *Pennsylvania History* 63, no. 1 (Winter 1996): 5–16.

Grele, Ronald J. "Whose Public? Whose History? What is the Goal of the Public Historian?" *Public Historian* 3, no. 1 (Winter 1981): 40–48.

Halbwachs, Maurice. *The Collective Memory.* Translated by Francis J. Ditter Jr. and Vida Yazdi Ditter. New York: Harper and Row, 1950.

Halter, Marilyn. *Shopping for Identity: The Marketing of Ethnicity.* New York: Schocken Books, 2000.

Handler, Richard, and Eric Gable. *The New History in an Old Museum: Creating the Past at Colonial Williamsburg.* Durham: Duke University Press, 1997.

Hareven, Tamara K., and Randolph Langenbach. "Living Places, Work Places, and Historical Identity." In *Our Past Before Us: Why Do We Save It?* edited by David Lowenthal and Marcus Binney, 109–23. London: Temple Smith, 1981.

Harris, Frank. "From the Industrial Revolution to the Heritage Industry." *Geographical Magazine* 61 (May 1989): 38–42.

Harris, Howard, and Mark McCollough. "Introduction." In *Keystone of Democracy: A History of Pennsylvania Workers,* edited by Howard Harris and Perry K. Blatz, xi–xiv. Harrisburg: Pennsylvania Historical and Museum Commission, 1999.

Hayden, Dolores. *The Power of Place: Urban Landscapes as Public History.* Cambridge: MIT Press, 1995.

Hewison, Robert. "Commerce and Culture." In *Enterprise and Heritage: Crosscurrents of National Culture,* edited by John Corner and Sylvia Harvey, 162–77. London: Routledge, 1991.

———. *The Heritage Industry: Britain in a Climate of Decline.* London: Methuen, 1987.

High, Steven. *Industrial Sunset: The Making of North America's Rust Belt, 1969–1984.* Toronto: University of Toronto Press, 2003.

High, Steven, and David W. Lewis. *Corporate Wasteland: The Landscape and Memory of Deindustrialization.* Ithaca: ILR Press/Cornell University Press, 2007.

Hokanson, Drake. *The Lincoln Highway: Main Street Across America.* Iowa City: University of Iowa Press, 1988.

Hollinshead, Keith. "Heritage Tourism in an Age of Historical Amnesia." *World's-Eye View on Hospitality Trends* 11, no. 3 (Fall 1996): 15–19.

Hooper-Greenhill, Eileen. *Museums and the Shaping of Knowledge.* London: Routledge, 1992.

Horne, Donald. *The Great Museum: The Re-presentation of History.* London: Pluto Press, 1984.

Hospers, Gert-Jan. "Industrial Heritage Tourism and Regional Restructuring in the European Union." *European Planning Studies* 10, no. 3 (2002): 397–404.

Hovanec, Evelyn A. *Common Lives of Uncommon Strength: The Women of the Coal and Coke Area of Southwestern Pennsylvania, 1880–1970.* Dunbar, PA: Patch/Work Voices Publishing, 2001.

Hufford, Mary. "Introduction: Rethinking the Cultural Mission." In *Conserving Culture: A New Discourse on Heritage,* edited by Mary Hufford, 1–11. Urbana: University of Illinois Press, 1994.

Hume, Janice. "Changing Characteristics of Heroic Women in Midcentury Mainstream Media." *Journal of Popular Culture* 34, no. 1 (Summer 2000): 9–29.

Hurley, Andrew. "Narrating the Urban Waterfront: The Role of Public History in Community Revitalization." *Public Historian* 28, no. 4: 19–50.

Jackson, John Brinckerhoff. *Discovering the Vernacular Landscape.* New Haven: Yale University Press, 1984.

Jakle, John A., and David Wilson. *Derelict Landscapes: The Wasting of America's Built Environment.* Savage, MD: Rowman and Littlefield, 1992.

Jenkins, J. Geraint. *Getting Yesterday Right: Interpreting the Heritage of Wales.* Cardiff: University of Wales Press, 1992.

Jenkins, Philip. "Mis-Remembering America's Industrial Heritage: The Molly Maguires." Paper presented to the American Historical Association, Pacific Coast Branch, Vancouver, Canada, August 2001.

Jones, Barbara L., with Edward K. Muller and Joel A. Tarr. *Born of Fire: The Valley of Work: Industrial Scenes of Southwestern Pennsylvania.* Westmoreland, PA: Westmoreland Museum of American Art, 2006.

Kammen, Carol. *On Doing Local History: Reflections on What Local Historians Do, Why, and What It Means.* Nashville, TN: American Association for State and Local History, 1986.

Kammen, Michael, with Carol Kammen. "Uses and Abuses of the Past: A Bifocal Perspective." In *Salvages and Biases: The Fabric of History in American Culture,* edited by Michael Kammen, 282–303. Ithaca: Cornell University Press, 1987. Originally published in *Minnesota History* 48 (Spring 1982): 2–12.

Kemp, Emory L. "The Preservation of Historic Engineering and Industrial Works: History, Pertinent Literature, Status, and Prospects." *Public Historian* 13, no. 3 (Summer 1991): 131–37.

Kerstetter, Deborah, John Confer, and Kelly Bricker. "Industrial Heritage Attractions: Types and Tourists." *Journal of Travel and Tourism Marketing* 7, no. 2 (1998): 91–104.

Kirschenblatt-Gimblett, Barbara. *Destination Culture: Tourism, Museums, and Heritage.* Berkeley and Los Angeles: University of California Press, 1998.

Kitch, Carolyn. "'A Genuine, Vivid Personality': Newspaper Coverage and the Construction of a 'Real' Advertising Celebrity in a Pioneering Publicity Campaign." *Journalism History* 31, no. 3 (Fall 2005): 122–37.

Kraybill, Donald B. *The Riddle of Amish Culture.* Baltimore: Johns Hopkins University Press, 1989.

Kupfer, Charles. "Exhibit Review: Steel: Made in Pennsylvania." *Pennsylvania History: A Journal of Mid-Atlantic Studies* 75, no. 1 (2008): 119–21.

Lavenda, Robert H. "Festivals and the Creation of Public Culture: Whose Voice(s)?" In *Museums and Communities: The Politics of Public Culture*, edited by Ivan Karp, Christine Mullen Kreamer, and Steven D. Lavine, 76–104. Washington, DC: Smithsonian Institution Press, 1992.

Leary, Thomas E., and Elizabeth C. Sholes. "Authenticity of Place and Voice: Examples of Industrial Heritage Preservation and Interpretation in the U.S. and Europe." *Public Historian* 22, no. 3 (Summer 2000): 49–66.

Lennon, John, and Malcolm Foley. *Dark Tourism: The Attraction of Death and Disaster.* London: Continuum, 2000.

Leonard, Joseph W. III. *Anthracite Roots: Generations of Coal Mining in Schuylkill County, Pennsylvania.* Charleston, SC: History Press, 2005.

Levin, Amy K. "Why Local Museums Matter." In *Defining Memory: Local Museums and the Construction of History in America's Changing Communities*, edited by Amy K. Levin, 9–26. Lanham, MD: AltaMira Press, 2007.

Linenthal, Edward T. *The Unfinished Bombing: Oklahoma City in American Memory.* New York: Oxford University Press, 2001.

Linkon, Sherry Lee, and John Russo. *Steeltown U.S.A.: Work and Memory in Youngstown.* Lawrence: University Press of Kansas, 2002.

Logan, William, and Keir Reeves, eds. *Places of Pain and Shame: Dealing with "Difficult Heritage."* London: Routledge, 2009.

Low, Setha M. "Symbolic Ties That Bind: Place Attachment in the Plaza." In *Place Attachment*, edited by Irwin Altman and Setha M. Low, 165–85. New York: Plenum Press, 1992.

Lowenthal, David. *The Heritage Crusade and the Spoils of History.* Cambridge: Cambridge University Press, 1998.

———. *The Past Is a Foreign Country.* Cambridge: Cambridge University Press, 1985.

———. "Pioneer Museums." In *History Museums in the United States*, edited by Warren Leon and Roy Rosenzweig, 115–27. Urbana: University of Illinois Press, 1989.

Lule, Jack. *Daily News, Eternal Stories: The Mythological Role of Journalism.* New York: Guilford Press, 2001.

MacCannell, Dean. *The Tourist: A New Theory of the Leisure Class.* Berkeley and Los Angeles: University of California Press, 1976.

Maher, Neil M. *Nature's New Deal: The Civilian Conservation Corps and the Roots of the American Environmental Movement.* New York: Oxford University Press, 2008.

Malmsheimer, Lonna. "Three Mile Island: Fact, Frame, and Fiction." *American Quarterly* 38, no. 1 (Spring 1986): 35–52.

Marchand, Roland. *Creating the Corporate Soul: The Rise of Public Relations and Corporate Imagery in American Big Business.* Berkeley and Los Angeles: University of California Press, 1998.

Marcus, Irwin M. "Museum Review: Migration, Milling, Mining: The Johnstown Heritage Discovery Center and the Windber Coal Heritage Center." *Pennsylvania History* 68, no. 4 (Winter 2002): 85–93.

Marstine, Janet. "William Gropper's 'Joe Magarac': Icon of American Industry." In *The Gimbel Pennsylvania Art Collection from the Collection of the University of Pittsburgh*, edited by Paul Chew. Greensburg, PA: Westmoreland Museum of Art, 1986.

Marx, Leo. *The Machine in the Garden: Technology and the Pastoral Ideal in America*. New York: Oxford University Press, 1964.

Massey, Doreen. *Space, Place, and Gender*. Minneapolis: University of Minnesota Press, 1994.

McCollester, Charles. *The Point of Pittsburgh: Production and Struggle at the Forks of the Ohio*. Pittsburgh, PA: Battle of Homestead Foundation, 2008.

McKay, Ian. *The Quest of the Folk: Antimodernism and Cultural Selection in Twentieth-Century Nova Scotia*. Montreal: McGill-Queen's University Press, 1994.

McKinney, Gary S. *Oil on the Brain: The Excitement and Boom in Northwestern Pennsylvania After Oil Was Discovered*. 3rd ed. Chicora, PA: Mechling Books, 2008.

Mellon, Steve. *After the Smoke Clears: Struggling to Get By in Rustbelt America*. Pittsburgh: University of Pittsburgh Press, 2002.

Mellor, Adrian. "Enterprise and Heritage in the Dock." In *Enterprise and Heritage: Crosscurrents of National Culture*, edited by John Corner and Sylvia Harvey, 45–75. London: Routledge, 1991.

Melosh, Barbara. "Speaking of Women: Museums' Representations of Women's History." In *History Museums in the United States*, edited by Warren Leon and Roy Rosenzweig, 183–214. Urbana: University of Illinois Press, 1989.

Miller, Donald L., and Richard E. Sharpless. *The Kingdom of Coal: Work, Enterprise, and Ethnic Communities in the Mine Fields*. Philadelphia: University of Pennsylvania Press, 1985.

Miller, James S. "Mapping the Boosterist Imaginary: Colonial Williamsburg, Historical Tourism, and the Construction of Managerial Memory." *Public Historian* 28, no. 4 (Fall 2006): 51–74.

Miner, Curtis. "Museum Review: The Senator John Heinz Pittsburgh Regional History Center." *Pennsylvania History* 63, no. 4 (Autumn 1996): 511–24.

Mires, Charlene. *Independence Hall in American Memory*. Philadelphia: University of Pennsylvania Press, 2002.

Modell, Judith, and Charlee Brodsky. *Envisioning Homestead: A Town Without Steel*. Pittsburgh: University of Pittsburgh Press, 1998.

Mooney-Melvin, Patricia. "Harnessing the Romance of the Past: Preservation, Tourism, and History." *Public Historian* 13, no. 2 (Spring 1991): 35–48.

Moore, Niamh, and Yvonne Whelan, eds. *Heritage, Memory and the Politics of Identity: New Perspectives on the Cultural Landscape*. Burlington, VT: Ashgate, 2007.

Mosher, Bill, exec. prod. *Born of Fire: How Pittsburgh Built a Nation*. Westmoreland, PA: Westmoreland Museum of American Art, 2006.

Mulrooney, Margaret M. *A Legacy of Coal: The Coal Company Towns of Southwestern Pennsylvania*. Washington, DC: National Park Service, 1989.

Norcliffe, Glen. "Mapping Deindustrialization: Brian Kipping's Landscapes of Toronto." *The Canadian Geographer* 40, no. 3 (1996): 266–72.

O'Boyle, Shaun, photographer, and Geoff Managh, introduction. *Modern Ruins: Portraits of Place in the Mid-Atlantic Region*. University Park: Penn State University Press, 2010.

Perrot, Mark, photographer, and John R. Lane, Introduction. *Eliza: Remembering a Pittsburgh Steel Mill*. Charlottesville, VA: Howell Press, 1989.

Perry, Daniel K. *"A Fine Substantial Piece of Masonry": Scranton's Historic Furnaces*. Scranton: Pennsylvania Historical and Museum Commission/Anthracite Heritage Museum and Iron Furnaces Associates, 1994.

Pfeuffer-Scherer, Dolores. "'Let Her Works Praise Her in the Gates': Elizabeth Duane Gillespie's Public Life of Service." Paper presented at the Pennsylvania Historical Association Annual Meeting, October 17, 2008, Bethlehem, PA.

Pitcaithley, Dwight T. "Historic Sites: What Can Be Learned from Them?" *History Teacher* 20, no. 2 (February 1987): 207–19.

Prentice, Richard C., Stephen F. Witt, and Claire Hamer. "Tourism as Experience: The Case of Heritage Parks." *Annals of Tourism Research* 25, no. 1 (1998): 1–24.

Reschly, Steven D., and Katherine Jellison. "Shifting Images of Lancaster County Amish in the 1930s and 1940s." Paper presented at The Amish in America Conference, Elizabethtown College, June 2007.

Richards, J. Stuart. *Death in the Mines.* Charleston, SC: History Press, 2007.

Richter, Amy G. *Home on the Rails: Women, the Railroad, and the Rise of Public Domesticity.* Chapel Hill: University of North Carolina Press, 2005.

Roberts, Paul, ed. *Points in Time: Building a Life in Western Pennsylvania.* Pittsburgh: Historical Society of Western Pennsylvania, 1996.

Rojek, Chris, and John Urry. "Transformations of Travel and Theory." In *Touring Cultures: Transformations of Travel and Theory,* edited by Chris Rojek and John Urry, 1–19. London: Routledge, 1997.

Rose, Gillian. *Feminism and Geography: The Limits of Geographical Knowledge.* Minneapolis: University of Minnesota Press, 1993.

Rosenzweig, Roy, and David Thelen. *The Presence of the Past: Popular Uses of History in American Life.* New York: Columbia University Press, 1998.

Roydhouse, Marion W. *Women of Industry and Reform: Shaping the History of Pennsylvania, 1865–1940.* Mansfield: Pennsylvania Historical Association, 2007.

Savage, Kirk. "Monuments of a Lost Cause: The Postindustrial Campaign to Commemorate Steel." In *Beyond the Ruins: The Meanings of Deindustrialization,* edited by Jefferson Cowie and Joseph Heathcott, 237–56. Ithaca, NY: ILR Press, 2003.

Sears, John F. *Sacred Places: American Tourist Attractions in the Nineteenth Century.* New York: Oxford University Press, 1989.

Serrin, William. *Homestead: The Glory and Tragedy of an American Steel Town.* New York: Times Books, 1992.

Shackel, Paul A. "Introduction: The Making of the American Landscape." In *Myth, Memory, and the Making of the American Landscape,* edited by Paul A. Shackel, 1–16. Gainesville: University Press of Florida, 2001.

Shackel, Paul A., and Matthew Palus. "Remembering an Industrial Landscape." *International Journal of Historical Archaeology* 10, no. 1 (March 2006): 49–71.

Sheffler, Judith. "'. . . there was difficulty and danger on every side': The Family and Business Leadership of Rebecca Lukens." *Pennsylvania History* 66, no. 3 (Summer 1999): 276–310.

Shopes, Linda. "Building Bridges Between Academic and Public History." *Public Historian* 19, no. 2 (Spring 1997): 53–56.

———. "Oral History and Community Involvement: The Baltimore Neighborhood Heritage Project." In *Presenting the Past: Essays on History and the Public,* edited by Susan Porter Benson, Stephen Brier, and Roy Rosenzweig, 249–63. Philadelphia: Temple University Press, 1986.

Short, J. R., L. M. Benton, W. B. Luce, and J. Walton. "Reconstructing the Image of an Industrial City." *Annals of the Association of American Geographers* 83, no. 2 (1993): 207–24.

Silverstone, Roger. "Museums and the Media: A Theoretical and Methodological Exploration." *International Journal of Museum Management and Curatorship* 7, no. 3 (1988): 231–41.

Slavishak, Edward. *Bodies of Work: Civic Display and Labor in Industrial Pittsburgh*. Durham: Duke University Press, 2008.

——. "Photo Ops: Centralia and the Flattening of History." Paper presented to the Pennsylvania Historical Association Conference, October 18, 2008, Bethlehem, PA.

Smith, Henry Nash. *Virgin Land: The American West as Symbol and Myth*. Cambridge: Harvard University Press, 1950.

Speakman, Joseph M. *At Work in Penn's Woods: The Civilian Conservation Corps in Pennsylvania*. University Park: Penn State University Press, 2006.

Stanton, Cathy. *The Lowell Experiment: Public History in a Postindustrial City*. Amherst: University of Massachusetts Press, 2006.

——. "The Past as a Public Good: The U.S. National Park Service and 'Cultural Repair' in Post-Industrial Places." In *People and Their Pasts: Public History Today*, edited by Paul Ashton and Hilda Kean, 57–73. London: Palgrave Macmillan, 2009.

Staub, Shalom. "Cultural Conservation and Economic Recovery Planning: The Pennsylvania Heritage Parks Program." In *Conserving Culture: A New Discourse on Heritage*, edited by Mary Hufford, 229–44. Urbana: University of Illinois Press, 1994.

Stranahan, Susan Q. *Susquehanna: River of Dreams*. Baltimore: The Johns Hopkins University Press, 1993.

Strohmeyer, John. *Crisis in Bethlehem: Big Steel's Struggle to Survive*. Bethesda, MD: Adler and Adler, 1986.

Summersby-Murray, Robert. "Interpreting Deindustrialised Landscapes of Atlantic Canada: Memory and Industrial Heritage in Sackville, New Brunswick." *Canadian Geographer* 46, no. 1 (Spring 2002): 48–62.

Taber, Thomas T. III. *Williamsport Lumber Capital*. Muncy, PA: Lycoming County Historical Society, 1995.

Tarr, Joel A., ed. *Devastation and Renewal: An Environmental History of Pittsburgh and Its Region*. Pittsburgh: University of Pittsburgh Press, 2003.

Taska, Lucy. "Public History Review Essay: 'Hauling an Infinite Freight of Mental Imagery': Finding Labour's Heritage at the Swindon Railway Workshops' STEAM Museum." *Labour History Review* 68, no. 3 (December 2003): 391–410.

Thayer, Robert L. Jr. "Pragmatism in Paradise: Technology and the American Landscape." *Landscape* 30, no. 3 (1990): 1–11.

Thelen, David. "Introduction." In *History as a Catalyst for Civic Dialogue: Case Studies from Animating Democracy*, edited by Pam Korza and Barbara Schaffer Bacon, v–viii. Washington, DC: Americans for the Arts, 2005.

Thompson, Tok. "Heritage Versus the Past." In *The Past in the Present: A Multidisciplinary Approach*, edited by Fabio Mugnaini, Padraig O Healai, and Tok Thompson, 197–208. Brussels: Edit Press, 2006.

Tilden, Freeman. *Interpreting Our Heritage*. Chapel Hill: University of North Carolina Press, 1957.

Treese, Lorett. *Railroads of Pennsylvania: Fragments of the Past in the Keystone Landscape*. Mechanicsburg, PA: Stackpole Books, 2003.

Tye, Larry. *Rising from the Rails: The Story of the Pullman Porter*. New York: Henry Holt, 2004.

Van Auken, Robin, and Louis E. Hunsinger Jr. *Images of America: Lycoming County's Industrial Heritage*. Charleston, SC: Arcadia, 2005.

Walbert, David. *Garden Spot: Lancaster County, the Old Order Amish, and the Selling of Rural America*. New York: Oxford University Press, 2002.

Walker, J. Samuel. *Three Mile Island: A Nuclear Crisis in Historical Perspective*. Berkeley and Los Angeles: University of California Press, 2004.

Wallace, Michael [Mike]. "The Politics of Public History." In *Past Meets Present: Essays About Historic Interpretation and Public Audiences,* edited by Jo Blatti, 37–53. Washington, DC: Smithsonian Institution Press, 1987.Washington, DC: Smithsonian Institution Press, 1987.

Wallace, Mike. *Mickey Mouse History and Other Essays on American Memory.* Philadelphia: Temple University Press, 1996.

Walsh, Kevin. *The Representation of the Past: Museums and Heritage in the Post-Modern World.* London: Routledge, 1992.

Wanhill, Stephen. "Mines—A Tourist Attraction: Coal Mining in Industrial South Wales." *Journal of Travel Research* 39 (August 2000): 60–69.

Ward, Mary Frances. *The Durable People: The Community Life of Curtin Village Workers, 1810–1922.* Howard, PA: Roland Curtin Foundation for the Preservation of Eagle Furnace, 1987.

Ward, Stephen V. *Selling Places: The Marketing and Promotion of Towns and Cities, 1850–2000.* New York: Routledge, 1998.

Warren, Kenneth. "Steel." In *Modern Ruins: Portraits of Place in the Mid-Atlantic Region,* photography by Shaun O'Boyle and introduction by Geoff Managh, 38–40. University Park: Penn State University Press, 2010.

Watson, Sheila, ed. *Museums and Their Communities.* London: Routledge, 2007.

Weeks, Jim. *Gettysburg: Memory, Market, and an American Shrine.* Princeton: Princeton University Press, 2003.

Weible, Robert. "Lowell: Building a New Appreciation for Historical Place." *Public Historian* 6, no. 3 (Summer 1984): 27–38.

Weible, Robert, and Francis R. Walsh, eds. *The Popular Perception of Industrial History.* Lanham, MD: American Association for State and Local History Library, 1989.

West, Bob. "The Making of the English Working Past: A Critical View of the Ironbridge Gorge Museum." In *The Museum Time-Machine: Putting Cultures on Display,* edited by Robert Lumley, 36–62. London: Routledge, 1988.

West, Emily. "Selling Canada to Canadians: Collective Memory, National Identity, and Popular Culture." *Critical Studies in Media Communication* 19, no. 2 (June 2002): 212–29.

West, Patricia. "Uncovering and Interpreting Women's History at Historic House Museums." In *Restoring Women's History Through Historic Preservation,* edited by Gail Lee Dubrow and Jennifer B. Goodman, 83–95. Baltimore: Johns Hopkins University Press, 2003.

White, Hayden. *The Content of the Form: Narrative Discourse and Historical Representation.* Baltimore: Johns Hopkins University Press, 1987.

Wiener, Lynn Y. "Women and Work." In *Reclaiming the Past: Landmarks of Women's History,* edited by Page Putnam Miller, 199–223. Bloomington: Indiana University Press, 1992.

Williams, Paul Harvey. *Memorial Museums: The Global Rush to Commemorate Atrocities.* New York: Berg, 2007.

Williams, Raymond. *The Long Revolution.* London: Chatto and Windus, 1961.

Winfield, Betty Houchin. "The Press Response to the Corps of Discovery: The Making of Heroes in an Egalitarian Age." *Journalism and Mass Communication Quarterly* 80, no. 4 (Winter 2003): 866–83.

Wolensky, Kenneth C. "Coal." In *Modern Ruins: Portraits of Place in the Mid-Atlantic Region,* photography by Shaun O'Boyle and introduction by Geoff Managh, 66–69. University Park: Penn State University Press, 2010.

Wolensky, Kenneth C., Nicole H. Wolensky, and Robert P. Wolensky. *Fighting for the Union Label: The Women's Garment Industry and the ILGWU in Pennsylvania.* University Park: Penn State University Press, 2002.

Wyckoff, William. "Postindustrial Butte." *Geographical Review* 85 (October 1995): 478–96.

Youngner, Rina. *Industry in Art: Pittsburgh, 1812 to 1920.* Pittsburgh: University of Pittsburgh Press, 2006.

Zelinsky, Wilbur. *The Cultural Geography of the United States.* Englewood Cliffs, NJ: Prentice-Hall, 1973.

Zelizer, Barbie. "Reading the Past Against the Grain: The Shape of Memory Studies." *Critical Studies in Mass Communication* 12, no. 2 (June 1995): 214–39.

Index

CPSIA information can be obtained
at www.ICGtesting.com
Printed in the USA
LVHW111713071219
639768LV00002B/188/P